Dawn Cook Ronr

*Antique American*

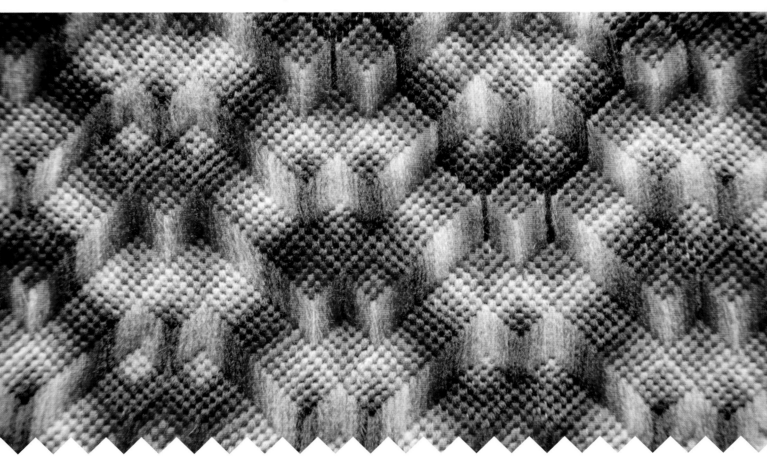

*Needlework Tools*

Schiffer Publishing Ltd

4880 Lower Valley Road • Atglen, PA 19310

Library of Congress Control Number: 2017955771

Cover and interior design by RoS
Title page photo: KGL
Type set in MrBlaketon/Verlag/Warnock Pro

ISBN: 978-0-7643-5549-3
Printed in China

Published by Schiffer Publishing, Ltd.
4880 Lower Valley Road
Atglen, PA 19310
Phone: (610) 593-1777; Fax: (610) 593-2002
E-mail: Info@schifferbooks.com
Web: www.schifferbooks.com

For our complete selection of fine books on this and related subjects, please visit our website at www.schifferbooks.com. You may also write for a free catalog.

Schiffer Publishing's titles are available at special discounts for bulk purchases for sales promotions or premiums. Special editions, including personalized covers, corporate imprints, and excerpts, can be created in large quantities for special needs. For more information, contact the publisher.

We are always looking for people to write books on new and related subjects. If you have an idea for a book, please contact us at proposals@schifferbooks.com.

OTHER SCHIFFER BOOKS ON RELATED SUBJECTS:

Arts and Crafts Embroidery, Laura Euler, ISBN 978-0-7643-4409-1

The Little Guide to Mastering Your Sewing Machine: All the Sewing Basics, Plus 15 Step-by-Step Projects, Sylvie Blondeau, ISBN 978-0-7643-4970-6

Contemporary International Tapestry, Carol K. Russell, ISBN 978-0-7643-4869-3

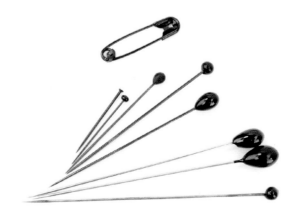

This book is dedicated to
Michael, Nora, and Ian

## Acknowledgments

There are several people who were invaluable in the process of completing the manuscript for this book. Their knowledge, encouragement, and support are deeply appreciated. Thank you to Pat L. Nickols, Ann Hermes, Barbara Garrett, and Florence McConnell.

The photos are an important part of this book. Thank you to the owners of personal collections who so graciously allowed me access to their treasures. I extend sincere appreciation to: Pat L. Nickols, E. L. "Tex" Johnson, Kathryn Lesieur, Florence McConnell, and Lynn Evans Miller.

A special thank you to the museum staff, and their volunteers across America who facilitated study appointments, and the transfer of photographs. Their generous time helped make collection objects accessible and available in this book:

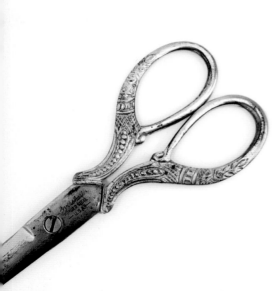

Chester County Historical Society, West Chester, Pennsylvania

Mingei International Museum, San Diego, California

Salem Academy and College, Salem, North Carolina

Schwenkfelder Library & Heritage Center, Pennsburg, Pennsylvania

Smithsonian National Museum of Natural History, Department of Anthropology, Suitland, Maryland

Winterthur Museum & Library, Winterthur, Delaware

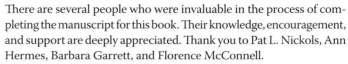

# Contents

**Introduction**..................................................6
*Raw Materials and Entrepreneurial Spirit*

**1.** Needles and Thread..............................8
   *Needle Storage, Threaders, Emeries, Winders, Waxers,
   Thread Stands, and Boxes*

**2.** Pins and Pin Storage ...........................48
   *Papers, Boxes and Poppets, Folders, Discs, Cushions, and Balls*

**3.** Thimbles and Thimble Holders ...............86

**4.** Bodkins, Awls, and Stilettos.....................96

**5.** Scissors and Cutting ............................102

**6.** Sewing Rolls, Reticules, Bags, and Waist Pockets .............110

**7.** Sewing Sets......................................154
   *Chatelaines, Baskets, and Boxes*

**8.** Clamps.............................................182

**9.** Threadwork......................................190
   *Crochet, Tambour, Knitting, Tatting, and Cording*

**10.** Hoops and Darning...............................200

**11.** Closures and Fasteners..........................206
   *Buttons, Snaps, Hooks, and Zippers*

**12.** Measuring, Marking, Patterns, and Templates....................214

**Notes** ..................................................228
**Bibliography** ......................................234
**Index** ...............................................236

# *Introduction*

## Raw Materials and Entrepreneurial Spirit

Do you ever find yourself looking at something, wondering how it came to be? Who made these buttons? Why are some pins black? Why do you need or want more than one needle and thread?

As long as I can remember I have been fascinated by textiles, sewing, embroidery, and the needlework tools required to create such beauty. My first sewing box was clear plastic, filled with colorful threads, black-handled Wiss scissors, and a yellow tape measure. I also had an assortment of colorful embroidery floss and I embroidered many dresser scarves in amongst my naively sewn scrappy doll clothes. As I got older and took sewing in home economics classes I was still fascinated with the textiles and tools. I enjoyed hand sewing and was confident enough to pack my hand sewing supplies and sew on the school bus.

In high school I frequented the library, where I found numerous books and magazines related to sewing and embroidery. By this time my sewing box was overflowing with more gadgets and tools: multiple scissors, complete sets of crochet hooks, and an assortment of buttons. It was the beginning of a collection that expanded as I explored the history of sewing and embroidery. Initially I was collecting anything old that was sewing-related.

I also expanded my personal library of needlework tool reference books, but always found a gap in the story of the American pieces in my collection. While I admired and added to my collection with French gold and ivory sets, English sterling, and German Black Forest pieces, it is the American items I always come back to.

Information on the American pieces in my collection was found in pieces and bits from many sources. My personal research and findings, specific to the American needlework tool story, became the basis of this book. I visited museums and private collections as part of the research process. Utilizing primary resources including journals, US patents, antique books, and letters, the research here builds on existing information to document American needlework tools into a single volume. As with any topic an author is passionate about, limiting the scope of the book was a challenge. New discoveries and theories present themselves on a

regular basis, and this book is by no means the end of a journey. I hope this research becomes the basis for deeper studies into the entrepreneurs and tool makers that help build the American needlework story.

The strong link between women's history and needlework tools is a fascinating part of the story. A young girl's future depended on a strong marriage. A young woman who could not use a needle was considered unmarriageable. An unmarried woman was a burden to her family. The 1834 issue of *The New England Farmer* mentions the marriageability of local young women in the report on the needlework exhibited at the Worcester Cattle Show: "A wife could not be dowered better, and when an agency for marriage contracts shall be established here, the young ladies who have received premiums from this Society, should occasion the largest demands by the broker upon those who may have the good fortune to secure such prizes."

To complete their needlework, women needed a source for their supplies. The availability of raw materials and entrepreneurialism in America were also drivers in the production of needlework tools. In many cases encouragement from the government to decrease dependence on foreign goods advanced the technology in sewing and embroidery just as it did for other industries.

The entrepreneurial spirit was always encouraged in America. Independence from foreign goods was promoted and rewarded. In some cases tools, equipment, and processes were copied from the maker's previous home country; others were cutting-edge developments. United States patents were granted to both men and women over a period of more than 200 years as they sought to innovate American sewing and embroidery while profiting along the way.

Ivory and bone were readily available through the nineteenth century. The whaling and cattle industries provided ample raw materials for many needlework tools like bodkins, stilettos, clamps, crochet hooks, and knitting needles. By the beginning of the twentieth century whale baleen became scarce and its use was discontinued. At about this time changes in the cattle industry also

impacted needlework tools. Cattle were being slaughtered at earlier ages, and the bones were not strong enough for tools. Cattle shin bones were imported from Argentina for use in American manufacturing. In the 1960s when plastics that imitated ivory and bone were readily available, those replaced the use of the real thing.[1]

Metal deposits were always an attraction for explorers to North America, and were drivers in many of the needlework tools produced here. The use of metal in needlework tools was almost always a preference due to its durability and appearance. Designers, inventors, and entrepreneurs looked around them for available raw materials. Most early American iron works extracted iron ore from bog iron deposits. The first American iron works was built in the seventeenth century at Falling Creek near Richmond, Virginia.[2] Early operations were called iron plantations. Over time, the iron works' relocation closer to urban manufacturing areas and evolving technologies made the process more cost effective and efficient. Iron tools were stronger than bone but more expensive and could not be made at home.

Many sterling silver American needlework tools are found. The 1859 discovery of silver at the Comstock Lode in Nevada boosted the interest in silver in America.[3] The height of the silver craze was during the fifty-year period from 1870 to 1920. With the passing of the Coinage Act of 1873, increased global supplies of silver together with technological innovation caused silver prices to drop. The affordability of silver made it possible for American silversmiths to offer a wide array of silver sewing implements.[4]

Design influences left their mark not only on architecture, furniture, and artworks, but also on needlework tools. For instance, during the Art Nouveau movement of 1890–1905, flatware lines sometimes included thimbles and sewing tools. The design influence extended beyond the flatware to those items.

I invite you to explore the story of American needlework tools and find a better understanding and perspective of what America contributed to the world of sewing and embroidery.

*I invite you to explore*
the story of American needlework tools
and find a better understanding and perspective of
what America contributed to the world
of sewing and embroidery.

# 1 Needles and Thread

## Needles

The needle was possibly one of the first tools devised by mankind, and has been an indispensable tool ever since.[1] It has been modified and improved over the centuries but the basic eye, shaft, and point has not substantially changed. The quality of a needle is essential for all stitching.

Needle predecessors were wood, flint, or bone awls used about 26,000–20,000 BCE. These tools had a sharp point that was used to pierce animal hides. Sinew was used to lace hide clothing together. The awl eventually evolved to have a notch, and later an opening or eye. The first needles were made, like awls, of thorns or sharpened bones. The first metal needles with eyes were found in Iraq dating to 3600 and 3200 BCE.[2]

Throughout the centuries the process of making hand sewing needles has evolved from a labor-intensive multistep hand process to an automated mass production process. Historical materials include bronze, iron, steel, and copper alloy. With hundreds of needle types today, present-day materials can include high-tech Teflon™ coatings, and precious metal electroplating.

Needle making was introduced to England by Flemish refugees living there. The English needle-making industry dates from the 1550s and employed cheap labor, in the form of women and children as young as three working in the long multistep manual process from converting wire to finished needles. Needle makers were paid a higher wage because of "Pointer's disease," pneumoconiosis caused by inhaling particles of stone and metal while grinding metal needles.[3] Small English shops with a master, his family, a few journeymen, and apprentices continued until the middle of the eighteenth century.

The seventeenth-century American estate of John White, a tailor in Salem, Massachusetts, lists a needle case and five needles equal to 5% of the total value of his estate.[4] Due to their expense, the proper care and storage of needles was essential for any early American home or business.

Hand sewing needles were manufactured in the American colonies. In 1775, Jeremiah Wilkinson, of Cumberland, Rhode Island, made needles from wire. In 1775 colonists were encouraged and offered a bounty to the person who could make the first pins and needles equal to those made in England. Needles were important tools to the American economy and part of the resistance to depending on imported goods. The American needle industry struggled and wasn't established on a semipermanent basis in America until 1852.[5] Demand for machine sewing needles drove the American production of needles for the growing sewing-machine market. Hand sewing needles continued to be popular imports.

American shopkeepers in the eighteenth and early nineteenth centuries bought imported English needles in bulk then counted out a specific quantity for a customer. The needles were hand wrapped in acid-free paper. The size and maker could be hand written on the outside of the small package, if it was marked at all. In nineteenth-century England, the English were producing ninety percent of the world's hand sewing needles. American needle makers advertised their goods as equal to if not superior, and free from rust, compared to the quality imported from Europe.[6] Yet the American needle industry struggled.

Pre-1840 hand sewing needles on acid-free paper wrapper, 1.25" needles. *Collection of the author.*

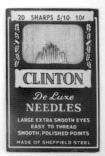

Hand sewing needle packages, left to right: 19th-century bundle of Milward & Sons hand sewing needles with original yellow thread tie; Dix and Rands all paper package; Crowley's with fabric interior; War Time Package Lighthouse brand with fold-down paper window; Clinton needles with clear window package. *Collection of the author.*

In the nineteenth century and earlier, children learned to sew at very young ages, often before age five. *The Ladies' Work-Table Book* from 1844 states, "No one can look upon THE NEEDLE, without emotion; it is a constant companion throughout the pilgrimage of life. We find it the first instrument of use placed in the hand of budding childhood, and it is found to retain its usefulness and charm, even when trembling in the grasp of fast declining age."

It is difficult to place a date on a hand sewing needle. If the needle is in original packaging, additional clues are available to arrive at an approximate date. American distributors did not repackage imported needles; most consumers were convinced the imported needles were superior.

It is important to keep in mind that packaging can be reproduced to look old. Needles can also be placed in old or new packaging. Printed artwork was also reused for decades after the initial illustrated event. Needle quality varied and still does today.

At the turn of the twentieth century Americans were purchasing 300 million English hand sewing needles in a variety of styles and designs. No attempt was made by Americans to seriously challenge the British needle industry. On the basis of the 1900 US Census records, those sales levels equate to almost four needles a year for every man, woman, and child in America.[8] English needle manufacturers were careful to

| Year | Package Information[7] |
|---|---|
| Pre-1840 | Folded in acid-free paper with hand writing or printed on white labels |
| 1840 | Trademarks are rarely seen |
| 1860–1940 | Labels with the name and address of the shop |
| 1860–1940 | Elaborate label printing |
| 1900 | Needles were fixed into a small piece of cloth inside the package |
| 1920 | Small opening in the package to see the needle eye |
| 1930 | Needles inserted into waxed paper |
| 1930 | Small window made of clear celluloid over the needle eye |
| 1960 | Blister packs, entire needle visible |

Low-quality needles exhibit rough texture along the length of the needle and inside the needle eye. Rough textures on needles drag and wear thread fibers during stitching causing thread breaks and damage to textiles. *Collection of the author.*

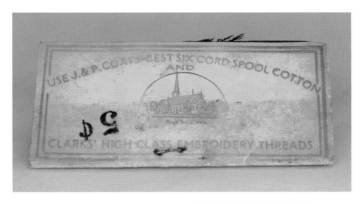

Printing on English needle packaging is an example of joint ventures between American and English manufacturers of the needles and thread. This package retains the original five-cent price. *Collection of the author.*

The needle is now ready for its eye. Manual dexterity and keen sight are necessary for this operation, and women are usually employed on it. The correct position of the needle in the eye-punching machine is insured by a central guide plate, which fits into the groove on the blade; at the will of the operator, the punch descends and passes through the blade into a hole in the central guide-plate.

But one needle can be punched at a time and every eye must be in precisely the proper place and of the exact size required.

On a daily average a girl will punch 7,000 needle-eyes or more than a dozen a minute. The operators sit facing the windows and in close proximity thereto so as to get good light. One illustration shows a long row of them carefully intent on the work, the character and effect of which is more graphically presented in the other illustrations.

10

This page from the "Evolution of a Singer Needle" tells some of the role women played in the manufacture of sewing machine needles. One girl will punch at least 7,000 needle-eyes per day. Note the male foreman illustrated standing behind the row of women. *Collection of the author.*

Informational booklet printed by the Singer Manufacturing Company. It details the importance of good needles for sewing machines. It also describes the American process for manufacturing sewing-machine needles. *Collection of the author.*

secure US patents for their needles and packaging. The English had also contracted American distributors in the nineteenth and early twentieth centuries with joint ventures.[9]

The American needle industry finally got a foothold in the mid-nineteenth century with the rise of the sewing-machine industry. The sewing machine is essentially an American product, and one of its most important features is the needle. It is estimated of all the operative labor involved in the construction of the sewing machine, six to eight percent of the process in the nineteenth century was making the machine needle.[10]

Sewing-machine needles were needed for the home and industrial markets in various designs requiring numerous US patents. The increasing demand for needles was incentive to automate a previously manual process. The American needle industry in the year 1900 required a labor force that included approximately 2,200 adults and 140 children.[11]

We take sewing needles for granted today. Almost all sewing needles in America are now imported. Hand sewing is a hobby rather than a necessity. High-quality needles are readily available and relatively inexpensive.

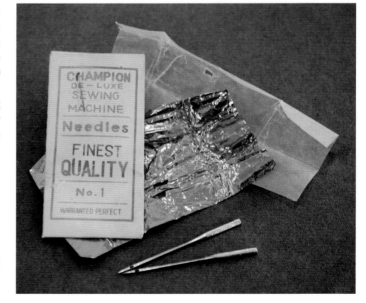

Open package of Champion sewing machine needles. Two needles are first wrapped in a lead sheet, then in wax paper, and then placed in the final printed wrapper. *Collection of the author.*

Sewing-machine needle packages: Left – Boye Needle Co, Chicago, Illinois, contains two needles in paper; Middle – B. Eldredge, Belvidere, Illinois, contains six needles in paper; Right – Champion Needles made of nickel-plated Swedish steel in Japan (interior lead wrapper) marked, "Warranted Perfect." *Collection of the author.*

Interior printing on Boye sewing machine needle package giving advice on potential sewing-machine stitch issues. *Collection of the author.*

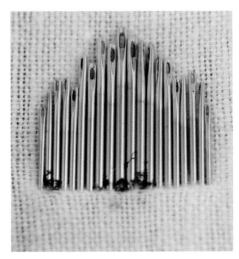

Interior needle packaging circa 1920 showing wool packaging fabric intended to minimize corrosion. However, moisture has accumulated at the edge of the wool, causing corrosion that prevents removal of the needle from the fabric. *Collection of the author.*

If your sewing machine skips stitches or breaks the thread, it is very seldom the fault of the needle. The shuttle is the heart of the sewing machine. When a machine is out of order it is at that point the trouble is usually found. The needle carries the thread into position and the shuttle must pick the thread off the needle and pass through the loop in forming the stitch. A perfect shuttle without sharp edges is necessary to do good work. A worn shuttle cannot be repaired.

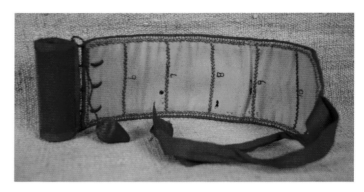

Leather needle roll with red silk binding. The cream wool lined interior is embroidered with numbers six to ten indicating needle sizes. Decorative feather stitch borders and silk ribbon ties. Matching red emery is attached to the roll end with thread. Three small sewn loops are for holding a bodkin. 3" × 6". *Collection of Tex Johnson.*

## Needle Storage

Needles, small simple tools in centuries past, were expensive due to their labor-intensive manufacturing and, given their small size, were easily lost. Keeping needles safe and close at hand was essential for women and men for centuries. Out of this need came containers specifically designed for storing needles. There is a wide array of needle storage options, from simple to complex, plain to highly ornamental.

Containers for needle storage take the form of needle cases and needle books. Needle books are made like a book with front and back covers; between the covers are wool pages to hold the needles. The wool pages were thought to prevent rust due to lanolin, a wax found in wool that repels moisture. A needle case could be made of hard material like metal, wood, shell, or porcelain.

Soft storage for needles includes books made of textiles, often having multiple interior wool flannel pages to hold the needles. American examples are typically colorful and creative. Textile covers include velvet, silk, cotton, and wool. An alternate cover material is leather. The outside covers are often embellished with paint, embroidery, beads, or ribbons. The inside-lining textiles are sometimes chosen in high contrast to the exterior, providing visual interest as well as practical storage.

*The Workwoman's Guide* from 1838 provides instructions for making a folding or roll-up needle case. The interior is made of a soft wool twill penciled off in sections for each desired needle size. The exterior and binding are made from wide satin ribbon. The penciled lines and needle size numbers were sometimes embroidered. Needles were placed by size in their marked sections stored in the wool twill. Roll-up needle cases are only a little wider than the length of a needle, about two inches or less. The length is determined by the number of needle sizes marked off, about ten inches or less.

Even after manufacturers began to sell needles prepackaged (post-1840), needle workers continued to create more-artistic needle storage methods. This practical need and creative desire continues today. In Victorian and Edwardian times, needle books were popular women's gifts. In sewing schools, students and pupils exchanged gifts like needle books. Homemade needle books were sold at fundraising bazaars and exchanged at clubs and social gatherings. Popular women's needlework magazines have been publishing patterns for needle books since the nineteenth century.

Sewing patterns from the nineteenth century were not detailed or specific. They provided layout ideas and possible decorations. Often, a single small black-and-white sketch was provided. Needle workers purchasing patterns in the nineteenth century were experienced at hand sewing and didn't need or expect much more than a paragraph describing materials with rudimentary instruction.

Embroidered covers on needle books include queen, cross, flame, and satin stitch as well as needlepoint. They are sometimes dated with a name or initials. Some are bound in narrow goods like ribbon or woven tapes. Others are simply hinged with thread or ribbon. Linings include silk and cotton fabrics.

Ring needle books are created similar to crochet buttons. The rings are made of horn, bone, brass, or plastic. Once covered in crochet the interior of the ring has decorative thread spokes, beads, or added thread patterns. The covered discs are joined together to make a larger circle for the front and back of the needle book. The front and back are hinged together, with wool needle pages sandwiched in between. This style is usually unlined. The outer edge is often tied with matching ribbons embellished with additional crocheted trim.

Silk embroidered roll embellished with glass beads and silk twist edging. The cream wool interior is embroidered with the numbers five through eleven indicating needle sizes. A small clasp is hidden at the rounded edge of the roll, the stitched thread loop to close the roll is hidden in one of the flowers. The one-inch emery is silk with cotton thread embroidery. 1.5" × 9". *Collection of the author.*

Blue faux silk roll layered with lace and embroidered ribbon flowers. Two snap closures secure the interior wool pages. Shown with a metal bodkin and brass thimble. 3" × 4.5". *Collection of the author.*

Painted velvet needle book with hand-sewn thread hinges and closure. It is lined in pink silk with cream wool needle pages. A note was enclosed inside, believed to be that of the maker. Dated June 30, 1831, it reads, "To Miss L. A. Emery, This little article, though in itself trifling, will not I hope be altogether valueless, when considered as a token of the approbation and affectionate regard of your teacher. L. A. Lee." 1.5" × 2". *Collection of Kathryn G. Lesieur.*

Perforated-paper counted-thread needle books. The 1849 example is bound in silk ribbon with matching closure and corner embellishments. The 1877 example is less ornate and executed on a less fine perforated paper. Left: 3" × 3". Right: 1.5" × 3". *Collection of the author.*

Ring needle book opened to show the front and back covers. One side is beaded in the ring centers; the others are thread woven. The hinge and closure are made from narrow wool braid in a color that matches the thread. The interior wool pages are cut to the shape of the cover and finished with a buttonhole-stitched edge in matching cream thread. 3" × 3". *Collection of the author.*

Bone and brass rings were sold carded for use in needlework projects. The brass rings are strung on a thread and were possibly purchased in bulk then strung on a ribbon for storage. A needle or crochet hook was used to stitch and join the rings. *Collection of the author.*

Dated 1898, the ring needle book example has wool pages that extend beyond the rings. The edge is cut in a complex pinked shape. A silk ribbon holds the layers together. 1.5" × 3". *Collection of the author.*

Interior wool needle book pages. The pink thread is a basic buttonhole stitch about a quarter inch deep and an eighth inch apart. The same pink thread is used in joining the rings. The pages in the blue book are cut to match the shape of the cover. The scalloped edge is finished in cream thread with a shallow buttonhole stitch. *Collection of the author.*

Wool Irish stitch needle book dated 1843. Opened to show the front and back embroidery with the initials H K. The pink-stitched center is the fold line. Green silk bound edges and cream wool needle pages. Probably owned by Hanna (Kriebel) Schultz (1823–1914), whose grandparents were Caspar Yeakle and Anna (Yeakle) Yeakel, of the Chestnut Hill Yeakles. 4" × 8" opened. *Schwenkfelder Library & Heritage Center, Pennsburg, Pennsylvania.*

Interior view of the Irish stitch needle book that was probably owned by Hanna (Kriebel) Schultz (1823–1914), whose grandparents were Caspar Yeakle and Anna (Yeakle) Yeakel, of the Chestnut Hill Yeakles. Paper cut embellished page and cream wool needle pages. 4" × 8" opened. *Schwenkfelder Library & Heritage Center, Pennsburg, Pennsylvania.*

This page from the August 1861 *Peterson's Magazine* is the complete set of instructions for the pictured "Hanging Pincushion and Needle-Book." The last line of the instructions states, "This forms a pretty little article for a fancy fair sale, as it may be made very showy; it is also very easy to execute." 7" × 9". *Collection of the author.*

The top of the needle pages is embroidered in a delicate floral spray. The three graduated pages have matching finished edges stitched in a single strand of silk thread. Every other edge stitch is deeper into the wool edge. 2.5" × 1.5". *Collection of the author.*

The most common material for the needle pages is wool flannel, which is a lightweight 100% wool. Sometimes referred to as doctor flannel, wool flannel was used in households for many purposes. Numerous ladies' magazines recommended the use of wool flannel for cleaning, medicinal, and cosmetic treatments; a necessary material to have close at hand in the home, it was readily available to use for needle storage.

The edges of the wool needle pages are finished to prevent raveling. Edge finishes include pinking with special scissors, embroidered, hemmed or bound. Some are also further embellished with embroidery in highly contrasting thread. The most common edge stitch is an embroidered blanket stitch.

Wool felt needle books were made in many forms. Popular shapes include various human forms dressed in felt clothing. Shapes from nature include leaves and flowers.

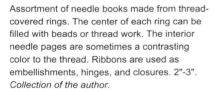

Assortment of needle books made from thread-covered rings. The center of each ring can be filled with beads or thread work. The interior needle pages are sometimes a contrasting color to the thread. Ribbons are used as embellishments, hinges, and closures. 2"-3". *Collection of the author.*

The top of these needle pages is embroidered with an asymmetrically placed stem of flowers. The edges are finished in matching brown thread in a fan stitch variation. 2.5" × 1.5". *Collection of the author.*

This colorful all-wool needle book is bound in commercial wool braid. The interior wool pages are each a different color including reds, purple, and blue. The pinked edges prevent raveling. The closure is a single china button with a thread loop closure. 3" × 6". *Collection of the author.*

Character-shaped wool felt needle books embellished with buttons, ribbon, lace, and embroidery. The boy is 5.5" tall. *Collection of the author.*

The interior view of the female needle book holds wool needle pages, a thimble, pins, safety pins, and thread winders. 7.5". *Collection of the author.*

An assortment of wool needle books with embellishments including embroidery, ribbons, and snaps. 6" leaf. *Collection of the author.*

Perforated paper can be cut to any shape. The rough edges in this example are covered in silk ribbon. The initials E. H. could be the maker, the recipient of a gift, or in memory of a loved one. Pink roses sometimes symbolize joy, grace, sweetness, or happiness. 3" × 3". *Collection of the author.*

### Paper Needle Books

English needle makers packaged their products in paper needle books. Some of the book papers were embellished and finished to look like leather. One example, shown in the 1886 Bloomingdale's catalog was imported from Blood's brand. The "All The Year Around Plush Needle Case" is described as a handsome silk plush case, satin lined, containing five papers of Blood's needles, bodkins, and darning needles. The purchase price was thirty-five cents. A similar book containing five papers of Milward's needles and a pocket had a combined cost of thirty-nine cents.[12] The needles were all imported, sometimes the outer needle book packaging was a joint venture with an American company.

Handmade paper needle books include perforated card, paste board, and Bristol board. Bristol board is heavy paper often used for watercolor painting. Pasteboard is thin yet strong; it was often cut into shapes and covered with fabric for the front and back covers of needle books. Perforated paper is pierced in regularly spaced increments manufactured in various thicknesses strong enough to carry cross stitches.

The perforated paper grid, simulating an even-weave linen or canvas, was often cross stitched from charted designs. Designs included sentiments like "Remember Me" and "Forget Me Not." The paper is heavy and can be cut in most any shape. It does not require a frame or hoop when stitching. The scale of the paper is measured by the number of perforated holes per square inch. It was available in fourteen, fifteen, and sixteen holes per square inch. The pieces of paper can be cut into shapes without fear of unraveling. Shapes and layers are stitched together to create the covers for needle books. Beaded embroidery was encouraged in women's magazines because the small glass beads did not fade like threads.

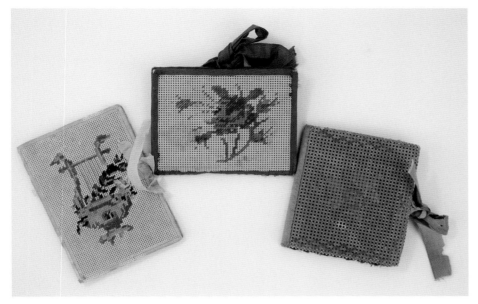

Perforated-paper needle books embroidered with cotton thread. The designs were stitched from charted patterns. The lyre is bound in cream silk ribbon that is also used as the closure tie. The center rose book is bound in blue silk. The book on the right was painted with a silver metallic finish that has tarnished. The blue silk binding and tie closure have also faded. About 3" × 2". *Collection of the author.*

Stationery shops of the mid-nineteenth century sold Bristol board cards with decorative perforated borders. The edges could be left as purchased or embellished with needlework. The center could be printed, stamped, painted, or embroidered. Bristol board can also be used for watercolor. Many nineteenth-century girls' schools offered training in watercolor painting. Subjects were often botanical with sentimental meanings. To form a needle book, two pieces were used to create the front and back covers, and wool felt pages were sandwiched in between to create the needle pages. Additional finishes include thread lacing, silk ribbons, beads, and inking.

Thread was used as a decorative feature in paper needle books. Not only could colored thread be embroidered into designs, it could be wrapped at pinked edges to create decorative designs. Special care was taken to hide the beginning and ending threads to make the inside cover just as attractive as the outside. Once again the front and back pieces were attached at the top with a ribbon, including the interior wool flannel pages.

Pasteboard was covered with fabric hand sewn around both sides of the board. Sometimes padding like quilt batting is placed under the fabric to soften the finished covers. The edges could be finished with decorative stitches or bound in ribbon. The pasteboard provided a firm surface for the front and back covers of the needle book. One edge of the book was bound to create the spine incorporating the wool needle pages.

The penciled rose stem was covered in delicate water colors. The perforated edges are stitched in red silk thread. The covers and interior pages are hinged together with silk ribbon. 3" × 2". *Collection of the author.*

Perforated paper offers a variety of options for finishing. Additional perforations could be added, and stitching threads could be laced into patterns. 3". *Chester County Historical Society, West Chester, Pennsylvania.*

The interior pages were creatively finished. Some examples use contrasting wool colors; others are neutral. Some of the needle page edges are pinked; others are densely embroidered. 3". *Chester County Historical Society, West Chester, Pennsylvania.*

The backs of the needle books are not always as ornate as the fronts. Some include only a small part of what was used on the front. The pink thread example has an inked sentiment on the back, "Tho lost to sight to memory dear." 3". *Chester County Historical Society, West Chester, Pennsylvania.*

The interior of this paper needle book is inscribed "From P Emlen – Christmas 1840." 3". *Chester County Historical Society, West Chester, Pennsylvania.*

A variety of fabric-covered needle books include cotton, silk, painted silk, velvet. The center book includes colorful wool needle pages with pinked edges. 1" – 3". *Collection of the author.*

Fabric covered needle books include leather, woven silk ribbon, and chintz. 1.5" – 3". *Collection of the author.*

Beaded needle books, probably Victorian. Interiors are lined in cream silk with cream wool needle pages. Thinly beaded with no built-up beading techniques. 3" × 3". *Collection of the author.*

In the late nineteenth and early twentieth centuries, Native Americans beaded needle books and sold them to tourists at popular vacation destinations like Niagara Falls. The base material is thin paper board covered with colorful fine wool. Wool colors often included red, purple, and blue. The beads were often clear, incorporated into loops, thick dimensional flowers, and leaves. Needle pages were in contrasting wool colors with pinked edges. During the same time period, similar beading was popular with Victorian ladies. It is unclear if the Native Americans learned the beading motifs and techniques from missionaries, or if they are adaptations of Native American beading. Other beaded sewing souvenirs, such as pincushions, are discussed in chapter 2.

Needle books made of natural materials are often one of a kind. Shells are one example that offers many variations. Often the shell was pierced with holes to form the hinge to open and close the case. Wool pages were fastened into the hinge when it was sewn. Other embellishments include piercing around the outer edge of the shell. Ribbons could be woven through the holes and bows added for further trimming.

In the twentieth century, paper needle books decorated with creative lithography were sold, often for use as advertising giveaways. This practice reached its peak in the twentieth century. The paper needle books were often printed in one country while the small packets of needles glued inside were made in another country. Paper needle books usually have the country that did the printing inked near the crease on the back cover. American distributors chose cheap needles imported from Japan and Czechoslovakia for use in advertising needle books. The needle packages were glued to the interior of the book; some needle books included a threader. While rarely American made, the products and objects of advertisements were. Advertisements included banks, insurance companies, grocery stores, and dry goods products. In some cases the company stamped their name and address on the back of the needle book. In other examples the sponsoring company was printed at the same time as the lithographic cover.

This needle book is made of birch bark embroidered with dyed moose hair. The lavish silk bows hinge and close the needle book covers. The interior has wool needle pages. 3.5" diameter. *Collection of the author.*

Detail of embroidery stitches made with dyed moose hair. 0.25" leaf stitch. *Collection of the author.*

Beaded needle book, probably Native American. Blue wool base fabrics bound in glazed cotton. Interior wool needle pages are red wool. 2.5" × 3" without handle. *Collection of the author.*

Shell needle case hinged with sinew-like material. The wool needle pages are hand bound in silk ribbon and joined to the hinge with thread. The case closes with a blue silk ribbon tie. 3" × 1.5". *Collection of the author.*

Needle book with photo transfer on lightweight metal cover and an interior of red wool needle pages. The front is marked, "The Twins of Poor Lo." The infants are on Native American cradle boards. It is possible this was sold as a souvenir piece. 3" × 4". *Collection of the author.*

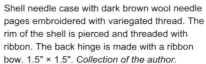

Shell needle case with dark brown wool needle pages embroidered with variegated thread. The rim of the shell is pierced and threaded with ribbon. The back hinge is made with a ribbon bow. 1.5" × 1.5". *Collection of the author.*

Needle books provided a direct vehicle for advertisements to reach women. One example is the Woman's Benefit Association needle book circulated around 1914. Bina West was a twenty-five-year-old school teacher when she founded the Woman's Benefit Association in 1892. Within three years they had 10,000 members. Created to benefit women and managed by women, it is still in existence today. At the time, American women had few rights, including the inability to purchase life insurance.[13] The needle book contains a variety of fine hand sewing needles serving as a vehicle to inform American women regarding new financial options.

The Nineteenth Amendment to the US Constitution (ratified on August 18, 1920) granted all women the right to vote. The 1928 presidential election season included a record number of women registered to vote. Able to exercise their vote on topics such as prohibition, women's-rights candidate Herbert Hoover courted the women's vote. Such critical national women's issues were also the subject of needle book advertising.

Not all needle books advertised such important information and products for American women. Common advertising examples are coal for heating the home, appliances, and grocery products. Also advertised are specific features of a needle manufacturer highlighting the superior features of the needles: self-threading, gold eye, and size assortments.

Later twentieth-century needle books include advertising as well as women's rights messages. The needles were still packaged and marketed specifically to women. Smaller packaging with fewer needles, the needle books are still sold and kept in travel kits and home sewing supplies.

Needle book sold to raise funds for the disabled. 1.5" × 2". *Collection of the author.*

This Virginia Slims cigarette advertising paper needle book was directed at women, the most common consumers of hand sewing needles. In this example the needles included were not household needles. They were large, coarse, heavy sailmakers' needles. Printed on the inside cover, "Made by Highly Skilled Crafts*MEN* in West Germany." 3" × 4". *Collection of the author.*

Promotional needle books for advertising. Left: Woman's Benefit Association filled with fine-sized hand sewing needles, 2.5" × 3.5"; the Herbert Hoover for President needle book has a request to "Work and Vote for the Republican Party," 2.5" × 4"; Virginia Slims needle book advertising cigarettes with the famous line, "You've Come A Long Way, Baby," 3" × 4". *Collection of the author.*

Paper advertising needle books included everyday places like grocery stores and banks. Some advertising was specific to products like coffee. The interiors have papers of needles glued in and sometimes also include an inexpensive needle threader. The backs are stamped or printed with contact information and the location of the business. Many were printed outside America. *Collection of the author.*

Bone needle cases sometimes had smooth exteriors with threaded lids. Others were carved with bands or ornate designs. The mass produced American examples are very plain. 0.25" × 2". *Collection of the author.*

## Hard Storage Containers

Hard storage containers for needles include open-ended vessels, tubes, and cylinder shapes with or without lids. The containers can be very plain or highly ornate. Materials include wood, precious metal, shell, and bone. The open-ended style of needle storage was worn at the waist, sometimes on a chatelaine, which was impractical as needles could easily slip out. Once out of vogue, styles executed in precious metals were often sent back to jewelers for reworking that included a closure in the latest style. Wood, shell, and bone containers did not always survive the effects of time. Cylinder sizes vary as some are styled to also contain larger bodkins, stilettos, and other sewing implements. Much later in the twentieth century, materials included plastics like Bakelite.

Wood needle cases can be smooth or heavily carved cylinders. Some smooth cylinder styles are big enough to also hold bodkins in addition to needles. One style of wood needle case was made in the shape of a person, decoratively painted in character themes such as pilgrims, colonial ladies, or clowns. Wood cases are unlined so needles are more likely to be damaged by moisture and abrasion from the raw wood. To access the needles, one end of the needle case is threaded or pulls open. Maker marks are sometimes on the bottom of the needle case.

American needle cases were sometimes made from silver and they could be highly decorative. Silver mining in the United States began on a large scale in the mid-nineteenth century. With the passing of the Coinage Act of 1873, global supplies of silver increased and technological innovation caused silver prices to drop. The affordability of silver made it possible for American silversmiths to offer a wide array of silver sewing implements. Design influences of the era like the Art Nouveau movement of 1890–1905 dictated designs.

Technology in other industries were sometimes translated to needle storage. The design for the rotating cylinder in a machine gun was adapted to a sterling needle case referred to as a mitrailleuse style. In 1884 William Gardner, of London, England, was issued US Patent 304,926. The needles are dispensed through a small hole in a disc that spins around the top of the cylinder to match the desired needle size. The American sterling versions are rare due to limited production. Mass-produced inexpensive imported examples by British patent holder Ernest Jahncke are commonly found.

Plastic became available in the early twentieth century. New Yorker Leo Baekeland invented the first synthetic plastic in 1907. Leo called the material Bakelite™ and also coined the term "plastic." Bakelite was advertised as the material of a thousand uses. The 1925 trademark filing is the letter B above the symbol for infinity.[14] Bakelite sewing items are highly collectible.

Pennsylvania wooden painted needle cases. 3" – 4" long. *Collection of Tex Johnson.*

Mitrailleuse-style needle case end. The round top turns like a dial for selecting different-sized needles. The small hole is where the needle slides out. 0.5" × 2". *Collection of the author.*

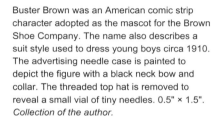

Buster Brown was an American comic strip character adopted as the mascot for the Brown Shoe Company. The name also describes a suit style used to dress young boys circa 1910. The advertising needle case is painted to depict the figure with a black neck bow and collar. The threaded top hat is removed to reveal a small vial of tiny needles. 0.5" × 1.5". *Collection of the author.*

Some styles of wooden needle cases were mass produced then painted to represent characters. On the left, the original box for "Mary Ann" does not include a manufacturer's mark and may have been a cottage industry. The figure in her yellow hat has a hand-painted appearance. The two figures on the right represent pilgrims. 0.5" × 3". *Collection of the author.*

## Needle Threaders

To solve the problem of passing thread through the tiny eye of a sewing needle, inventors came up with new products. An early solution for threading the eye of commercially made needles was redesigning the needle's eye. Some hand sewing needles were designed with self-threading eyes. The eye of the needle was designed to be a small hook that the thread could be pulled into. This style is still available today but is not fail proof. Many sewers prefer the use of a separate threading tool.

Other solutions to simplify the threading of a needle included a loop or hook device that was inserted into the eye of the needle. Thread was inserted into the hook or loop and pulled back through the needle eye. Twentieth-century paper needle books often included aluminum needle threaders with a fine wire loop that was inserted through the needle eye.

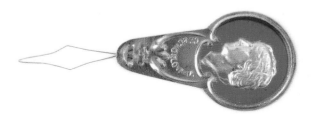

Needle threader with fine-gauge wire and stamped female in profile. Also stamped to show it was made in Czechoslovakia. The advertising needle threader has a very fine hook to pull the thread through the eye of the needle. 1.5" × .5". *Collection of the author.*

Examples of the calyx on berry emeries include felt or decorative stitching with green yarn or thread. Loop materials include rings and thread. 1" – 1.5". *Collection of the author.*

Variety of emeries from solid silk, watered silk, holly berry printed silk, and painted dots on cotton and silk. Largest measures 2" × 1"; the smallest is 0.5". *Collection of the author.*

Assortment of berry emeries. Milk glass Westmoreland dish in the shape of hands. 7" × 8". *Collection of the author.*

Emeries are not always red or pink. These examples were probably made to match a sewing set or roll. All made of silk, two have thread-stitched calyxes and two have applied fabric tops. 1" – 1.5". *Collection of the author.*

## Emeries

Emery is mineral grit or powder used for polishing and is a common filler for sewing emeries. Emery by volume is heavier and coarser than common fillings for pincushions. Needles and pins were inserted and pulled out of the emery to polish and remove light oxidative rust from needles and pins. The needle and pin points were cleaned but not necessarily sharpened. A needle or pin will rust if left inserted in the emery. A common shape for a sewing emery is a strawberry or small pillow. The emery is almost always smaller than a pincushion when they come in pairs. By the 1890s emeries were seldom used as needles and pins had become so inexpensive they were thrown away when damaged or worn out. Emeries continue to be sold today, but mostly as a decoration, and are sometimes found with useless plastic bead filler.

Patriotic emery made from a three-inch length of ribbon folded in half. The sides are hand stitched as is the closure at the top. The top has a narrow ribbon bow to cover the hand-sewn gathers. The box is possibly the original, and it could have been made for a fund-raising fair. 0.5" × 1.5". *Collection of the author.*

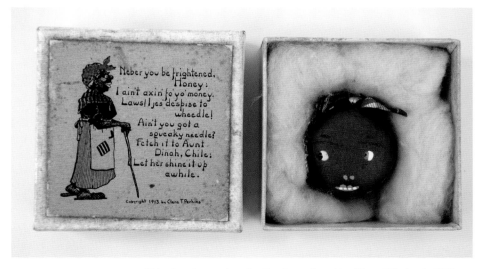

This stereotype cartoon is offensive and would not be sold today. In 1913, it was not unusual to see items like this readily available. The original box label, "Never you be frightened, Honey: I aint axin' fo' yo' money. Laws! I jes despise to wheedle! Aint you got a squeaky needle? Fetch it to Aunt Dinah Chile; Let her shine it up awhile. Copyright 1913 by Clara T. Perkins." 3" box. *Collection of the author.*

The Corticelli Thread Company registered a cat carrying a spool knave as their logo. The bottom of the box is printed with a detailed etching on the silk mills in Florence, Massachusetts. The thread color and number is printed on the short side of the box. 3" × 5". *Collection of the author.*

## Thread

Like the needle, thread was essential for sewing. Thread has been made by hand since humankind decided to join hides for clothing. The drop spindle was the primary spinning tool used to create thread for clothing and fabric from Egyptian mummy wrappings to tapestries to ropes and sails for ships for almost 9,000 years. The spinning wheel, commonly associated with the art of spinning, was not introduced to Europe until the late Middle Ages/early Renaissance. Cotton was first spun by machinery in England in 1730. Like sewing needles, prior to mass production, thread was precious enough to recycle on thread winders or thread reels for reuse.

A substitute for thread was human hair. Hair was used for embroidery and jewelry in the late eighteenth and early nineteenth centuries. Civil War soldiers often left a lock of hair at home. If they did not return, the hair was made into jewelry. Women's magazines like *Godey's Lady's Book* featured articles on the use of hair for embroidery. Instructions were to wind twenty-four inches of hair onto bobbins. Some of the embroideries became mourning pieces when embroidered with the hair of loved ones.[15]

Samuel Slater immigrated to the United States in 1768, arriving with memorized secrets from the British textile industry. By 1793 Slater and his Quaker partner, Moses Brown, opened their first factory in Pawtucket, Rhode Island. Samuel's wife, Hannah (Wilkinson) Slater, invented a type of cotton sewing thread in 1793, becoming the first American woman granted a US patent.[16]

The first American water-powered silk thread mill was built in 1810 in Mansfield, Connecticut, by Rodney and Horatio Hanks. In 1821 Hanks built another mill across the street from the first building. A larger mill was then built in 1854. The business passed through the Hanks family and was rebuilt after fires. The mill operated until 1928.[17] It was purchased by Henry Ford in 1930 and reconstructed at the Greenfield Village in Dearborn, Michigan.

In 1837, supporting efforts to be independent of foreign imports, the United States Congress purchased and distributed manuals on sericulture. In hopes of quick riches, many people purchased mulberry trees. Subsequent frosts destroyed plantations of trees. Attempts to cross French gypsy moths with the silkworm moth resulted in an accidental release of pest gypsy moths. The gypsy moth has since expanded its range and become a serious forest pest in America.[18]

The Corticelli Silk Mills started in 1838 in Florence, Massachusetts. Due to the difficulty in America of growing mulberry trees to feed the silkworms, silk cocoons were imported beginning in 1846. The need for smooth threads in sewing machines in 1852 helped the industry succeed. In 1852 Isaac Singer, after trying the thread in one of his sewing machines stated, "I shall want all you can make."[19]

By 1895 Corticelli offered a free pattern book for sending in three two-cent stamps to cover postage. The patterns for crochet, knitting, and tatting all used their thread products. The free patterns were intended to promote sales. One of their advertisements claiming the superiority of silk thread tells of a flood in 1874 that

Willimantic Star Six Cord box features the red-star trademark prominently on the top of the lid. In small type in the lower left corner of the box The American Thread Company is noted with the term "SUCC'R." This most likely indicates the box was printed after Willimantic was bought by the conglomerate American Thread in 1898. 3" × 6". *Collection of the author.*

washed the mill away, scattering thread for miles. In 1901, a large quantity of the thread was found at the bottom of a pond. It was washed, dried, and tested to be unimpaired. This unprecedented durability allowed Corticelli to proclaim that manufacturers, tailors, dressmakers, and women everywhere should not be penny wise and pound foolish. They further state vegetable-based thread becomes worthless.[20]

In 1854, a group of Hartford, Connecticut, investors, led by Austin Dunham and Lawson Ives, bought the old Jillson cotton mill for what was to become the Willimantic Thread Company. The company used expertise of production managers from a nearby mill to manufacture thread for sewing machines. Prior to this time, thread wound on spools came only in black or white; colored thread was available only in bulk skeins. From the beginning the Willimantic Company offered spooled thread in a wide variety of colors, appealing to two growing markets: America's emerging ready-to-wear clothing industry, and the rising popularity of home sewing machines. Thread was dyed like textiles; it often contained allergenic and carcinogenic additives.[21]

The invention of the sewing machine provided vast markets for higher-quality, consistent sewing threads. New technologies supporting the improved quality of thread in sewing machines included twisting plies together and the use of spools to hold the thread. Several US patents were issued to American inventors for factory equipment to improve sewing-machine thread quality. Judges at the 1876 Centennial Exposition in Philadelphia stated, "The American invention of the sewing machine was the inauguration of the sewing-silk manufacture of America, in the forms and proportions which it now holds."[22]

In 1864 Englishman Clark had built a mill in Newark, New Jersey. In 1870 English rival Coats opened a mill in Pawtucket, Rhode Island. In 1896, the Coats & Clark Company was formed with the merger of Scottish firms and American mills in 1896. In response, several other English firms merged to form the English Sewing Cotton Company. There was fierce global competition

within the thousands of cotton and linen thread products and accusations of price fixing. In March 1898, the English Sewing Company purchased the Willimantic Linen Company and twelve other independent thread and yarn companies, merging them into the American Thread Company operating in Willimantic, Connecticut.[23] The company name, American, and manufacturing presence in the United States gave the appearance of an American product to consumers.

The American Thread Company reached their production peak in the 1890s. They were the largest employer in Connecticut, employing 3,200 workers.[24] As one of the world's largest producers of cotton thread they manufactured 90,000 miles of thread each day. One of the first illuminated factories in America, it allowed twenty-four-hour-a-day operation.[25] By 1913 the US Government filed restraint of trade lawsuits under the Sherman Antitrust Act against the thread companies.[26] Even with a modified structure of ownership, foreign interests continued to hinder America's ability to compete.

Innovations in thread manufacturing led to thread being sold to consumers on wooden spools. The first manufactured threads were sold in hanks. Once home, the hanks were wound onto thread barrels, thread winders, and reusable spools.

Large wooden spool production facilities were built in Maine, near supplies of white birch trees' tight-grained hardwood. The spool companies built mills, drying sheds, boarding houses for loggers, and dwellings for mill workers with their families. Three thousand cords of white birch were required annually to produce work for a crew of sixty men employed at the mill. An additional 700,000 feet of lumber was used to construct shipping boxes for the thread spools. In 1892, the Merrick Thread Company turned out 69,500,000 single spools. The state of Maine produced 800,000,000 spools annually. When production at the mills first started, workers received one dollar a day, each day they worked. Employees who could not work due to rain or other bad weather were not paid.[27]

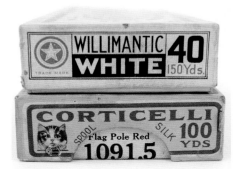

American thread companies struggled to compete with foreign competition. They advertised their American mills, promoted popular colors, and catered to consumer needs. Some retailers had wooden display cabinets to store thread inventories. Others placed the manufacturer's boxes on shelves with the short end facing out. The companies used every side available to promote their products. *Collection of the author.*

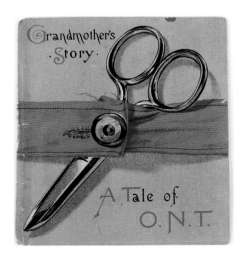

This small booklet is a fictional account of Clark's ONT Thread use throughout one woman's life. It was possibly a free marketing piece for potential customers. 3" × 3". *Collection of the author.*

The Clark box is a little misleading as the year 1812 is the date the company first produced twisted cotton threads in Great Britain. The bottom of the box promotes English Milward's sewing needles. There is no mention of any American location on the box. The thread use for machine and hand sewing is emphasized. 3" × 6". *Collection of the author.*

The J.&P. Coats thread box lists USA on the front of their box, even though they were an English company. This box was printed pre-1896 before the Coat's & Clark merger. The border printing on the lid of the box includes an American ruler in "United States Standard Measure." 3" × 6". *Collection of the author.*

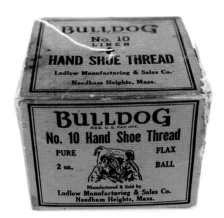

The center of the Clark's ONT Thread booklet shows where the pages are sewn together. The story has us at the point of a potential marriage proposal. Rather than presenting her with a box of chocolates, the booklet implies thread is better. 3" × 3". *Collection of the author.*

Ludlow started using the Bulldog Thread trademark around 1915. The linen thread in this package was pulled from the inner ball through a hole in the lid. This protected the thread from being soiled. This weight was advertised for leather repairs. It is unwaxed and had to be treated prior to use in a machine. Linen thread generally wears longer than cotton thread and is still popular today for bookbinders, shoe repair shops, and historical costumes for reenactors. 3" cube. *Collection of the author.*

Embroidery Thread and Yarn with Usage

| Type | Composition | Use | Comments |
|---|---|---|---|
| Crewel Yarn | Wool | Embroidery | 2 ply |
| Tapestry Yarn | Wool | Needlepoint | 4-ply twist |
| Floss | Cotton | Embroidery | 6 strand |
| Floss–Other | Silk, Linen, Rayon | Embroidery | Mixed ply |
| Matte | Cotton | Embroidery | 5-ply twist |
| Darning Yarn | Cotton | Mending, Darning | Mixed ply |

Wooden spools were labeled with ink impressions or applied paper labels. As much information as possible was put on the spool. The tops and bottom of the spool were marked. The spools were made in many sizes, and some wood spools were stained colors. 1" spool assortment. *Collection of the author.*

A scientist for American company DuPont developed nylon in the 1930s, with thread production and distribution beginning in 1938. The all-man-made thread was heavily marketed to the fashion industry. It replaced silk for stockings and sewing.[28] In 1940, DuPont developed Orlon, which became very popular for knitting. So began the introduction of other synthetic threads: polyester, Terylene, and blends. Synthetic fibers are used alone and are sometimes mixed with natural fibers.[29]

In addition to sewing threads, the industry supported the needs of embroiderers. A variety of embroidery thread and yarn is manufactured with specific features for use in various forms of needlework. Thread is a long fiber of cotton, wool, silk, or rayon used mainly in sewing. Yarn is a continuous length of several fibers interlocked.

Darning thread was primarily cotton. When lighter-weight thread was needed, cotton floss which separated by ply was available. Silk threads were sometimes used when a lightweight mend was needed. In a pinch, human hair can be used as darning thread.

Thread winder made of carved horn. The edges of the horn can be sharp and file marks can be seen on the surface where attempts were made to smooth the edges. Winding the thread in a pattern adds to the decorative nature of the winder. 1.5". *Collection of the author.*

Some wooden thread winders were made specifically for fitted wooden sewing boxes. The shapes vary; in these examples the thread winds around the narrow part of the winder. The winders slide into the tray for storage. Top: 1.5"; Bottom: 1.5" × 3". *Collection of the author.*

## Thread Winders

Thread winders were used to store thread before thread barrels and spools were available. Thread manufacturers did not sell thread on wooden spools until the mid-nineteenth century. Winders were made in a variety of designs and materials. The simplest winder can be created by folding a small piece of paper. More desirable are decorative thread winders that provided function and beauty. Some fitted needlework boxes contained thread reels, barrels, and winders to fit every thread storage need. American designs are commonly wrought from wood, horn, or silver. Sterling thread winders in the 1900s were made by numerous American silver companies. Shapes were frequently variations of a small center with four arms. Thread winders were popular as sweetheart gifts and were also sold as souvenirs.

The smooth surface of precious metal and mother-of-pearl thread winders were popular for silks and fine threads that easily snag. They were decorative and often custom made.

In America, thread reels were also called spools. After 1825, the purpose of the thread reel was to hold the newly available commercially produced wooden spools of thread. Thread reels were decorative end caps that covered the ends of commercial wooden spools. The ornamental reels were sometimes of carved mother-of-pearl or bone. Their purpose was purely decorative to cover what was considered the unsightly wooden spool end. The decorative ends unscrewed from a fine threaded metal rod. Serving no practical purpose, the decorative spools were also popular for the compartments in sewing boxes through about 1875.

In the twentieth century, thread spools were sometimes carried in sterling barrels. The barrels had tiny holes for the thread to feed through. They were decorative but also kept the thread clean and stationary so they could not roll away.

To cover what was considered an unattractive wooden spool and label, accessories were sold to embellish the spools. The end unscrews; the center rod is inserted through the center of the spool. The end disc is threaded on the rod to secure the spool. 0.75" × 1". *Collection of the author.*

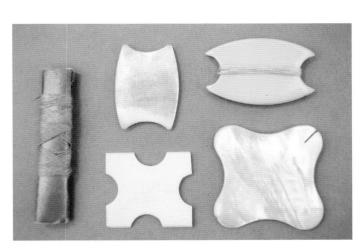

Thread winders can be as simple as a piece of paper or of more-exotic materials. This paper example is gold to provide a small hint of elegance. 0.25" × 2". The mother-of-pearl barrel shape fits in small sewing sets. 0.5" × 1". The four-armed winder is made of cow bone. 1" square. The beige barrel shape is made of celluloid and meant to simulate the grain of ivory. 0.5" × 1". The four-petal mother-of-pearl winder has a small slot for the end of the thread. 1.5" square. *Collection of the author.*

Decorative mother-of-pearl top of a thread spool cover. When displayed, the wooden portion of the spool is barely visible. Many styles were made for fitted boxes and in small sets. 0.75". *Collection of the author.*

Thread waxer inside a wooden poplar Shaker sewing box. One end of the ribbon is secured in the wax shape. The other end of the ribbon is threaded through the side of the basket and secured with a bow. 0.5" wax. *Collection of the author.*

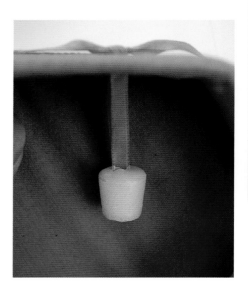

Thread waxer in the shape of a cat. Probably in the original cotton-lined box it was sold in. 1" × 2". *Collection of Kathryn G. Lesieur.*

## Thread Waxers

The needlework tool designed to hold wax for applying to sewing thread is called a waxer. Prior to the manufacturing process that twisted plies of sewing thread for strength, it was waxed for more-uniform stitches. After cutting a length of thread it was pulled through the wax, coating the full length. Home sewers waxed with beeswax or white wax to strengthen and keep the thread from tangling. Ear wax was another possibility for waxing thread. Some fitted sewing boxes contain tiny ear spoons. Sometimes the ear spoon is affixed to the end of the bodkin.

Sterling-topped waxers held colored wax formed in the shape of berries or grapes. The silver top formed the leaves with a small loop for attaching to chatelaines or stringing on a ribbon. Wax could be refreshed or added new under the silver leaf cap. Multiple waxers in colors were desirable for use on colored thread. Colored wax was not used to coat white thread. Some waxer coloring is applied only on the surface of the wax, and as the thread is pulled through the wax cake the colored surface becomes marred, uncovering the natural wax beneath.

A style of waxer with a china doll covered with wax from below the waist is often called a "Frozen Charlotte." The origin of the Frozen Charlotte story is the 1843 poem "A Corpse Going to a Ball," written by Maine resident Seba Smith. A version of the poem was set to music and became a popular ballad.[30] The story, and song, tell of a young woman on a sleigh ride with her beau. She didn't wear an outer wrap and freezes to death by the time they arrive at their destination. Little china dolls embedded in sewing wax appear frozen in place, like Charlotte in the story.

Demand for waxers decreased after 1860 when thread manufactures improved their manufacturing process. Waxers are still made and used today for a diverse selection of threads.

Sterling top on a berry-shaped wax base. A small loop is in the center for hanging the waxer on a ribbon or tassel or suspending on a chatelaine clasp. 0.5". *Collection of the author.*

Souvenir thread waxer with original box from Plymouth, Massachusetts. The box reads, "This Plymouth Rock of Bayberry sweet Will wax your thread For sewing neat." The original cotton lining is tinted blue to simulate water around the "rock" of wax. Box: 1" × 2". *Collection of the author.*

Group of waxers includes a fruit with sterling top and tassel, 0.5"; grape cluster with ribbon top, 0.5" × 1"; Frozen Charlotte with ribbon bodice, 0.25" × 1". *Collection of Kathryn G. Lesieur.*

Mother-of-pearl discs for holding wax. The decorative discs have a center rod that was inserted through a cake of wax. The threaded-base receptacle screws onto the center rod. Wax was easily replaced when needed. 0.75" × 0.5". *Collection of the author.*

Peach thread waxer suspended on a ribbon. The peach coloring is only on the surface of the berry shape. Once the thread was pulled through the wax, the colored surface is marred. 0.5". *Collection of the author.*

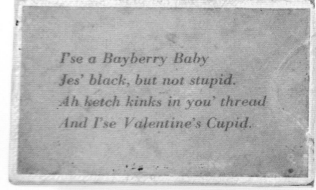

Black China Frozen Charlotte in a heart-shaped wax cake. The original red bow matches the red ink of the box lid. The lines in the heart wax cake are from thread being pulled through the wax. The lid reads, "I'se a Bayberry Baby Jes' black, but not stupid. Ah ketch kinks in you' thread And I'se Valentine Cupid." 1" × 2". *Collection of the author.*

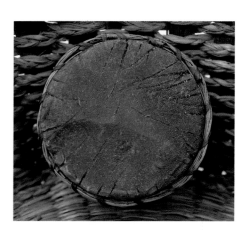

Used wax cake in a small woven basket tied to the inside of a larger sewing basket. The lines around the circumference are from thread being pulled through the wax. 2.5". *Collection of the author.*

Frozen Charlotte with a ribbon bodice. China doll set in wax. 0.5" × 3". *Collection of the author.*

Variation in stacked thread stands includes the number of drawers, finial materials, wood veneers, knob materials, and pincushion pedestals. In all examples but the largest, the thread portals are bone. There are three to five thread portals to a side at the top of each stand. This style is sometimes incorrectly labeled Shaker. Largest: 12" × 9" × 18". Smallest: 6" × 4.5" × 5.5". *Collection of the author.*

## Thread Stands and Boxes

The American distribution of thread wound on wooden spools began by 1830. The Industrial Revolution automated much of the spool-manufacturing process. The appearance of wooden thread spools was not initially accepted as suitable for show in a ladies' drawing room; thus, decorative ways to hide or enhance thread spools were created.[31]

One style of American thread stand was the wooden stacked-drawer type, with two to more than five levels. The top level features small circular openings or "port-holes" for the end of thread to feed through. The openings for the thread are lined with bone, ivory, or mother-of-pearl for the thread to glide through when pulled. The spools are stored out of sight inside the upper compartment on posts. There are typically eight to twelve thread spool posts, each aligned with a port opening. Additional features can include the use of multiple woods, multiple drawers, foldaway mirrors for reflecting candlelight, and pincushions mounted on

the top. The stands are sometimes decorated with finials and knobs of ivory, bone, or wood. This drawer style with graduated tiers is often attributed to the American Shakers as an item sold to "the World." This Shaker attribution is antidotal; no primary source has been found to corroborate the story. It is possible a few were owned by Shaker members.

The example shown in this chapter with bone finials, three levels, two drawers, and one thread level was acquired with full provenance. As with many American sewing items it passed through the family through the maternal line. This thread stand was originally a gift from a mother to a daughter in about 1910. The Boston family was very comfortable financially, and the box had light, if any, use. Their summer home was in Stonington, Connecticut. The family had hired help for generations. The ladies of the house made girlhood samplers and did light embroidery as adults.

Tambour door spool holder cupboards. The door styles include vertical and horizontal doors. Patented in 1879. 9" × 5" × 11". *Collection of the author.*

Interior of the tambour door spool holder cupboards. Metal rods hold the spools in place on each pullout shelf. The pincushions are padded with sawdust. 9" × 5" × 11". *Collection of the author.*

The thread spools are clearly visible on the round thread stands. There are many variations on the center post and the circular wooden discs holding the spools. The center example is made of empty wooden spools stacked and glued in place. Gold paint at the thickest part of the spool adds a little elegance. Left: 9" tall, 6" base. Center: 8" tall, 4" base. Right: 8" tall, 7" base. *Collection of the author.*

Wooden thread boxes were distributed by thread manufacturers like British company Coats and Clarks. The Bloomingdale's catalog from 1886 offers a "Neat Ebony Box containing 8 spools cotton, thimble, and pincushion" for fifty cents. These are sometimes mistaken for American thread boxes.

William H. Conant of Hillsboro, New Hampshire, patented a spool holder cupboard in 1879. His design incorporated a drawer base, tambour doors, pullout shelving, a pincushion, thimble holder, and metal pins to hold thread spools. It is unclear if other tambour door styles were also made by him. The back of the cabinet has a sticker, "No. 34, Novelty Spool Case, Patent Apr. 29, 1879."[32]

Less decorative are round thread stands with metal rods to secure wooden thread spools, which are also seen in many variations. The wooden spools are still visible but are kept organized. The thin metal rods go through the wooden circles and are secured in the round wooden base. Double tiers can hold up to twenty-four thread spools. Another wood style in mahogany has a single drawer and dates to around 1900. All of the round styles are topped with a pincushion.

Thread stand with removable metal rods that secure each spool from the top down. The center pincushion has an impression for holding a thimble. A small drawer is large enough to hold needle packages or perhaps a small scissor. 5" × 6". *Collection of Tex Johnson.*

Multiple spools fit on each rod. The rods are held in place with wooden ends and a loop handle. 6" × 8". *Collection of Tex Johnson.*

Metal spring arms extend from the center post to hold the thread spools in place. The lid is topped with a thimble post. 6" × 10". *Collection of Tex Johnson.*

The lid is removed to expose the wool patchwork pincushion inside. 6" × 7". *Collection of Tex Johnson.*

Thread spools are held in place by rods in a portioned wood frame. The top of the thread stand is a green velvet pincushion. 6" × 4" × 12". *Collection of the author.*

Walnut three-level thread stand with thread storage in the center. A note found in the lower drawer reads, "This spool cabinet was made by Ray Whipple in the 1930s. Ray was Ashley's Postmaster for years and was also an osteopath. He made two of the spool cabinets for momma Edith Jenkins. She gave one to Aunt Nell. This one was Nell's. Earlene has the one mom had." The middle section lifts off to hold up to five spools of thread. The top drawer measures less than 2". 7.5" square, 11" tall. *Collection of the author.*

Thread stand with center post for a thimble. Four corner posts for thread surround a sturdy center pillar pincushion. 8" × 10" × 10". *Collection of the author.*

Locking walnut thread cabinet with ivory inlay for the lock and thread portals. The hinged lid opens to reveal two rows of rods to hold spools. 6" × 12" × 7". *Collection of the author.*

Detail of the hand inset ivory inlay. Diamond 0.5" × 1". *Collection of the author.*

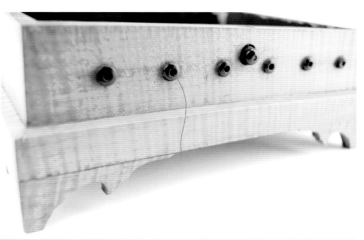

Tiger maple thread box with six thread portals. Interior partition to secure thread spools on rods. Lid has inlay of walnut and mahogany. 8" × 6" × 4.25". *Collection of the author.*

Detail of tiger maple thread box; detail of ebony thread portals. 0.25" diameter. *Collection of the author.*

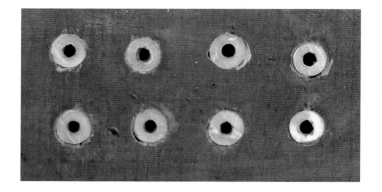

Stacked thread box with mother-of-pearl thread portals. The red velvet pincushion provides a lid covering the thread spool posts. The lower-level thread portals are inlays, but no holes are drilled through the wooden drawer face. 8.5" × 8.5" × 8.5". *Collection of the author.*

Detail of the mother-of-pearl thread portals. Portal size 0.375". *Collection of the author.*

Wrought-iron thread stand with three tiers and a top pincushion. The red-painted edge was added by a previous owner. 7" × 21".
*Collection of Pat L. Nickols.*

The Shakers made and sold a round wooden thread stand. The round base has spool-height metal pins for the thread spools. The center post supports a rather large, round pincushion divided into sections by eight threads. The stands were often sold with sewing accessories like wax cakes, and emeries suspended from the pincushion with ribbon. The bottom is marked with Shaker and the community of origin. In the 1908 Shaker sales catalog from Alfred, Maine, a spool stand is listed for $1.60. It includes a velvet needle book as well as wax and emery balls suspended by ribbons; however, thread spools were not included.

Ornate iron thread stands were patented in the early twentieth century. William Henry Simmons holds US Patent 39,515 for a double-tiered thread stand. Granted on September 8, 1908, the patent drawing shows a metal stand with two metal tiers topped by a pincushion. Each tier holds six spools. Other similar styles include three tiers variations in the metal.

Portable wooden thread boxes were made with handles on the top for portability. The boxes were large enough to hold a project and numerous thread spools, yet small enough to carry. Some boxes are just big enough to hold a ball of crochet thread and hook. They have a small eyelet or port for the thread end to pass though. The largest handled style has slender legs and stands on the floor like a piece of furniture. Added features include interior sliding trays and spool posts. Some were made as home or school wood shop projects.

Revolving metal thread stand with original corduroy covered pincushion. 6" × 4".
*Collection of the author.*

Mustard-yellow painted thread box with lower drawer. Worn pincushion has lost its filling. The top level has four ivory thread portals. The box was assembled using very fine square-headed nails. 7" × 5" × 6". *Collection of the author.*

Thread stands from the Shaker community in Alfred, Maine. Each base holds six spools of thread. The stands were sold with accessories suspended from the center pincushion. Left: 5" base, 6.5" tall. Right: 5" base, 5.5" tall. *Collection of the author.*

Bottom marking on the stand base. 1.25" mark. *Collection of the author.*

Metal rods hold six spools of thread from the top down. A small drawer is large enough to hold a few needle packages or small scissor. Replacement pincushion. 4" × 4" × 7". *Collection of the author.*

Trio of wooden thread cabinets with handles. Left: Nails on the top row hold six thread spools per side. The partitioned drawer pulls out from either side. 14" × 8" × 10". Center Back: Two lids flip back from the center, revealing two rows of spool thread storage. The bottom is bent wood, creating a gently curved bottom. 10" × 14" × 8". Right: Lids flip back from the center to hold a ball of yarn or spool of crochet thread. The end of the thread is threaded through a small thread portal in the center. 6" × 5.5" × 8.5". *Collection of the author.*

Floor stand with two slender legs that branch out to four. Each side has a lift lid that opens to reveal a row of thread spool holders. The handle makes it convenient to move around the house. 25" × 24" × 10". *Collection of the author.*

Two slender legs branch to four at the base of this thread cabinet. The drawer opens to reveal a sliding tray and posts for holding spools of thread. The two side units have flap lids that open for storage of yarn or crochet cotton. The handle makes it convenient to carry around the house. 30" × 8" × 24". *Collection of the author.*

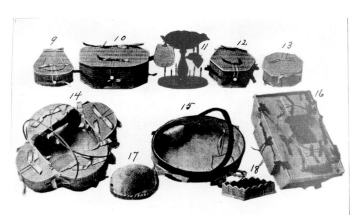

Page from "Catalog of Fancy Goods," Alfred, York County, Maine. Fannie C. Casey, Trustee and General Manager 1908. 8" × 5.75". *Collection of the author.*

Plaited straw sewn in the shape of a bee hive. Lined with a metal cone, the thread is pulled through the top. 2.5" × 3". *Collection of Kathryn G. Lesieur.*

# Pins and Pin Storage

## Pins

Pins, like needles, were equally essential to everyday life and have been in use for centuries. Also, like needles, early examples were made from natural materials like thorns, slivers of bone or wood, fish bones, and feather shafts. The word "pin" is derived from words like *pinna*, which comes from Latin and means feather. The French word *epingle* derives from the Latin *spinula*; a thorn.[1] In contrast to the pins of today, early pins might not have a large pin head; the sharp sliver could move completely through the object it was intended to hold together. Pins were used to temporarily join two pieces of fabric together, hold on a hat, or secure papers. Pins were used in the home and in business offices.

Modern pins have three parts: a sharp tip, narrow body, and a head for guiding the pin. Early metal pins were formed by hand one at a time. The first metal pins had each individual pin head attached separately from the shaft. A pin head consisted of two coils of wire soldered on the top of the shaft.

During the War of 1812, pins were so scarce the price for a pin package was $1.00, approximately a day's wages for a carpenter.[2] The American pin-manufacturing industry was more successful than the hand sewing-needle industry. Pins were a luxury to the poor in America until they were mass produced and distributed in the mid-nineteenth century. Machine-made pins were less expensive and more reliable than labor-intensive handmade pins.

The invention of making solid-headed, one-piece wire pins by machinery is generally attributed to Lemuel Wellman Wright, of New Hampshire, in the year 1824. However, he opted to patent his machine in England. He set up manufacturing in England and the technology failed to create a good point on the pins. Modifications were made too late to save the business. It was reopened in 1833 and England had the first successful machine-made solid-headed pins.[3]

The Howe Manufacturing Company of Connecticut was one of the first to automate American pin manufacturing. Founder John Howe had his first US patent in 1832. In 1836, his business, located in Birmingham, Connecticut, was manufacturing coil-headed pins. By 1840 he converted to machinery producing solid-head pins. The machinery and process improved to being able to produce seventy pins per minute. Howe and others went on to invent machinery and processes to stick pins in paper and package more than five hundred packages a day.[4] Prior to mechanization, women were paid to do piece work pinning from home. Home tasks included "pinning" the pins to the paper packages from which they were sold until the process was later automated.

Waterbury, Connecticut, was the heart of brass manufacturing in America. The Oakville Pin Company was founded in 1852 by Green Kendrick. The company employed thousands of local residents.[5] With the belief great riches could be made manufacturing pins, several companies sprung up in America. They used numerous types of machines and processes that often produced inferior pins. The overproduction of inferior pins by 1858 caused a collapse of the industry leaving only two companies in operation, in the cities of Poughkeepsie and Birmingham.[6]

Spiral pin head detail, formed from two pieces of wire. The second piece was coiled around the end of the shaft. Dating pins is nearly impossible. *Collection of the author.*

Wooden Oakville pin labels. Left: Bottom label, 3". Center: Bottom label, 2". Right: Top view with pin papers circling the central pincushion, 2.5". *Collection of the author.*

As seen from the top of the pin, the separate pin head is applied to the pin shaft. The dark dot in the center is the top of the pin shaft. 0.0625" per pin. *Collection of the author.*

This lump of coal has a hollow opening with a coiled paper filled with pins. It was probably given as an advertising gift to customers. The two-digit phone number was used in the time when callers gave the operator the number and were manually connected through a switchboard plug. 2" × 1.5". *Collection of the author.*

Assortment of mourning pins to use in dressing during mourning dressing. It was preferable that every part of the pin be black or darkly colored. 0.5"–3". *Collection of the author.*

## Mourning Pins

Black pins were a social requirement for mourning when wearing nineteenth-century garments. The head and shaft of the needle were required to be black. Black pins blended with black mourning attire: veils, ribbons, and arm bands. The shine of brass or steel pins was socially unacceptable in mourning practices. In 1886, the Bloomingdale's catalog sold a box of American Mourning pins for seven cents. In the same section, "Kirby's Best English" pins sold for twelve cents a paper. Regular straight pins in the same catalog sold for two cents a paper. Prices are similar in the Montgomery Ward & Company catalog of 1895. The pin section of the catalog is larger and includes straight pins in sizes 2, 3, and 4. A paper generally held about 240 pins. Toilet pins are generally long (over 1.5 inches) and are used for clothing, corsages, and sometimes curtains. Hat pins are generally seven to nine inches long, and most have highly decorative ends.

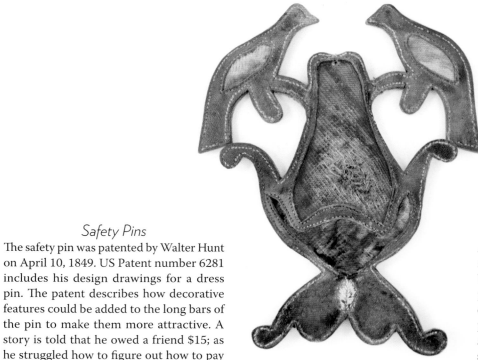

Leather wall pincushion. Bird shapes with green velvet pincushion centers flank a central well-worn red velvet pincushion. The heavy leather was sewn in layers. 5.5" × 7" × 0.25". *Collection of the author.*

## Pin Storage

A supply of pins warrants safe and secure storage. Numerous options were available: boxes, discs, cushions, wool pages, stuck paper, and soft balls. The primary goal of each storage option is to safely secure the pin, prevent rust, and provide easy access. As pin-manufacturing techniques advanced so did the competition. The increased competition advanced pin packaging and marketing approaches.

### Safety Pins

The safety pin was patented by Walter Hunt on April 10, 1849. US Patent number 6281 includes his design drawings for a dress pin. The patent describes how decorative features could be added to the long bars of the pin to make them more attractive. A story is told that he owed a friend $15; as he struggled how to figure out how to pay the debt he twisted a thin wire in his hand. Examining the twisted wire he discovered the wire could be clasped and unclasped while retaining its shape. Once issued, he sold the patent to W. R. Grace Company for $400 and was able to pay off his debt. Additional patents for improvement to the original safety pin have been successful through the twentieth century.

### Stuck Paper

Initially pins were "stuck" or pinned into paper by women and children. One report includes mention of a comb type tool that was passed through a tray of loose pins. The pins trapped between the teeth of the comb were then inserted into a colored crimped paper.[7] Papers of pins were sold into the twentieth century. Home sewers created decorative silk holders for the folded papers filled with pins. Some pin papers were coiled and inserted into wooden holders. The paper sheets were printed with advertising. Once inserted into a silk holder the advertising was not seen again.

Decorative gold plated safety pin with embossed front. 0.5". *Collection of the author.*

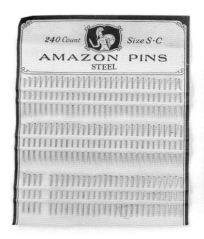

Amazon pin papers; 240 count and 72 count for five cents. 3" – 5". *Collection of the author.*

Wooden Oakville pin circles hold coiled pin papers securely in place. Two of the pin paper holders have velvet pincushions in the centers. The center example shows how difficult it is to neatly replace used pins. 1.5" – 2.5". *Collection of the author.*

Papers of pins from Wallace and Sons holding ninety brass pins, 6" × 15". Guardian paper with ninety brass silk pins and original ten-cent price sticker, 3" × 6". The compactly folded Washington paper holds 400 pins, 5" × 12". *Collection of the author.*

Assortment of silk pin papers from Clinton, counts: 120, 150, and 180. 3" – 5". *Collection of the author.*

Delta Steel Pins matchbook style paper of pins. The front cover is tucked in to show how the pins are readily available for use. Thick felt holds the base of the pin in place. 4" × 1.5". *Collection of the author.*

Walnut poppet for securely holding pins inside. The base hinge and top loop closure are made of narrow black cord. The bottom hinge is covered with a silk ruffle and thread tassel. The interior pink pincushion is filled with wool. The closure loop closes with a thread knob. 1.5" × 1". *Collection of the author.*

## Pin Boxes and Poppets

Pin boxes were made of wood, paper, metal, glass, porcelain, and bone. Covered containers for pins are sometimes referred to as poppets. The pins were loose inside the box, and the lid was secured with a clasp or latch.

In the mid-nineteenth century, factory-made pins were available in paper and metal boxes. A business owner could have their business and contact information printed or stamped on the paper or box. These business names should not be confused with the manufacture of the pins.

Pin cubes were popular in America. The squares were often used for advertising that could be viewed under the pin heads. The pins were often German, but the advertising was for American businesses.

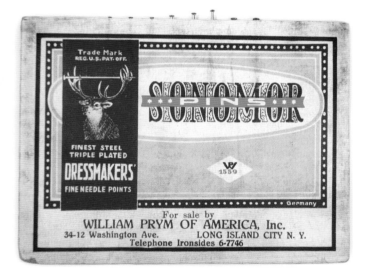

Sonomor steel dressmakers' pin paper. 3" × 4". *Collection of the author.*

Sonomor Dressmakers' Pins sample card. Includes eight pin sizes with corresponding illustrations on the outer package. They were sold by the pound, ⅛-, 1-, and 5-pound boxes. 3" × 4". *Collection of the author.*

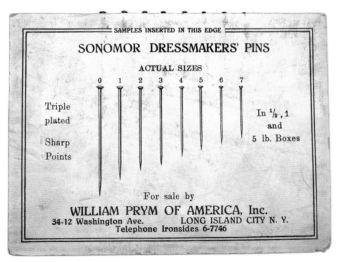

Half-pound box of Siren Dressmakers' Pins, sold by the Star Pin Company of Derby, Connecticut. 6" × 3" × 0.5". *Collection of the author.*

Quarter-pound Clinton Silk Dressmakers Pins, size 17. Brilliant blue textured paper covering the plain paper base. 5" × 3" × 0.5". *Collection of the author.*

Paper pin cube, "Made in United States of America," holds glass-headed black and white pins. Toilet Pins were used for dressing and kept on dressing tables. The plaid paper package was possibly an attempt to simulate Tartan ware from Scotland. This set includes additional dressing table supplies like hairpins to accompany the coiled paper of straight pins. 2.5" × 0.5" × 3". *Collection of the author.*

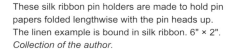

## Pin Folders

Pin folders were made at home to store pins after they were removed from the manufacturer's packaging. The folders store flat, making them easier to travel with than a pincushion. Pin folders are often made of silk and lined with wool. In between the cover and lining is a layer of batting. Some edges of the folder are embellished in feather stitch. The supply of pins can be sorted by size and color. Pin folders are often bound in silk ribbon and closed with a ribbon tie.

These silk ribbon pin holders are made to hold pin papers folded lengthwise with the pin heads up. The linen example is bound in silk ribbon. 6" × 2". *Collection of the author.*

Folded pin papers stored in a metallic finished leather envelope. Lined in silk satin with a brass stamped owl closure. Brown ribbon bows secure the ends. 5" × 2" × 0.5". *Collection of Kathryn G. Lesieur.*

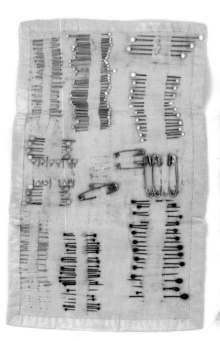

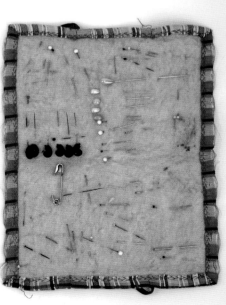

Wide silk rolls made to hold pins. Folded flat and tied closed with ribbons, they are easily stored. Crazy quilt style with crochet edge and embroidery, 5" × 6". Pink floral watered silk bound in pale ribbon, 6" × 4" folded. Blue floral with pink feathered stitch edge, 6" × 3" folded. Red plaid silk with bands of red silk ribbon. 6" × 7". *Collection of the author.*

Silk rolls opened to show pins and linings. The left pin roll has the pins carefully arranged by type and color. The lining is silk; there is no interlining. The pale ribbon binding is applied. 6" × 12". The red plaid roll is lined in fluffy wool batting. The front is brought to the inside to create a binding. It is embroidered down with a feather stitch. 7" × 10". *Collection of the author.*

Pin discs promoting the purchase of life insurance. One side shows a mother and infant; the reverse side has an advertising pitch for Prudential Insurance. In between the printed paper discs is thick wool felt with pins inserted with just the head visible. 1.5" × 2". *Collection of the author.*

Side view of the Prudential pin discs. With use, the center felt layer begins to separate as new pin holes are made. 1.5" × 2". *Collection of the author.*

## Pin Discs

Pin discs gained popularity at the beginning of the nineteenth century. Pin discs are generally solid circles of bone, ivory, wood, mother-of-pearl, tortoiseshell, or fabric-covered pasteboard one half to two inches in diameter. Variations on the disc shape include rectangles, clover, and other sentimental shapes like hearts. Sandwiched between the top and bottom discs are layers of wool or cotton joined by a narrow strip of ribbon or woven trim. Pin discs made through the twentieth century were often included in fitted sewing boxes. Later twentieth-century examples of pin discs are made of paper with a felt center and include advertising. The advertising examples were given to customers as gifts for listening to a sales presentation.

Side view of pin discs shows the difference in the filling materials and edge treatments. *Collection of the author.*

The eight-pointed star motif is beaded embroidery with glass seed beads the size of a pin head. The selvedge edge of the ribbon is hand stitched to the edge of the beading. 1.5". *Collection of the author.*

Wood pin disc with green velvet sides. Claims to be made from the wood shingles from the Ford Mansion in Morristown, New Jersey. General George Washington headquartered there during the winter of 1779 – 1780. The reverse side shows the house. The pins are inserted horizontally into the side of the pin disc. 2" × 0.5". *Collection of the author.*

Wood pin disc, reverse side.

Assorted fabric-covered pin discs. The fronts and backs are hand sewn together. The linen circle on the top left is embroidered with the letter "D" and embellished with a bow. The reverse side is plain matching linen: 1.5" diameter. The silk striped heart has a contrasting silk stripe fabric on the reverse side. It holds replacement pins: 2" × 2.25". The cotton-covered heart has the same large-scale print on the front and back: 2". The silk print circle in the lower right has a matching solid silk on the reverse side: 2.25". *Collection of the author.*

KC Baking Powder advertising pin disc. Originally manufactured in Chicago, Illinois, the brand was purchased by Clabber Girl in 1950. This example would be pre-1950. Well used, it has stood up even though made of paper. 1" × 2.5". *Collection of the author.*

Cow horn pincushion mounted on a fabric-covered wooden base. The top edge of the horn is decoratively cut to enhance the attached fabric cushion. 6". *Collection of the author.*

## Pincushions

Perhaps the most well-known form of pin storage is the pincushion. Pincushions were often made of textile and needlework pieces. They range in style from basic small squares or cubes to complex shapes covered in elaborate embroidery. Used alone or mounted on boxes, clamps, bags, rolls, or stands, the design of a pincushion is often creative and one-of-a-kind.

Popular granular fillings for pincushions are bran, ground walnut shell, sawdust, and emery powder. Fiber stuffing includes wool and cotton. There are many theories as to the best filler to extend the life of pins and needles. Wool or emery is thought to deter rust. Preferences vary by the style of the pincushion, the climate it will be used in, and the cover material. Additional filler might include a magnet, sewing weight, or card stock for a stiffer cushion.

Dating pincushions can be difficult. Often small, they are frequently composed of small amounts of fabric that could have been saved for a long period of time so the date of the fabric manufacture does not indicate the date of the pincushion. The creation of pincushions was also a socially acceptable pastime for women over past centuries. Popular for centuries as gifts and fund-raising events, they are often treasured for sentimental reasons. Many pincushions were not used; the sentimental

Bound in narrow tape, and topped in pink cotton this pincushion also serves as a needle book. An assortment of pins and needles, both machine and hand, remain in the cushion. 4.25" × 2.25". *Schwenkfelder Library & Heritage Center, Pennsburg, Pennsylvania.*

Silk-lined interior of the tape bound pincushion. Red velvet needle page. 4.25" × 2.25". *Schwenkfelder Library & Heritage Center, Pennsburg, Pennsylvania.*

This Penimaid package is pins and a pincushion all in one. Manufactured in Winstead, Connecticut, the unique packaging was patented. The pins were stuck in the reverse side. 1.5" × 6". *Collection of the author.*

The reverse side of the Penimaid package shows the wool felt interior where the pins were placed. The black thread around the center was a previous owner's solution when the package sides started to fail. 1.5" × 6". *Collection of the author.*

Monument-styled pincushion with six columns. Heavily weighted, it may have been used in a tailor's shop or as a store fixture. The center pincushion was originally bright red velvet. It lifts off, revealing a small cup large enough for a tape measure or other small articles. 10" × 12". *Collection of the author.*

value exceeded the need for practical use. It is common for a needle worker to own several pincushions, some for practical use, others as keepsakes. Pincushion styles followed the popularity of needlework and fashion of the era.

Men were also in need of pincushions. Tailors, sailors, and soldiers also needed a place for pins and needles. They are not always distinguishable from other pincushions but are generally larger and less ornate. Very large pincushions were used in dressing rooms for clothing and hat pins. Retail businesses providing alterations and tailors also used pincushions.

One style of square or rectangular silk pincushions was decorated with a design composed by the heads of the pins. Sometimes referred to as "pin stuck" cushions, the designs were ruined if the pins were removed and used. These were made and given to commemorate weddings and births.[8] Popular over centuries, many styles and sizes were created. Often the pins were arranged with a simple verse with trim along the outer edges. Mary Andere in her book *Old Needlework Boxes and Tools* writes of an eighteenth-century Boston baby presented with a cushion pinned with "Welcome, Little Stranger, Though The Port Is Closed." Other pinned verses found in America are "Peace, Prosperity and Joy Attend the Little Girl or Boy," "God Assist the Mother Through her Danger, And protect the Little Stranger," and "May the Dew of Heaven Shine Upon The Appearing Flower." The January 1860 *Godey's Lady's Book* provides instructions for an "Infants Pincushion" featuring the following lines:

> *May thy fragrance ever be*
>
> *Like the rosebud in the tree*
>
> *With a luster more sublime*
>
> *And thy every virtue shine*

Pincushion stuck or pinned with pins to create a design. Similar cushions were made in England and America. Dated 1823, it was probably presented to an expecting or new mother as a gift. 7". *Lynn Evans Miller Collection.*

Embroidered pincushions include queen stitch, needlepoint on canvas, cross stitch, and other types of decorative embroidery. The queen stitch, also known as the rococo stitch, is found in needlework as early as the seventeenth century. Queen stitch pincushions were made in New England. In addition to pincushions, the queen stitch was used on wallets and sewing rolls. Worked in silk or wool, geometric symmetrical designs were created in colorful threads. The pincushions are diverse in design and color. Additional embellishments are added like beads, ribbon, and yarn.

Pincushions were often made at home. They were made for personal use, gifts, and fund-raising events. The 1860 publication of *Treasures of Needlework* advertised their patterns and projects would "Yield profit to the Fancy Fair."

After the Civil War, demeaning pincushions were created, exhibiting derogatory stereotypes. These images were also present in mass media: Aunt Jemima and Topsy from Uncle Tom's cabin. Prejudiced attitudes in America are nothing new. Culturally acceptable depictions of segments of our diverse culture changed over time as people became more informed.

Pin heads are used in this example to form the initials of the giver and recipient. A small 1" emery is shown with the pin keep. 6" × 4" × 0.5". *Collection of Kathryn G. Lesieur.*

A double-sided embroidered pincushion. One side consists of a light-blue silk ground with an Irish stitched carnation motif in light blue, red, pink, dark blue, green, yellow, and lavender silk. The reverse side consists of multiple panels of silk, composed of a wide cream stripe with damask woven tulip motifs, contrasted with a salmon-pink silk with interwoven white silk dashes. Attached at the top is a 2.50" long peach silk ribbon loop. 7.5" × 4" × 0.625". *Schwenkfelder Library & Heritage Center, Pennsburg, Pennsylvania.*

Pincushion in the shape of a small box. The sides are embroidered and bound individually, then assembled by hand stitching through the bindings. Embroidered motifs include birds, berries, and flowers in a variety of stitches. The corners are embellished with silk bows. 3". *Schwenkfelder Library & Heritage Center, Pennsburg, Pennsylvania.*

Top view showing the queen stitch top in a geometric arrangement. 3". *Schwenkfelder Library & Heritage Center, Pennsburg, Pennsylvania.*

Pine needle pincushions woven in two different styles. Colored wool fabric tops. 3". *Collection of the author.*

Pine needle pincushion bottoms. The birch bark bottom on the right still displays what is probably the original twenty-five-cent price. 3". *Collection of the author.*

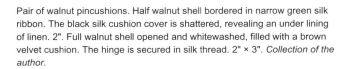

Pair of walnut pincushions. Half walnut shell bordered in narrow green silk ribbon. The black silk cushion cover is shattered, revealing an under lining of linen. 2". Full walnut shell opened and whitewashed, filled with a brown velvet cushion. The hinge is secured in silk thread. 2" × 3". *Collection of the author.*

Homemade tomato pincushion, red and green velvet with a green satin ribbon. 3" × 1.5". *Collection of Tex Johnson.*

Glass jar overflowing with an assortment of tomato pincushions. The pincushions are made of velvet, cotton, and satin. Some have attached emeries. 3" – 4". *Collection of the author.*

Perhaps one of the most recognizable pincushions is the tomato. The History of the North-West Soldiers' Fair Treasurer's Report, published in 1864 by the US Sanitary Commission, lists tomato pincushions sold at fund-raising fairs in 1863. In the nineteenth century, folklore encouraged households to keep a tomato on the mantel to ward off evil spirits or bring good luck. Being a seasonal fruit, in many parts of America, stuffed-fabric representations of the tomato were made. The plump filled fruit became a place to stick loose pins and needles. In the *New England Stationer and Printer Annual Bulletin* of 1903, Walden's Stationer and Printer advertised a tomato pincushion for use on an office desk. The non-scratch bottom protects the surface of highly polished desks. A tomato pincushion, sometimes with an emery strawberry,

has become a twentieth-century staple in most sewing baskets.

In the Victorian era (1837–1901), seashells were popular materials for needlework tools, including pincushions. Objects made from natural shells mean no two are alike. Like other crafters, the Shakers of Maine also gathered shells from the Maine shore.[9] The Shaker shell pincushions were not advertised in their catalogs and are not marked.[10] The shells were cleaned and holes were made at the back of the shells for threading the ribbon hinges. Small velvet pillows were inserted and glued between the shells to make the pincushion.

Pincushions were sometimes modeled after common objects, even the human form. Chairs, balls, and animals; the only limit was the maker's imagination. The use of pasteboard framework covered in fabric made all kinds of shapes and sizes possible. Wood examples were also made, some very detailed. Carved wooden parts are also sometimes combined with fabrics to add detail that cannot be achieved with fabric alone.

Trio of pincushions made of seashells. The stuffed interiors are made of velvet. The two largest shells show signs of wear. 3". The smallest shell is also filled with a velvet pincushion but is in like-new condition. 1". *Collection of the author.*

Top view of scalloped pincushion showing the pierced holes with threaded bow tie hinge. 3". *Collection of the author.*

Cultural stereotypes depicted in pincushions. The figure on the left in the red hat has a pincushion skirt that also holds a cloth retractable tape measure. 3" × 6". The child with a melon, sitting on the pincushion, has no markings. 3". The Asian figure is a bobble head on a spring. The back of the body is a full pincushion. 3" × 6". The figure under the real cotton boll has a labeled base, "Educational Souvenir ATLANTA, GA. Hollander Novelty Co. Pearl River La." 4.5" × 2" × 2". *Collection of the author.*

Cowry shell with the top cut off exposing the interior of the shell's two naturally formed sections. One section is stuffed with a red velvet pincushion, the other left open for small sewing accessories. Possibly made for the souvenir trade. 2" × 4". *Collection of the author.*

Pincushion in the shape of a sled, made with a wooden base and green velvet top. The front runner is made to swivel, just like a real sled. A ribbon would be threaded through the front sleigh blades. 8" × 1.5". *Collection of the author.*

Black velvet elephant with red silk pincushion saddle. Beaded eye and white felt tusks. 4.5" × 3.5" × 2". Large elephant is cream silk or rayon pincushion, machine stitched with embroidery embellished seams. Velvet saddle with added embroidery. Soft filling. 8" × 5" × 4". The turtle is hand sewn and filled with bird seed or rice. The eye is painted on and the legs are black wool felt. 4" × 3.5" × 1". *Collection of the author.*

Jockey or sport cap of blue and gold cotton. The bill and base are paperboard. The filling is lightweight, possibly wool. The pins can be inserted in the stuffed portion or inserted vertically along the seams. It is all hand sewn. 3.5" × 2" × 2". *Collection of the author.*

Strawberry cushion made with pins as berry seeds, 2.5" × 2.5". The carrot is painted and topped in green ribbon. 0.5" × 5". The berry has a decorative band embellished with feather stitch and topped with embroidered green wool. 2". *Collection of Kathryn G. Lesieur.*

Paperboard chair covered in a striped brown silk. It is trimmed in hand-applied multi-toned gimp. The seat of the chair lifts to store small sewing implements and threads. The seat is padded to serve as a pincushion. Small decorative puffs are added with light-blue glass-headed pins. The piece of paper ephemera hand tacked with thread reads, "May Your Life be Peace." Slight wear on the lower left edge, where perhaps a left-handed owner frequently picked it up. All hand sewn. 4.5" × 7" × 3". *Collection of the author.*

Petite pincushion with miniature wooden head and jointed arms. The dress is made of blue velvet, trimmed in lace. 0.5" × 2". *Chester County Historical Society, West Chester, Pennsylvania.*

Embroidered silk top for a foot stool or pedestal-styled pincushion. Cream silk ground with embroidery in green, peach, and brown. The edge is bound in silk ribbon and embellished with embroidery stitches. Origin is noted as Washington Township or vicinity, Berks County, Pennsylvania. Possibly made by or for Lydia (Schulz) Yeakel Miller Delong. 2.5" tall. *Schwenkfelder Library & Heritage Center, Pennsburg, Pennsylvania.*

Side view of the embroidered foot stool styled as a pincushion. The sides are wrapped in peach silk and embellished with cording. Three carved wooden legs support the top. Origin is noted as Washington Township or vicinity, Berks County, Pennsylvania. Possibly made by or for Lydia (Schulz) Yeakel Miller Delong. 2.5" tall. *Schwenkfelder Library & Heritage Center, Pennsburg, Pennsylvania.*

Advertising pincushion foot stool topped in velvet. The four thin metal legs are elegantly styled. The advertising bottom is printed, "The York Furniture Company 10 West Market York PA." 3.5" × 2.5". *Collection of the author.*

Tufted pillow pincushion with woven tape sides. The hanging loop is crochet and included in the final seam. The tufts are tied with cotton thread. 3" square. *Collection of the author.*

Trio of chair pincushions. The souvenir example is made of a piece of wooden branch. The seat is made of a tomato pincushion. Handwritten on the back rest is "Marvel Cave Notch Missouri." Marvel Cave was opened in 1894 as a tourist destination. The location later had the Silver Dollar City theme park built around the cave entrance. This pincushion was probably sold as a tourist souvenir. 2.5" × 5.5". The center chair is made from clothes pins, perhaps recycled broken pieces. The seat is a hand-sewn cushion tacked in place with thumb tacks. 2" × 2" × 4". The example on the right is possibly made of wood from cigar boxes. Part of a logo can be seen in the wood on one side. The posts are capped with decorative tacks. 2" × 2" × 4". *Collection of the author.*

Burgundy velvet pincushion made by covering a recycled food can. Embellished with tatting border and motifs. 3". Eight-petal flower with two colors of velvet. The center is mauve silk and the binding is a red dot cotton. The hanging loop is made of woven braid. The back is cotton covered paper board. 5". The velvet butterfly is embroidered in several colors with cotton floss. One side of the wings forms a needle book; the other side is a pin keep. 3" × 3". *Collection of the author.*

The silk pincushion with a flared top has a silk thread pompom on each corner. Each side of the cushion is a different color of silk. 2". The large pincushion bound in red wool is weighted in the interior base. The top is embellished with a crochet circle. 6" × 3" × 4". The pincushion in front has a brocade base and plaid top. 2" × 2.5". *Collection of the author.*

Paperboard chair covered in fabric. The curved back has a pocket for a thimble. The padded pincushion set lifts to reveal storage. To lift the cushion, a variegated thread covered ring is attached on the front. 3" × 6". *Antique Sewing Chair – Round Seat – 2012-35-387, Mingei International Museum, Gift of Pat L. Nickols.*

Detail of the front thread-covered ring on Antique Sewing Chair. Single crochet stitches in variegated thread cover the ring that is used as a handle to lift the seat of the chair. 1". *Detail: Antique Sewing Chair – Round Seat – 2012-35-387, Mingei International Museum, Gift of Pat L. Nickols.*

Sawdust-filled satin pincushion embellished with fish scales. The embroidery thread is possibly silk used in a stem stitch and French knots. 4" × 3". *Collection of the author.*

Detail of flowers and leaves formed by stitching fish scales to the silk ground fabric. The flowers are formed with several graduated sized scales with trimmed edges. The leaves are single scales cut to shape. 0.25" scales. *Collection of the author.*

The use of exotic embroidery materials was popular in the Victorian era. Fish scales, beetle wings, and feathers became components in embroideries. Embroidery was used to embellish many accessories, including pincushions and needle books. Volume 3 of *Cassell's Household Guide* of 1869 includes instructions for collecting, preparing, and tinting fish scales; embroidery attachment techniques; and patterns for articles like pincushions.[11] *The Needlework Dictionary* of 1882 suggests the scales be as fresh as possible. Fish with iridescent scales like carp, perch, and goldfish were recommended. The scales were scraped from the fish, tail to head. They were then soaked in cold water until soft, placed between plain papers, and pressed to dry. When dry, the scales were then punched with a sharp needle, making two small holes at the base. Instructions are provided for making birds, butterflies, daisies, chrysanthemums, and leaves.[12]

Pincushions were also made from repurposed broken household items, referred to as make-dos. The term "make-do" implies making do with what you have to fulfill a need. Softball-shaped pincushions were mounted on glass bases of broken candlesticks and oil lamps. Tins from canned food were cleaned and then covered with decorative fabrics and trim. Makers were highly creative in their combinations of repurposed household items and decorations.

Trio of make-do pincushions made from the bases of broken lamps and candle sticks. The wooden candlestick (middle) is topped with a half puzzle ball made of black velvet and red wool. Small wool pompoms cover the intersections where the melon shapes meet. 4" × 6". The brown velvet cushion (left) is faded from the original red. The velvet is covering a straw ball that shows much use. A matching hand-stitched strip of velvet band attaches the pincushion to the base. 4" × 7.5". The yarn-wrapped ball cushion (right) has an inserted accent of red ribbon. The yarn ball covers another rolled ball of yarn. It is attached to the glass base with ream cording in a beautifully knotted pattern. 5" × 8". *Collection of the author.*

Wool strawberry make-do mounted on a glass lamp base. The leaves are made from wool that has worn and now looks like embroidery. Hand sewn and gathered to the base. 3" × 8". *Collection of Tex Johnson.*

Make-do pincushion composed of a china doll head, wool remnants, and a lace apron. The apron is pinned in place with glass-headed pins. The arms and hands are all fabric, made like a cloth doll. The scale of the head to the body gives the example a rather primitive look. 4". *Collection of Tex Johnson.*

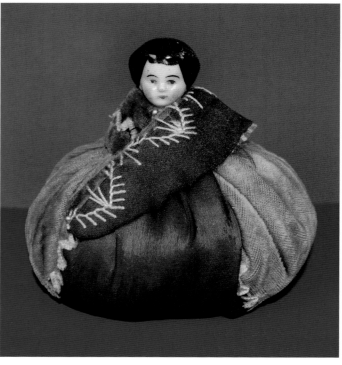

Make-do pincushion composed of a china doll head and crazy quilt remnants. 4". *Collection of Tex Johnson.*

Regional American styles of pincushions have been identified in Pennsylvania. Teardrop pincushions with pompom yarn corners and star pincushions were often made of fabric scraps. They frequently incorporate wool yarn embellishments. Ball styles include round shapes formed by connected squares. Puzzle balls were made of wool, cotton, or silk. Comprising thirty-six oval shapes, each set of three was joined to create a shape like the wedge of an orange.[13] The wedges were attached at the tips to form a ball. Bird shapes were also made, sometimes to perch on the top of wooden thread spools. Another style popular in Lancaster County is wool plush work combined with double cross stitch on canvas. There are also whimsy pincushions of beads strung on wire woven to form a cup holding a silk pincushion.[14]

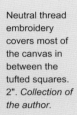

Graduated sizes of tufted pincushions. Sawdust filled, made in two and three bright wool colors in each cushion. Ranging in size from 8" down to 2". *Collection of the author.*

Neutral thread embroidery covers most of the canvas in between the tufted squares. 2". *Collection of the author.*

Silk pillow pincushion rimmed in lace, sitting in a raised beaded cup. The silk has shattered but the tiny ribbon bows remain. The small glass seed beads were threaded onto thin wire that was then woven to form the raised beaded cup. Said to be from Katarina Bucher Betchel of Pennsylvania. c. 1850. 2" × 3". *Collection of the author.*

Triangle drop pincushions in two sizes. The silk plaid example is made from three squares of silk and tufted at the corners with silk tassels. 3" per side. The knitted braid example is made from two short strips of braid forming triangular facets. The corner tassels are made of wool yarn. In both examples the seams are embroidered in feather stitching. 1" per side. *Collection of the author.*

Plaid silk bird with thread tassel embellishments. Hand sewn and embellished with feather stitch embroidery. 3" × 1.5" × 0.5". *Chester County Historical Society, West Chester, Pennsylvania.*

Sculptural pincushions made by folding squares of fabric on the diagonal and sewing triangles. The straight edges are tacked together in the center to form a circle of triangles. Made in a variety of scraps, there are twelve triangles made in six different fabrics, embellished with wool pompoms. The center example is dark-blue velvet made of six triangles, 3" × 2.5". The colorful example on the right is made of eight triangles in four prints, 3.5" × 3.5". The top is a fabric ruffle and strip of fabric for hanging. 3.5" × 3.5". *Collection of the author.*

Bottom view of the sculptural pincushions. The example on the left has a small circle of fabric hand tacked over the center. *Collection of the author.*

Light-brown and black velvet star pincushion. Black silk bows embellish each light brown star tip. A center button tacks the front and back together. Filled with a light and soft material. A black silk hanging ribbon is in the center. 9" × 0.5". *Collection of the author.*

Cotton-stuffed eight-pointed star with hand-sewn seams. The center is hand tacked with a few hand stitches. The attached note reads, "Mothers & Mary B. from some lady in Harwood About 1850." 5". *Collection of the author.*

Four-pointed shape in cotton pincushion bordered in an applied silk ruffle. The blue ruffle is tacked in the center. The hanging ribbon is hand sewn on a center side. Each point has a thread tassel. Firm filling, possibly cotton. 3" × 3" × 0.5". *Collection of the author.*

Pieced six-pointed star pincushion made of twelve pieces of fabric in six prints. Wool tufts of yarn embellish the tips and valleys. 7" × 0.5". *Collection of the author.*

Tufted detail of six-pointed star. The yarn was looped through the cotton fabric, wrapped, and bound in a thread band. The wool yarn was unraveled creating a wavy, feather-like texture. 0.5". *Collection of the author.*

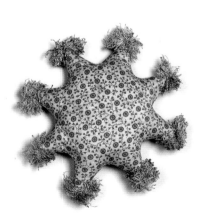

Eight-pointed red and off-white cotton print pincushion. Each point is tipped with a thread tassel. The record indicates the tassels were originally green, now faded to beige. The handwritten note with the pincushion reads, "Grandmother Brecht's Mother's – 101 years old in May 1926." According to the donor, this would indicate the pincushion belonged to Catherine Ernst Brecht (1825–?), wife of John G. Brecht (1806–1881). They resided in Montgomery County, Pennsylvania. 7". *Schwenkfelder Library & Heritage Center, Pennsburg, Pennsylvania.*

Square pillows assembled to resemble a sphere. Stuffed wool and cotton fabrics. Wool pompoms are stitched at each corner. Wool yarn hanging loop. 4" diameter. *Collection of Tex Johnson.*

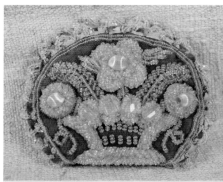

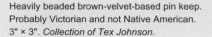

Heavily beaded brown-velvet-based pin keep. Probably Victorian and not Native American. 3" × 3". *Collection of Tex Johnson.*

Detail of layered beading on the top edge of a finished pincushion. Possibly Native American beaded for the tourist trade. Clear glass seed beads. *Collection of Tex Johnson.*

Native Americans on reservations beaded pincushions for the tourist market. As early as 1830 there were reports of the Seneca in New York creating beautiful pincushions. The Iroquois beadwork designs also catered to tourists visiting near the reservations. One visitor recorded, "tastefully . . . wrought! The same pattern is never repeated; the ornaments are poetically conceived, and executed with a richness of imagination which our manufacturers lack, accustomed as they are, to reproduce a thousand times the same design. To the children of the Great Spirit, the flowers, the birds, and the trees, speak a language, which transcribe in the charming figures, more pleasing to our eye than any artificial invention."[15] Native

Americans sold their goods at concession stands around Niagara Falls, Goat Island, and Seneca, New York. Some of the designs are very similar to published designs in ladies magazines of the same era. It is unclear where the designs originated. One theory is that missionaries showed the Native Americans how to adapt their beading techniques to please the tourist markets. Other beadwork pincushions have floral embroidery motifs executed in moose hair.[16] Another style is similar to ceramic half doll pincushions. The Native Americans incorporated a colorful beaded doll on top of a velvet skirt-shaped base embellished with beads. The skirt is stuffed to form the pincushion and gathers at the waist of the beaded doll.

Native American beaded half doll, possibly made for the tourist market. Red velvet base with beads and sequins. The half doll is beaded in detail with tiny seed beads. A separate necklace and braid in the back add finishing touches. 3" × 4". *Collection of the author.*

Heart-shaped beaded pincushion on a red wool base. Possibly Native American beaded for the tourist trade. 3" × 3". *Collection of Tex Johnson.*

Six-petal beaded pincushion on a black velvet ground. Possibly Native American beaded for the tourist trade. 4". *Collection of Tex Johnson.*

The 1895 Montgomery Ward mail order catalog lists white metal pincushions with plush covers made in the shape of a shoe or basket. They were included in the catalog over several years. With postage, the pincushions sold for about fifteen cents.

Mosaic-pieced pincushions are composed of small pieces of fabric combined in a pleasing pattern to create a pillow. They are usually hand sewn; sometimes the fabric is wrapped over paper. The mosaic cushions were filled with wool, crushed nutshells, or sawdust.

Diamond silk paper-pieced pincushion. The placement of the blue diamonds creates an optical illusion sometimes referred to as "tumbling blocks." The outer ruffle is lightly tacked to the outer edge and not included in the seam. A ruffled circle is tacked at each corner. The attached note reads, "Cushion that Bessie's mother was making when she died Grandma Pottinger finished it." 5" × 8". *Collection of the author.*

Cotton, hand-pieced flowers made of seven hexagons, 0.75" per side. Small hanging loop of cotton fabric at the top. Stuffed in soft material, possibly cotton or wool. 3.5" across. *Collection of the author.*

Cotton, hand-pieced quarter-square triangle embellished with thread tassels. Stuffed in soft material, possibly cotton or wool. 2.5" per side. *Collection of the author.*

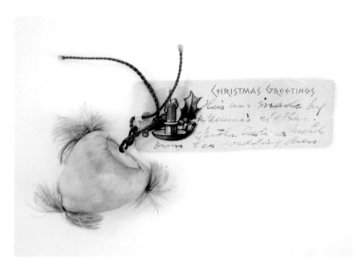

Hand-sewn heart-shaped velvet pincushions, firmly stuffed with sawdust. The trio of cushions is attached through the loops. 3" × 4". The large brown pin-cushion is tied with a velvet bow. 4" × 5". The two smaller examples are small enough to slide onto a child's thumb. The lower left example is theorem painted velvet. 1.5" × 2" and 2" × 2.5". *Collection of the author.*

Hand-sewn silk pincushion filled with wool. Fine wool thread tassels at each corner. The thread between the points is wrapped in heavier thread. The attached gift tag reads, "Christmas Greetings, This was made by Williams's mother. Martha Audra Nichols (sic) from her wedding dress." On the back is written, "Your Great Grandmother." 1" heart, 1" × 2.5" tag. *Collection of the author.*

Blue velvet heart pincushion with a red silk bow embellishment. Firmly filled. 1.25" × 1.5". *Collection of Kathryn G. Lesieur.*

Heart-shaped pincushions, symbolizing love, were popular since they were often given as a gift. The *Godey's Lady's Book* in January of 1834 provided instructions for this style. Two triangle shapes of linen were sewn together, leaving a small opening at the top for stuffing. The stuffing was bran, wool, or flannel. The reader was informed that cotton would not do. Once the opening was closed, the pincushion was covered in decorative fabric like silk or velvet. The two upper corners were then firmly tacked together. This formed the shape of the heart. Some sizes are perfect to be worn on the thumb like a ring. Small sizes could be made and filled with emery. Ribbons for hanging or embellishment were some-times added where the points came together.

Wooden shapes were also made into pincushions. Many are one-of-a-kind carved miniature versions of practical items like shoes and food items. Part of the wooden form is hollowed out and the pincushion placed in the hole.

Leather was used for pincushions. As pins would not easily pierce the leather, a top and bottom shape were attached with a silk ribbon. The silk ribbon gave the pincushion about a half-inch depth. The pins were inserted into the side of the cushion.

Carved wooden shoe with finely painted details. The front has silk ribbon added for the bow and lace. The top silk velvet pincushion was well used. 4" × 2" × 3". *Collection of Tex Johnson.*

The bottom of the shoe is dated 1900 and was made by Lucy Fletcher. The letters are scratched into the wood and painted in black. 4" × 2" × 3". *Collection of Tex Johnson.*

Painted silk slipper–shaped pincushion with attached emery. 2.5" × 1". *Collection of Kathryn G. Lesieur.*

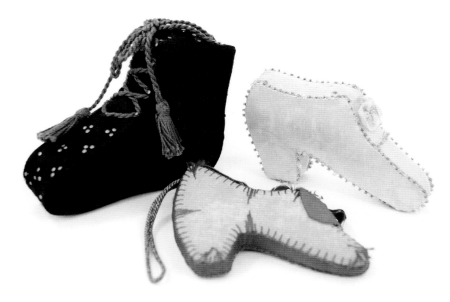

Trio of fabric-covered paperboard. The gusset is made from silk ribbon. The pins are stuck in the silk, sometimes in a pattern. The pins are sometimes stuck in the seam where the fabric and ribbon pieces meet. The faux shoe laces are sometimes twisted cord, ribbons or made of embroidery stitches. 4" – 3". *Collection of the author.*

Wooden shoe grouping, all with faux laces. In some examples the lace is threaded through an actual hole. In other examples, the ribbon or thread hooks around nail heads. The pincushions are firmly stuffed with wool or cotton. 4" × 3". *Collection of the author.*

Matched pair of painted shoes, no left or right. Decorative flower motifs are framed by white and gold straight-line painting. The green velvet cushions are well worn. The red silk bows are possibly original. 4" × 2.5". *Collection of the author.*

Decoratively painted wooden shoe pincushions. The black pair are glossy painted wing tips mounted on a painted base. 7" × 5" × 5". The white shoe has a replacement cushion and no base. 5" × 2" × 3.5". The red shoe is mounted on a matching heart base painted in the same colors and motifs. 7" × 4" × 5". *Collection of Kathryn G. Lesieur.*

One-of-a-kind wooden horseshoe pincushion topping a leg stand, ending with a shoe resting on a heart base. Red and gold paint add detailed embellishment of lacing and leaves. 3" × 4". *Collection of Kathryn G. Lesieur.*

Leather pincushions in a variety of shapes. The tops and bottoms are joined with silk ribbon stitched to the binding. The pins are inserted into the silk ribbon sides. The heart-shaped cushion doubles as a needle case with a hinged bottom. 3" – 4". *Collection of Kathryn G. Lesieur.*

Boot lace detail, showing the yellow thread as it wraps around black glass pin heads and crosses in the center. Less than 0.25" between pins. *Collection of the author*

The yellow-laced, pin-wrapped, leather boot pincushion is topped in silk. The top edge is ruffled in silk ribbon. 9" × 4" × 2". The small red leather boot has a red ribbon insert used in a side gusset. All hand sewn in fine silk thread. 3" × 0.5" × 2". The brass button boot also has an ivory silk ribbon gusset and a large bow at the boot top and toe. The leather sides are embellished with machine stitching. 6" × 3.5" × 0.5". *Collection of the author*.

Pair of shoe pincushions joined with a ribbon at the heels. Three clear acetate shapes are crocheted together to form the shoes. The toes are embellished with hand-painted flowers. The shoes are filled with silk like cushions to hold pins. Each shoe is 3" long. *Collection of the author.*

Leather pincushions in a variety of styles. The green velvet double-ended example is bound in the center with leather. The round disc has the same leather on both sides, joined with a yellow ribbon. The bell shape is bound and joined in blue silk ribbon. 0.5" × 4". *Collection of the author.*

Leather shoe pincushion with leather sole. Embellished with beads and a silk bow. The red wool pincushion cover is firmly filled. 4" long. *Collection of the author.*

A double-sided pin ball composed of a cotton ground with decorative silk embroidery. One side consists of a glazed brown cotton base with a floral motif in blue, pink, dark-green, gold, peach, and light-green silk embroidery. Encircling the pin ball's center is a 0.5" wide champagne color silk ribbon with peach silk herringbone embroidery. The ribbon is outlined in gold silk. 2.75" diameter. *Schwenkfelder Library & Heritage Center, Pennsburg, Pennsylvania.*

A double-sided pin ball composed of a cotton ground with decorative silk embroidery. A glazed brown cotton ground with an eight-point star comprising red, green, and blue silk and outlined in gold silk with a surrounding gold and peach silk border. Encircling the pin ball's center is a 0.5" wide champagne color silk ribbon with peach silk herringbone embroidery. The ribbon is outlined in gold silk. The maker is unknown. 2.3" diameter. *Schwenkfelder Library & Heritage Center, Pennsburg, Pennsylvania.*

Embroidery pieces ready to be made into pin balls. The linen examples still hold the basting lines marking where to stitch. The brown cotton ground is embroidered with silk flowers. It has been trimmed in preparation for covering the ball. 4.5" across. *Chester County Historical Society, West Chester, Pennsylvania.*

### Pin Balls

Pin balls, round in shape like a tennis ball, range in size from 1.5" to 3.5" in diameter. They were made joining two flat halves of finely knitted, embroidered, or woven needlework over a stuffed form. The two flat pieces were gathered up and joined in the center. They were firmly stuffed with cotton or wool; the center seam was covered with a metal ring or trim. They were popular additions to a chatelaine or could hang at the waist on an independent cord or ribbon. Some examples have the year and initials of the maker.

Thread-wrapped pin balls were made beginning in the eighteenth century.[17] It is possible they were influenced by seventeenth-century Asian temari balls. Early American examples are made of silk, or silk and metallic threads. The threads are wrapped and wound onto thread spokes to create patterns. Later examples are made of wool yarn or pearl cotton. Many examples are wrapped to the outer edge, with the circumference wrapped in silk ribbon. In some examples a ribbon extends several inches above the ball for hanging.

Pieced cotton, wool, and silk fabric pin balls were created in Lancaster County, Pennsylvania, from 1830 to 1900. They are colorful and frequently included additional trim like rickrack.[18] These were possibly made as an extension of quilting since some examples used a design called "nine patch" in quilting.

Crazy-quilt pin balls were made by covering a firmly rolled ball of cotton or wool. The small pieces of black velvet were laid on the preformed ball. Seams were hand sewn and decorative stitching was added over the seams.

Queen stitch pin ball with silver finishing pieces. One side of the chatelaine hook is heart-shaped; the other is engraved "J. Brinton 1795." 2" ball, 1" × 2.3" clip. *Chester County Historical Society, West Chester, Pennsylvania.*

Pin ball embroidered in Irish stitch. Each side has a cross-stitched square in the center. One side has the initials MH in the center of the square. The other side has a year partially worn off. The numbers "180_" remain. 2" diameter. *Chester County Historical Society, West Chester, Pennsylvania.*

A double-sided pin ball composed of brown velvet ground with decorative silk embroidery. One side consists of a dark-brown velvet ground with a grid pattern framed by a wreath motif in dark-green, red, orange, pink, and light-green silk. Encircling the pin ball's center is a 3/8" wide green cotton tape with orange silk herringbone embroidery. Attached at the top is a 22.00" long torn and knotted loop made of the same green cotton tape. Made by Lucina S. Schultz (1875–1892), as a young girl. She died at the age of seventeen. Lucina was the daughter of Joel S. (1832–1900) and Sarah K. (Schultz) Schultz (1836–1920), of East Greenville, Montgomery County, Pennsylvania. The ball is 2.25" diameter. *Schwenkfelder Library & Heritage Center, Pennsburg, Pennsylvania.*

A double-sided pin ball composed of velvet ground brown with a flower motif in the same-colored silk embroidery. Encircling the pin ball's center is a 3/8" wide green cotton tape with orange silk herringbone embroidery. Attached at the top is a 22.00" long torn and knotted loop made of the same green cotton tape. Attached at the top is a 22.00" long torn and knotted loop made of the same green cotton tape. Made by Lucina S. Schultz (1875–1892), as a young girl. She died at the age of seventeen. Lucina was the daughter of Joel S. (1832–1900) and Sarah K. (Schultz) Schultz (1836–1920), of East Greenville, Montgomery County, Pennsylvania. The ball is 2.25" diameter. *Schwenkfelder Library & Heritage Center, Pennsburg, Pennsylvania.*

Pin ball covered in the same cotton on both sides. Center is covered in homemade woven tape and pinned in place. 2" × 4". *Collection of the author.*

A double-sided pin ball composed of wool embroidery. This side consists of a light-green wool ground with an Irish stitch carnation motif in red, pink, yellow, orange, and cream wool; the year "1776" and the initials "S.K." were worked in cream wool block letters. Encircling the pin ball's center is a 0.625" wide salmon-pink silk ribbon that has been wrapped around the pin ball and pinned in place. Made by or for Susanna B. (Yeakle) Kriebel (1750–1808), wife of Andrew Y. Kriebel (1748–1830). They resided in Lower Salford Township, Montgomery County, Pennsylvania. The ball is 2" diameter. *Schwenkfelder Library & Heritage Center, Pennsburg, Pennsylvania.*

The reverse side consists of an exposed natural linen ground (due to loss of embroidery) with diamond harlequin design in multicolored wool. *Schwenkfelder Library & Heritage Center, Pennsburg, Pennsylvania.*

A double-sided pin ball composed of a silk ground with decorative embroidery. One side consists of a quartered ground comprised of brown, green, and blue silk base with a floral motif embroidered in silk in each quarter. Encircling the pin ball's center is a 3/8" wide peach silk ribbon with green silk herringbone embroidery. Unknown maker. The ball is 2" diameter. *Schwenkfelder Library & Heritage Center, Pennsburg, Pennsylvania.*

A double-sided pin ball composed of a silk ground with decorative embroidery consists of a quartered ground comprising brown, blue, and pink silk with a floral motif also embroidered in silk in each quarter. Encircling the pin ball's center is a 3/8" wide peach silk ribbon with green silk herringbone embroidery. Unknown maker. The ball is 2" diameter. *Schwenkfelder Library & Heritage Center, Pennsburg, Pennsylvania.*

Trio of pin balls showing red silk, queen stitch, and cotton covers in a variety of sizes. The two largest are banded in silver with hanging loops for a waist hook. The smallest is banded and made to hang from a ribbon. 2" – 4". *Collection of Tex Johnson.*

Variety of pin balls displayed in an antique redware bowl. *Collection of Kathryn G. Lesieur.*

Thread-wrapped ball in six thread colors around eight thread spokes. Both sides are wrapped in the same pattern. Banded around the outer edge with silk ribbon with a herringbone stitch over the top. 2" diameter. *Collection of the author.*

Brightly colored yarn and pearl cotton wrapped thread balls. Each with eight spokes and wrapped the same on each side. Each has a small yarn hanging loop. 2" – 3". *Collection of the author.*

Mosaic wool pin ball with seam covered in rickrack. Similar styles have been found in Lancaster County, Pennsylvania. 2" diameter. *Collection of the author.*

Crazy quilt pieced and embroidered pin ball. Pieces of wool, velvet, and silk fabrics covering a soft inner ball. 4" diameter. *Collection of the author.*

Pin ball made of tiny squares and triangles of cotton fabric pieced together around a globe-shaped sphere. An embroidered hanging loop made of red checked fabric is attached at the top. 2.5". *Courtesy Winterthur Museum, pin ball made by Anna H. Bomberger, 1860-1880, Warwick Township, Lancaster County, Pennsylvania; cotton, linen. Museum purchase with funds provided by the Henry Francis du Pont Collectors Circle, 2013.31.181.*

Thread-wrapped pin ball. Finely wrapped and banded around the middle with silk ribbon. The top of the blue ribbon is embroidered with a herringbone stitch in yellow thread. 2" diameter. *Collection of Kathryn G. Lesieur.*

Silk puzzle ball embellished with metallic thread at the outer seam lines. Small clusters of stitches embellish each intersection. A silk gold ribbon is at the top for hanging. 3" diameter. *Collection of the author.*

Pincushions formed over paperboard shapes. The large example is black wool bound in red wool braided tape embellished with a black crochet motif. It is weighted at the bottom and filled with wool at the top for pins. The tasseled example is made of silk fabric with silk thread tassels at each corner. The small example has a base shape similar to a thread winder. Two different fabrics form the top and bottom. 2" – 5". *Collection of the author.*

Velvet pincushion and pin ball connected with wool yarn. The seams of the ball are embellished with white herringbone stitches. 2" diameter ball. 2" × 4" pincushion. *Collection of the author.*

Silk puzzle half ball with embroidery over seams. Red ribbon embellishment at the top. Evidence of use as a pincushion remains in the silk fabric. 5" diameter. *Collection of the author.*

Woven poplar Shaker pincushion embellished with a red bow. The edges are finished in white kid leather. The cushion is made from red velvet. 5" diameter. *Collection of Tex Johnson.*

Peach or orange pin ball made from wool braided tape. Tied at the top with wool yarn, the fringe is formed by the unraveled braid ends. Each seam is embroidered with light-blue thread. Possibly filled with wool. 3" × 4". *Collection of the author.*

Crazy quilt pincushion sometimes referred to as a scissor rest or bodkin holder. Silk fabrics and embroidered seams. The tassels at the ends are unraveled silk fabrics. 6" long. *Collection of the author.*

Pin balls formed with pentagon shapes. Cotton-covered papers are hand stitched together to form balls. Pins are inserted into the seams, with only the pin heads visible. The final size of the ball is determined by the size of the side of the pentagon. 1.5" diameter. *Collection of the author.*

Examples of pin balls made from triangles. The largest example features two pin sizes. Glass-headed pins are at each point. The smaller pins are inserted along each seam line. The sides of the triangles are slightly concave, giving the final shape dramatic curves. 5" diameter. The tasseled example (left) has silk threads at the intersection of the silk triangle points. 3" diameter. The small example (right) is embellished with a single bow. 2" diameter. *Collection of the author.*

### Almost Balls

Later American versions of the pin ball were made as described in the 1855 *Godey's Lady's Book*, Vol. 51, page 168. Called a Harlequin Ball, it was made of velvet, silk, and satin shapes. The maker was to select bright colors as varied as possible. "Using twelve pentagon pieces, five are sewn round, one half of each; the points of every two meet and are sewed together. The space between is filled with four star pointed and one square piece—all different colors." The shapes were complex and would be difficult to join tiny inset seams in silk. An early twentieth-century pin ball variation is very similar, using pentagons but leaving out the more complex diamond and square shape.

Using a paper foundation, mosaic-paper-pieced techniques created other shapes, not quite balls. The shapes were formed by hand sewing together pentagons and triangles. The fabric is laced over the paper shape from the back with sewing thread. The paper-covered pieces are then hand sewn together to form the three-dimensional shape. The twenty triangle pieces join to form a regular convex icosahedron. The twelve pentagon pieces join to form a regular dodecahedron. The geometric shapes were sometimes filled with objects to make sounds; bells, tiny rattles, or dried peanuts in shells. Some instructions advise the use of odds and ends of wool. The seams are stuck with minnikin pins. Minnikins are the smallest of pins, less than half an inch long and four hundredths of an inch in diameter. Beads were sometimes added to the pins for added embellishment.

Multi-colored pin ball formed by hand sewing together fabric-wrapped paper triangles. The pins are inserted in the seam lines. Only the head of the pin is visible. 1.125" diameter. *Chester County Historical Society, West Chester, Pennsylvania.*

PIN-CUSHION.

nd of certain use. The cotton-box befor

Page from *Godey's Lady's Book* illustrating the pin ball made from paper piecing. The illustration shows the complex piecing required for the pattern to work. Published in *Godey's Lady's Book*, Vol. 51, page 168. *Collection of the author.*

Instruction page published in *Godey's Lady's Book*, Vol. 51, page 168. The illustration is all the maker had available to create the pincushion. No templates were provided. *Collection of the author.*

The HARLEQUIN BALL is a pin-cushion in patch-work, made of velvet, silk, and satin, in as many bright and varied colors as possible. The principal pieces, of which there are twelve, are pentagons, or five-sided figures. Five are sewed round, one for each half; the points of every two meet, and are sewed together, and the space between is filled in four pointed and one square piece, all also of different colors. Care should be taken that these colors blend well together. The top should be black, or some other tint that will harmonize with everything, whilst each one should be arranged with reference to those on each side of it. Green, amber, rich blue, claret, and violet, will go well together in the order in which we give them; or the claret and amber might change places. But put the violet in the place of the amber and the effect is destroyed; as, though it harmonizes with green, it does not with blue. When finished, it should be stuffed with ends of wool, and the joinings stuck with minikin pins.

# Thimbles

Thimbles are available in a variety of materials, including carved stone, leather, wood, mother-of-pearl, tortoiseshell, taqua and coquille nut, horn, bone, sterling and plated silver, brass, bronze, steel, gold, bone, and porcelain. Combinations of materials embellished with jewels are also used. The first thimbles were probably animal skin wrapped around the finger for protection. Leather thimbles are still made and used today. The first bronze thimbles were used around 3000 BCE.[1] More-recent materials include plastics, aluminum, and silicone.

There are four basic parts to a thimble. The top or dome is the closed end of the thimble. The sidewall of a thimble is sometimes textured. Texture is added by knurling. Knurling is a process where texture is added to a metal object to increase friction; this assists in picking an item up. However, not all thimbles are textured. On the sidewall, sometimes an additional band on the lower portion of the thimble is included where decoration or embellishment is added. Below the thimble band is sometimes a rim. The rim is a circular opening at the base of the thimble. Not all thimbles have rims.[2]

Children as young as three in the nineteenth century had thimbles. The book *Needlework for Student Teachers* provides lesson plans for what they term "Babies," defined as three- to five-year-olds. They are instructed to thread needles and wear thimbles in Step 1. The instruction is very specific. The thimble finger had to push the needle through the fabric up to the eye of the needle. The children were expected to darn their own stockings by age five.[3]

In colonial America, one of an apprentice silversmith's first tasks was to make a thimble. The style was tall tapered and utilized a steel cap. Thimbles were made individually and were not manufactured in quantities in America until 1794. American Benjamin Halstead established the first American thimble factory in 1794. He is likely the first *silversmith* who sought to specialize in thimble manufacturing versus thimble making. Halstead advertised in 1794 that he could manufacture to perfection and citizens should buy from him in support of American manufacturing interests. Prior to this, Americans relied heavily on imports from Europe.[4]

Brass thimbles were traded by Lewis and Clark with Native Americans in expeditions beginning in 1804. Needles and other sewing supplies were in the trader's personal inventory in addition to trade goods. The native Indians were more apt to pierce the thimble and then string a bead in the thimble for a tinkling necklace rather than use the thimble as a sewing aid. The brass thimbles may have been imports from Europe, possibly purchased in Saint Louis prior to embarking on the journey west.[5]

The Ketcham & McDougall Company was established in 1832 on Long Island, New York. In the mid-nineteenth century, manufacturing thimbles was their primary focus. Their factory was a group of three six-story buildings with a separate retail store. The retail store was known as "The Thimble House."[6] They stopped producing thimbles in 1932.[7] They are still in business today, making scientific instrumentation.

In 1839, George Washington Simons started a thimble company in Philadelphia, Pennsylvania. His brother joined him and they called the business Simons Brothers Company. He was also a business leader who embraced new technologies. By 1860, the company grew to employ sixty people. Still in business today, they manufacture jewelry, thimbles, and emblematic pieces in precious metals.[8] The Simons Brothers thimbles are fairly similar with dimpled sides and a decorative band. Their gold and silver thimbles were marked with "S" set in a shield on the interior of the thimble. Their alloy thimbles are trademarked S.B.C. set within the outline of a thimble on the interior of the thimble.[9]

In 1842, a protective tariff was passed that levied a thirty percent duty on all imported gold and silverware. This tariff helped the American precious metal industry compete with imports.[10]

In 1853 Henry Muhr emigrated from Germany and set up a watch repair shop. By 1892 his jewelry business, including thimbles, had grown to include his sons and two US locations, as well

Examples of mass-produced brass thimbles. The smallest example is a child's size. Children as young as three were taught to use thimbles. 0.5". *Collection of the author.*

Sterling thimble with decorative bands. The interior has the makers mark. 0.5". *Collection of the author.*

Leather thimble designed to cover the end of the finger, leaving the fingernail uncovered. Hand gathered with a small leather strip added to help secure the thimble. 1". *Collection of the author.*

Thimble with side attachment to assist in threading sewing needles. The side bar slides up, as does the hair-thin wire used to thread through the needle eye. When finished, all of the pieces slide down flush with the end of the thimble. Marked "Made in U.S.A." 0.5" × 1". *Collection of the author.*

Plastic and aluminum advertising thimbles. Advertising on thimbles was not limited to sewing-related topics. Companies include coal and fuel, flour, life insurance, and hosiery. They were inexpensively made and often given away free as promotional items. 0.5". *Collection of the author.*

as an office in Antwerp, Belgium. As H. Muhr's Sons, they manufactured watch cases, jewelry, and thimbles.[11]

Nathan Stern was a Muhr employee; by 1868 he established his own jewelry business that included thimbles. By 1871 he moved his company to New York. At that time the company showed forty-six patterns of thimbles in their catalog. His sons joined him in the business, which became known as Stern Brothers. Their trademark was a small "B" and "C" enclosed in a larger block letter "S." In 1913 Stern Brothers merged with the Goldstein Company. The new company became Goldstein, Stern and Company. The trade mark changed to a block "G" enclosing a smaller "S" and "C."[12]

There are several characteristics for identifying American thimbles. They are generally shorter with more-squared-off tops than examples from other countries. The size markings are small and precise. Their designs are conservative and the finish is high quality.[13]

American thimbles often have markings that are helpful in identifying thimbles. Unlike European countries, America has no hallmark or dating system for precious metals. American thimbles have patents, which are sometimes stamped on the thimbles. Another distinction for American thimbles is the precise size stamps visible on the exterior band. Other American marks of interest are .925 markings. In the 1860s the word "sterling" was introduced to indicate 92.5 percent fine-metal content. Some silver thimbles may be marked "coin," which is ninety percent pure. The term "coin" comes from the nineteenth-century practice by silversmiths to melt down silver coins to make small articles. The American silver marking system does not have a letter date; it has a sterling mark and a manufacturer's trademark.[14]

Many women prefer to own more than one thimble. For fine white work, some needle workers prefer light natural-substance thimbles like bone or ivory. For heavy work like wool darning a thick, heavy thimble is preferred.

There are numerous patents for thimbles, and new thimble patents continue today. Design variations include changes to the cap end, open ends with added thread cutters, and needle pulling and pushing devices, as well as shapes to accommodate fingernails. Some new thimbles are adhesive metal or plastic ovals applied directly to the skin like a bandage.

In the twentieth century advertising thimbles were popular in America, a recurring theme for sewing tools. Advertising thimbles were produced in America more than in any other country, particularly political thimbles. Advertisements were diverse and focused on products for the homemaker. For example, head lice remedies, fuel oil, and shoe repair services. Thimbles were also printed with political campaign messages for candidates and government promotions to buy war bonds. Door-to-door salesmen used them to leverage a potential customer's time listening to a sales pitch. The thimbles were cheaply made and were ordered from manufacturers in large quantities. An order for one million brass thimbles was not unusual.

Celluloid, Bakelite, and other plastics were popular in America from the late nineteenth century through today. In addition to advertising, ladies would sometimes add their own painting to decorate the smooth lower thimble band. Popular themes were cupids, flowers, and pastoral scenes from sterling thimbles. The advertising or painting easily wore off with use.

Some high-quality thimbles were used for advertising promotions. Ladies' magazines offered thimble premiums in an effort to boost subscriptions. In 1923, *Needlecraft Magazine* offered a lovely sterling silver thimble to readers who brought in four new magazine subscriptions. Lipton Tea offered a silver thimble if customers sent in a specified number of package labels.

Wooden set of nuts attached on a large leaf. The leaf is carved from a single piece of wood. The interior of one walnut is concave and holds pins. The other walnut has a velvet-covered thimble post. 10" × 3". *Collection of the author.*

Wooden carved snail with brass-hinged shell lid. The thimble sits on a red velvet covered post inside the snail shell. 4.5" × 2". *Collection of the author.*

## Thimble Holders

There are many forms of storage for thimbles. Thimble holders were made for home storage and the safe transportation of the small treasures. Thimble storage containers were often very creative in shape and form. They also protected the thimble from damage or loss. In early household inventories the holders are often referred to as caskets. It is unclear if the small caskets were specifically made to hold the thimbles or were found to be the right size for a thimble, jewelry, or other small treasures. The holders were made in a wide variety of materials, including silver, gold, brass, cast metal, wood, vegetable ivory (nuts), basketry, tortoiseshell, glass, ivory, leather, mother-of-pearl, beaded work, transferware, and plastics like celluloid. It is possible precious metal thimbles may have had custom holders made at the same time as the thimble.

The holders are sometimes referred to as thimble buckets, cages, or cases. A thimble bucket is open at the top like a water bucket and is sometimes velvet lined for protecting the surface. The bucket is one of the least-secure storage options because the open top allows it to easily slip out. A thimble cage is worn on a chain suspended on a chatelaine or necklace. The cage can be closed which secures the thimble from slipping out.

A popular thimble case depicts walnut shapes in metal or wood. The metal walnuts are often lined in velvet or other soft materials. They often include additional small sewing supplies like pins and needles. The nut is hinged on one end and closes with a small loop on the other end.

Wooden walnut holders are carved on the top and sides with a flat bottom for sitting on a table. The lid opens with a metal hinge and uses a small post that helps hold the case closed. The interiors are sometimes fabric lined. Some styles feature a stem or other realistic addition to the carved walnut shell. Other wood carvings also incorporated designs that could hold thimbles.

Wooden carved thimble holders. The snail shell opens to hold the thimble. The walnuts are stained dark and light. There is some variation on the shape of the shell and stem. The hinged shell lids open to hold the thimble in a small velvet-lined hole. 4.5" – 3". *Collection of the author.*

Wooden carved antelope standing on a rock shape. Painted in detail with glass eyes. The base holds a pincushion and thimble holder indention. 5" tall. *Collection of the author.*

89

Shell and brass pedestal basket. Possible a repurposed salt cellar it is the perfect size to hold a thimble. 2". *Collection of the author.*

Set of brass-banded shell thimble holders. Natural luster creates the beauty in the shell covers. The beaded and hinged brass bands are hand applied creating a finished edge. 5" × 1". *Collection of the author.*

Detail of the beaded brass band and two handles at the rim of the shell holder. 0.25" brass band closed. *Collection of the author.*

Shell and egg-shaped thimble holders made of brass or mother-of-pearl were hinged with brass closures. The edges are brass covered with some variations in pattern, clasp, and hinge styles. The shells come in a wide variety of sizes. Some were sold as souvenirs, marked to commemorate vacation destinations. The brass holders were durable but could tarnish and soil needlework. The shell styles were clean but fragile, subject to cracks and breaking.

Vegetable ivory thimble holders are carved from tagua or coquille nuts to simulate more expensive ivory. Because the nuts are small in size, more than one nut is used to make components for thimble holders. The nuts start out colored like ivory, darkening to shades of brown with age.

Some thimble holders are components of larger sewing sets. An example is the sweetgrass miniature-basket thimble holders. Sweetgrass baskets were woven by Native Americans for the tourist market. Other pieces in the sets include woven scissor sheaths, pincushions, and needle books.

Sewing kits and sets often included thimble holders in their design. Thimbles were easily lost in sewing boxes and baskets and so warranted a specific location for storage. Having a separate thimble holder kept the thimble safe and within quick reach for immediate use. Leather sewing rolls often have a small leather loop for the thimble to rest in an inverted position in the corner. Sewing rolls sometime have fabric-lined openings the size of a thimble for safe keeping.

American retail sources for thimbles included jewelers and pharmacies. They packaged the thimbles in tiny boxes that were sometimes velvet lined. The thimble didn't stand on its end; it lay on its side, often with a curved paper support. The paper boxes were not intended for long-term storage. Other styles include a leather or shagreen fish skin–covered box with a tiny latch. Some boxes were also covered in silk or velvet, making an elegant container for gift presentations. The thimble owner often opted to move the thimble to a durable thimble holder or directly into the sewing box.

Brass egg-shaped thimble holder with petite chain handle. The brass is embossed with Egyptian themed motifs. 2" long. *Collection of the author.*

Interior detail of lined thimble holder examples. The red velvet example is padded and fitted for the thimble on one side. The green velvet example is lined to provide some padding to the thimble. 1.5" – 3" long. *Collection of the author.*

Thimble holders from silk ribbon chatelaines. This style of chatelaine is worn at the neck. The three-sided silk-covered paper examples are left unsewn on one edge. By pressing the tip, the unsewn seam opens and the thimble can be accessed. The crochet example has just enough tension to hold the thimble in place. 2.25" long. *Collection of the author.*

Souvenir ship made from seashells. The main shell sail is decoratively painted with flowers and lettered "From Niagara Falls." The flag, anchor, post, roping, and figurehead at the bow and base are brass. Inside the boat is a fabric-covered post for the thimble to rest. 2.5". *Collection of the author.*

Figurehead from the box of the thimble holder ship. Probably intended to be a likeness of Neptune's face. 0.25" across. *Collection of the author.*

Trio of three-sided thimble holders. Each one is made of three pointed ovals hand sewn together in a buttonhole stitch. One side is left unsewn for the opening. The blue velvet example is embroidered in a feather stitch. The points are embellished with a bow. The green silk example is lined in pink and has a pink bow in the middle of the opening. The small example is heavily embroidered on all three sides. 6" – 3". *Collection of Kathryn G. Lesieur.*

Interior of a fitted wooden sewing box. Compartments include a pincushion, covered storage, bobbin shelf, and thimble holders. *Collection of the author.*

Metal wall sewing compendium with metal arm to hold most any thimble size. The soft metal is bent to size for the thimble. 1" thimble. *Collection of the author.*

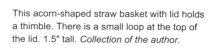

This acorn-shaped straw basket with lid holds a thimble. There is a small loop at the top of the lid. 1.5" tall. *Collection of the author.*

Silk-covered paper thimble holders. The brown silk example is made of ten diamond shapes, hand sewn together except for one side. The open side is the opening for the thimble. Each point is embellished with a blue silk bow. 3" long. The cream and beige example is hand painted. The pointed oval shapes are hand sewn together except for one side. The unstitched seam is the opening. 2". *Chester County Historical Society, West Chester, Pennsylvania.*

Pink-silk-lined leather loop inside a lined silk sewing box. 1" diameter loop. *Collection of the author.*

Retail packaging for a single thimble. Clinton brand, made of nickel. 1.25". *Collection of the author.*

Paper thimble boxes from retailers. Examples include opticians, jewelers, pharmacists, and dry goods businesses. The interiors have fabric-covered insertion papers to hold the thimble stable. 1.25". *Collection of the author.*

Silver thimble holders were popular after the fall in silver prices in the last quarter of the nineteenth century. A common style is a relief-embossed silver cylinder with a hinged lid. The interior has a silver post where the thimble rests. The holder and thimble were sold separately.

Thimble holders were sometimes homemade. Crochet patterns for thimble holders included hanging styles incorporating dried bird bones, using the wishbone, and hat-shaped holders with needle pages.[15] Another style is crocheted in the shape of a hat, with the thimble fitting in the hat's center. The hat brim folds back and is filled with needle pages.

Leather thimble holders in assorted styles. 1.25". *Collection of the author.*

Sterling thimble holders with hinged lids. The interior has a post for the thimble to rest on. 1.5" × 1". *Collection of the author.*

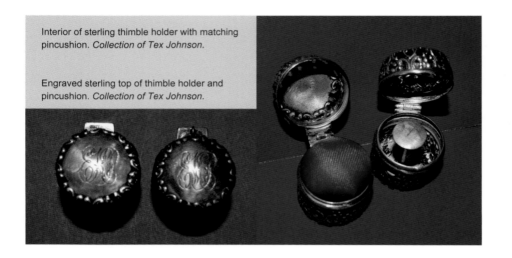

Interior of sterling thimble holder with matching pincushion. *Collection of Tex Johnson.*

Engraved sterling top of thimble holder and pincushion. *Collection of Tex Johnson.*

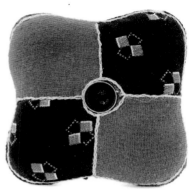

Thimble recessed in the middle of a pincushion. 3" square. *Collection of the author.*

Wishbone crochet thimble holder holds the thimble like a bucket. The ribbon forms a necklace to wear the thimble. 3" diameter. *Collection of the author.*

Collection of crochet hat thimble holders. The top is hinged with wool needle pages inside. The thimble is stored in the crown of the hat. 3" diameter. *Collection of the author.*

Shoe thimble holder also has needle pages. Pins are inserted around the circumference of the sole. 3" long. *Collection of the author.*

Pink silk drawstring bag divided in the center with embellished artificial flowers, fruits, and leaves. The drawstring top holds a painted thimble and the lower section is a pincushion. 2" × 3.75". *Chester County Historical Society, West Chester, Pennsylvania.*

Leather hat with blue silk ribbon bound seams. Details include a visor and tiny covered buttons. 2.75" × 1.75". *Chester County Historical Society, West Chester, Pennsylvania.*

Leather hat with blue silk bound seams. The bottom of the hat has a blue silk ribbon bound recessed area for the thimble to fit in. 2.75" × 1.75". *Chester County Historical Society, West Chester, Pennsylvania.*

# Bodkins, Awls, and Stilettos

## Bodkins

Before the invention of zippers, snaps, and other garment closures, bodkins were used by men and women as an essential tool in order to dress. Most garments before the nineteenth century required some type of lacing or drawstring in order to close. The lacing required the use of a bodkin, which is a slender, rigid, and dull-ended tool used to thread narrow textiles through small openings or casings in garments. A bodkin is sometimes referred to as a ribbon threader. Bodkins have been used for as long as sewing needles. They are made of the same materials as needles, including metals, bone, wood, shell, and plastic. Common bodkins made of bone were sold until 1945.[1]

Bodkins are made in two styles. The first style is similar to a large hand sewing needle with a large eye and a blunt or ball tip. The second style is long and flat with a rectangular opening in the top and a squared-off end at the bottom. Important features both styles have in common are a large opening at one end to hold the end of the lacing material and a blunt tip that won't catch or pierce the material as it is guided through the casing. Some have two openings at the top of the bodkin. The openings vary in size and shape.

Some women wore their bodkins as personal adornment. Customs varied by local practices and cultural beliefs. These bodkins, while practical, were generally precious metal and were sometimes engraved. When displayed, the uppermost bodkin hole could be adorned with a jewel or bead indicating a woman's wealth and status to the rest of society. Women would place a bodkin in their hair simply for quick access and convenience.

Predating use in America, bodkins were also used for "needle binding." Needle binding consists of looping thread in circles with the blunt-ended bodkin and could be used to create mittens and socks. Later methods preferred in America were knitting and crochet.[2]

In the eighteenth and nineteenth centuries bodkins were valuable and included in household inventories. They were the subject of court cases involving theft and breaking sumptuary laws.[3] *Black's Law Dictionary* defines sumptuary law as "Laws made for the purpose of restraining luxury or extravagance, particularly against inordinate expenditures in the matter of apparel, food, furniture, etc." Once mass produced, like sewing needles, bodkin values were greatly reduced as prices fell. Bodkins were then readily available to all households.

Packaged bodkins were sometimes sold in sets of assorted sizes where each bodkin had a number inscribed on it referring to the length. The number of the needle-style bodkin refers to the length of the bodkin. These packaged sets were designed for decorative display as well as use. The packaged sets included ornate bodkins of precious metals and engraving. Some individual bodkins in the later nineteenth and early twentieth centuries were manufactured with advertising etched the length of the shaft. Bodkins were also popular as souvenirs to commemorate vacation destinations and attendance at events such as the Panama Exhibition of 1915.

Ball-tip bodkins in assorted sizes. These examples were sold as a set and have double eyes. 2" – 2.5" long. *Collection of the author.*

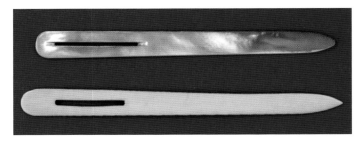

Bodkin and leather sheath given by the Singer Company at the Panama Exposition in 1915. Quarter-inch ribbon is threaded through the top of the bodkin. 3" long. *Collection of the author.*

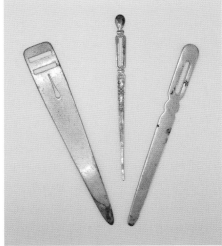

Variety of bodkin styles and sizes. 3" long. *Collection of the author.*

Precious metal bodkins. The example on top is 18-karat gold; the bottom example is silver. 2.5" – 3" long. *Collection of the author.*

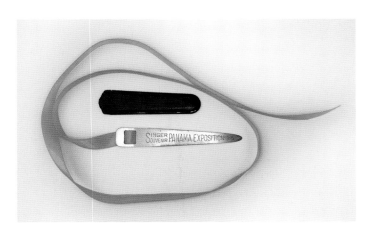

Bodkins made from natural materials. The top example is carved from shell. The bottom example is carved from bone. 3" long. *Collection of the author.*

MERRY CHRISTMAS

THESE RIBBON BEADERS, PINK AND BLUE,
I SEND TO YOU TO-DAY—
A TINY GIFT—WITH LOVE MOST TRUE
TO WISH YOU JOY ALWAY

Plastic bodkins added to an embellished Christmas card. The bodkins slide out from under the gold tape. 3" × 5". *Collection of the author.*

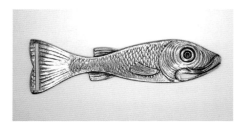

Sterling bodkin in the shape of a fish. The tail has a long narrow opening; the mouth has a round opening. 3.5" long. *Collection of the author.*

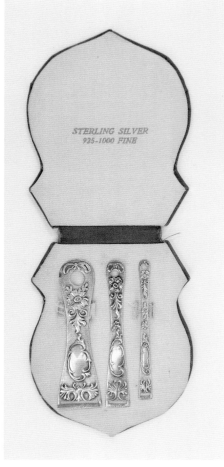

Matching set of sterling silver bodkins in a silk-covered case. 3" bodkin length. *Collection of the author.*

## Bodkin Holders

Bodkin holders protected bodkins from loss and damage. The holders came in a variety of styles, both practical and ornamental. Early styles resemble needle cases and were generally larger to accommodate the larger bodkin size. They were also commonly included in fitted needlework sets. Early-twentieth-century sets have a front and back cover and were manufactured specifically for holding three graduated sizes of bodkins. Some of the most creative bodkin holders are homemade and serve dual purposes.

The hard-cased cylindrical bodkin cases are made of wood, ceramics, and shell. Some cylindrical cases are also suitable for an assortment of needlework implements so they can be considered general-purpose containers. Porcelain, mother-of-pearl, and precious-metal ornamental styles reflect a higher social status of an owner.

American sterling bodkins were often sold in sets including bodkins in three or four graduated sizes. These sets came in a silk-covered shaped case with a hinged cover that opens like a book. Ribbon loops hold the bodkins in place. Ribbons were also used to tie the covers closed.

One homemade style of bodkin holder is sewn in the shape of a tube and is made from commercial wool braided tape or ribbon. The ends are tied closed and the side seams are embellished with embroidery. The embroidery stitch was chosen to provide a channel for the bodkin to slide into for storage. Filled with soft cotton or wool, the holder can also serve as a pincushion. With no primary pattern source known for the original intent, perhaps the popularity of the style is due to its multipurpose use as a bodkin holder, scissor rest, and pincushion.

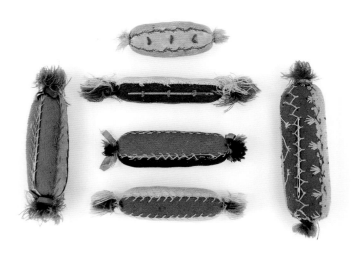

Bodkin holders made of wool knitted braid in multiple colors. The braid was sold to use on the bottom of skirts. Small lengths were left over from yardage needed for the hem of a nineteenth-century skirt. The short lengths were stitched together to form a tube. The hand-sewn seams are embellished with decorative stitches. The ends are tied closed with threads and ribbons. In some examples a loose bullion stitch is used to create the loops for the bodkin. 2.5" – 4" long. *Collection of the author.*

Bodkin holders made of wool knitted braid in multiple colors. These examples are not embroidered. A possible clue that the embroidery was added after the holders were made. 3" – 4" long. *Collection of the author.*

Bodkins were also stored inside sewing rolls. The bodkin is positioned to safely roll up for storage. 3" long brass bodkin. *Collection of the author.*

Detail of stitched loop securing the bodkin inside the sewing roll. The bodkin easily slides out of the loops for use. 0.25" loop. *Collection of the author.*

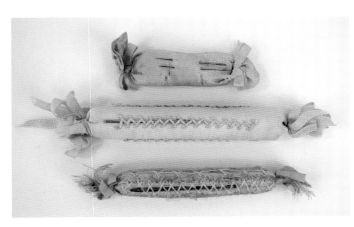

Bodkin holders made of silk ribbon and trim. The ends are tied closed with ribbons. The bodkins are held in place with decorative stitching. 3" – 5" long. *Collection of the author.*

Bodkin holders made of wool knitted braid in multiple colors. These variations include ribbon handles, creative embroidery stitches, and an oversized spiral style. 4" – 10". *Collection of the author.*

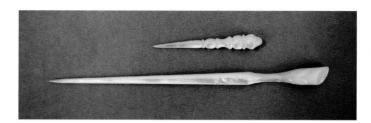

Awl made from shell, also referred to as mother-of-pearl. The tips are very sharp. 2" – 6" long. *Collection of the author.*

## Awls

An awl is a sharp, pointed handheld tool for piercing leather and textiles. The awl starts out wide at the handle and narrows to a pointed tip. Common materials for American awls include metal, bone, mother-of-pearl, and ivory. The handle section of the awl can be smooth or patterned.

Awls were necessary tools for men and women. The same tool is sometimes referred to as a fid. Most fids were generally larger and were used to work out knots in rope. Small sizes are very useful in embroidery, and this universal tool is useful for untangling knots in thread. The tip of the awl or fid can be inserted into a knot to loosen it for untangling.

Awl made by carving shell. Small impressions for finger placement are carved about 1" from the end. The tip is not as pointed as many bone awls. 4.5" long. *Collection of the author.*

Bone awls with various carved ends. The grain of the bone discolors with age and use. 3" – 4" long. *Collection of the author.*

## Stilettos

A stiletto is a metal awl with an attached handle where the metal-pointed awl rod is held in a decorative handle. The handles are made in a variety of styles and materials. Some American styles are made of bone. Other handle materials include wood and mother-of-pearl. In 1907, Charles Haynes of Newark, New Jersey, received US Patent 917,295 for an embroidery stiletto also called a fabric piercer.[4] His invention had an adjustable slide to limit the size of the hole made by the point. Other twentieth-century styles include one-piece sterling silver stilettos.

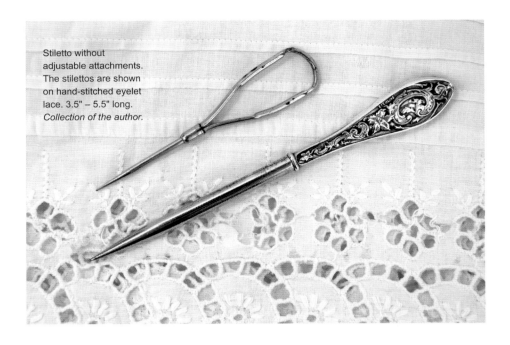

Stiletto without adjustable attachments. The stilettos are shown on hand-stitched eyelet lace. 3.5" – 5.5" long. *Collection of the author.*

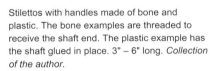

Stilettos with handles made of bone and plastic. The bone examples are threaded to receive the shaft end. The plastic example has the shaft glued in place. 3" – 6" long. *Collection of the author.*

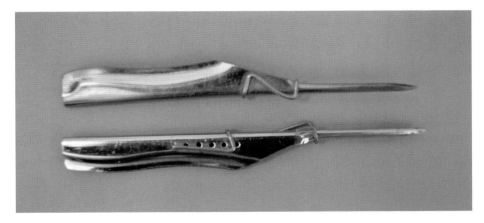

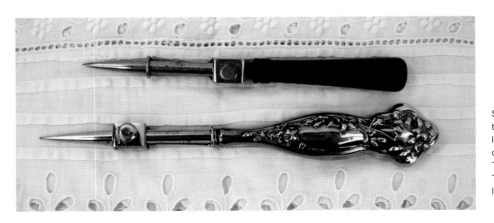

Adjustable punches for needle punch embroidery. Not to be confused with stilettos or awls. Yarn or thread is threaded through the shaft and the needle, coming out of the eye into the tip of the punch. The tip of the punch is inserted into fabric, creating a loop as it is pulled back out. Repeated loops create a decorative nap in the fabric. 5" long. *Collection of the author.*

Stiletto with attachments that adjust the depth the tip can pierce through fabric. The thumb screw loosens and the stop point can be moved up or down. The handle on the black example is wood. The sterling handle example has a steel shaft. The stilettos are shown on hand-stitched eyelet lace. 6" – 7" long. *Collection of the author.*

# Scissors and Cutting

## Scissors

Like many other industries in America, the manufacture of scissors was led by immigrants who brought their knowledge, skills, and drive for success. Connecticut, New Jersey, and Ohio became the center of scissor production in America. These locations offered water power, rail systems, and business incentives. More than seventeen companies were manufacturing scissors in America in 1930. Scissor companies competed on design, price, and durability.

American entrepreneurs were also importing scissors from England. Edward Andrews advertised in 1752 he had a "choice assortment of the newest and neatest goods from London including scissors." Other entrepreneurs, called cutlers, were manufacturing and selling scissors. The April 13, 1767 *New York Gazette* contains an advertisement for cutler Richard Sause. The ad states that he carries on the cutlery business in various branches, from grinding to finishing. Along with several styles of scissors, Sause's company sold razors, knives, swords, and many other types of sharp polished-metal items. Many shops also did repairs and provided sharpening services. Fine scissors for embroidery had to be imported.[1]

By 1830 the American cutlery industry was utilizing power machinery. However, the final fine grinding stage remained a labor-intensive manual process.[2] In 1835 German immigrant Rochus Heinisch enlarged his surgical instrument business to include scissors and knives. His sons joined him in the business, known as Heinisch's Sons Company. He patented a tailor's shear that was said to enable one man to do the work of four. In 1914 the company closed and was sold to Jacob Wiss. The Heinisch family continued to work in the business and remained friends with Wiss.[3]

In 1877, Fremont, Ohio, offered free natural gas to any business that would move there. Two scissor companies took advantage of the free gas offer. Clauss Shear Company and the Henkel Company grew there, merging in 1919 into one of the largest scissor companies in the world, employing thousands of local residents. At that time, they had the largest payroll in America. By 2004, after several integrations and mergers, Clauss was acquired by Acme United Corporation. The scissors are now made in China and offer a lifetime warranty.[4] The label states, "Choice of professionals since 1877" with the Clauss logo.

Beginning in 1848, J. Wiss & Sons Company of Newark, New Jersey, started operating out of a single room on a lathe powered by a dog on a treadmill. They grew to become the largest scissor company with the eventual purchase of their competitor, the Heinisch Company. They developed cutting-edge patents and manufacturing processes that continued to keep Wiss world renowned for quality and innovation. They were still at the top of the industry in 1948, when they expanded into garden shears. In the 1970s they patented the "New Quick Clip" that was popular with home sewers.[5] The Wiss Company was sold in 1976 to Cooper Industries and merged into Apex Tool Group in 2010.[6]

At the end of the nineteenth century, silver-handled scissors were fashionable. Silversmiths in America created numerous decorative handle designs. Most of the blades for these scissors were imported from Europe. Unger Brothers made and distributed scissors with German blades on American Art Nouveau–designed handles.

In the twentieth century, the J. J. Conway Company of Bridgeport, Connecticut, sold a comprehensive line of scissors. They held many patents for scissors. The "Eversharp" name in script along with the letters "USA" are found on their blades. Many designs featured ornate handles attempting to emulate fancy sterling models.

Retail stores sometimes contracted with scissor companies for private label scissors. Blades were marked with company advertising like Butler Brothers, who developed Ben Franklin Stores. Advertising scissors were also made for politicians.

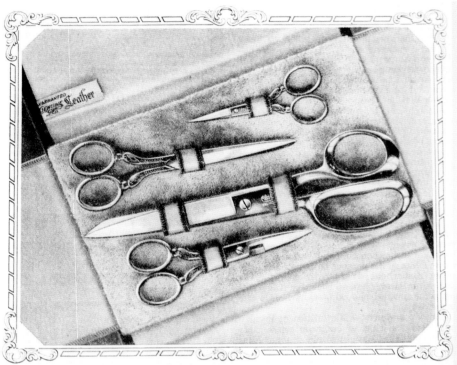

Clauss Cutlery advertisement from the June 7, 1924, edition of the *Saturday Evening Post*. It includes the Clauss logo. Clauss claimed they achieved preference once held by European cutlery. They promoted scissor sets, plain and fancy, as gifts. *Collection of the author.*

**Attractive and Useful Graduation Presents**

*Clauss Scissors in sets, both plain and fancy, are available at the better stores as graduation presents. The price range is wide. Every pair is fully guaranteed against all mechanical defects.*

Clauss Cutlery has very definitely won for itself the preference once held by goods made in Europe.

Women generally now recognize Clauss Scissors and shears as unequaled for sewing and manicure use.

They have also found that a single pair of scissors or shears in the house is not enough, and that it is better economy, and far more convenient, to have scissors which are right in size and weight for the work in hand.

*Clauss Cutlery is guaranteed against all mechanical defects. More than 6,000 responsible hardware, department and drug stores sell Clauss Cutlery. The complete line includes scissors and shears for every purpose, pocket knives, razors, manicure and pedicure implements.*

The Clauss Shear Co., Fremont, O.

# CLAUSS CUTLERY

SCISSORS · SHEARS · KNIVES · MANICURING SETS

Clauss logo from 1924 proudly displays "American Made." 2" printed in ad. *Collection of the author.*

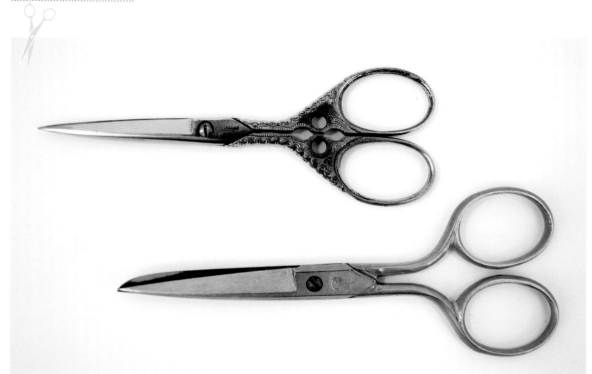

Examples of Clauss scissors; the Clauss name is found just above the screw in the mark position. 5" – 7" long. *Collection of the author.*

Wiss black handles scissors. The Wiss name is marked on the blades. 8" long. *Collection of the author.*

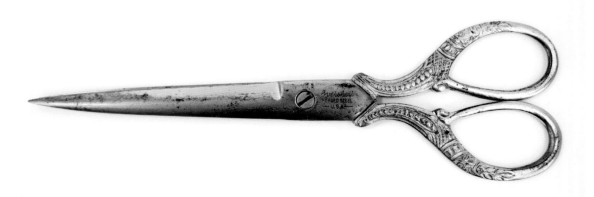

Eversharp Forged Steel scissors marked USA. Decorative handles. 9" long. *Collection of the author.*

Butler Brothers scissors. Retail stores sometimes contracted with scissor companies for private label scissors. Blades were marked with company advertising like Butler Brothers, who developed Ben Franklin Stores. 6" long. *Collection of the author.*

One style of specialty scissor is the buttonhole scissor. The scissors were designed with special blades and a gauge to set the cutting length. The purpose of the design was to prevent cutting through the end of the buttonhole into the garment.

Pinking shears cut a zigzag pattern instead of a straight edge. The zigzag edge helps prevent woven fabrics from fraying or limits the fraying of woven fabrics. Louise Austin of Whatcom, Washington, was issued US Patent 489406 for pinking shears on January 3, 1893.[7] The drawings included in the patent application included multiple cutting edges. Her invention replaced the use of labor-intensive pinking irons. The pinking iron was a metal rod with a pinked edge that was held against the fabric on a hard surface and struck with a hammer.

Samuel Briskman of Brooklyn, New York, held three patents for pinking shears by 1934. He formed the American Pinking Shears Corporation, which was later renamed Pinking Shears Corporation. His company milled the teeth into the blades and Wiss made the actual scissors. Both companies were able to brand and sell the pinking shears. Production peaked in the 1950s and decreased with the popularity of synthetic fabrics and serging machines.[8]

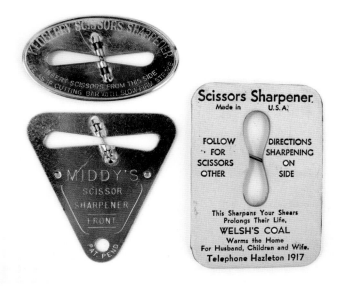

Various types of scissor sharpeners were sold for use in the home. The example on the right is an advertising piece from a coal company. It was probably given as a free premium to customers. 2" × 3". *Collection of the author.*

Scissors designed specifically to cut buttonholes. The screw adjusts to stop the blades from closing completely. By stopping the blades at a preset length, a buttonhole could not be cut too far. 7" long. *Collection of the author.*

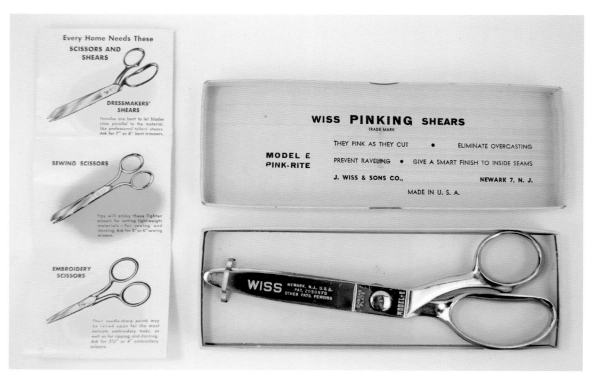

Boxed Wiss pinking shears. Pinking shears were designed to create an edge finish on fabric that would not ravel. The advertising insert in the box includes descriptions of related scissor options. 10" box. *Collection of the author.*

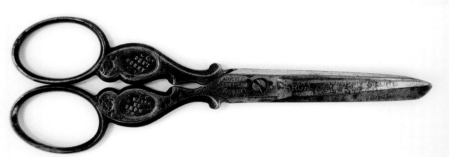

Krusius German scissors made as American advertising pieces. George Washington and Abraham Lincoln are shown on one side of the handles. 8" long. *Collection of the author.*

Krusius German scissors made for American company Broadway Department Stores, marked on the blades. The handles are marked "Don't worry" and "Watch us Grow." 8" long. *Collection of the author.*

Leather scissor case from L. Herder & Son Cutlers in Philadelphia. Founded in 1871. The family had several cutlery businesses in Philadelphia since 1847. It is unknown if the scissors are original to the case. The original case has compartments for four graduated-size scissors. 8" long × 2.5" wide. *Chester County Historical Society, West Chester, Pennsylvania.*

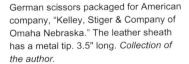

German scissors packaged for American company, "Kelley, Stiger & Company of Omaha Nebraska." The leather sheath has a metal tip. 3.5" long. *Collection of the author.*

Steel blade buttonhole cutter safely enclosed in a decorative brass shield. A scale is marked in the brass to indicate the size of the buttonhole. 4.5" long closed. 7" long extended. *Collection of the author.*

Detail of steel-blade brass buttonhole cutter. The slide is embossed with the company name and patent information. *Collection of the author.*

## Other Cutting Tools

Once a buttonhole is stitched, in order to be useful it has to be cut open. Initial tools were sharp metal pieces. Their precision left much to be desired and caused errors that required additional time to complete a satisfactory repair. Buttonhole scissors were an option but expensive in relation to alternative methods. Less expensive than specialty scissors, specialized tools were developed to cut the buttonholes.

T. B. Doolittle of Bridgeport, Connecticut, received US Patent 131085 for a buttonhole cutter on September 3, 1872.[9] The device is a wedge-shaped brass shield with a steel blade sandwiched inside. The razor-sharp blade slides in a groove along a scale of one to eight. The tool is held over the finished buttonhole, and the thumb plate slides the blade down, piercing the fabric to the width set on the scale and cutting the opening to the desired size with needed precision.

Stitches may need to be removed from a workpiece. The quickest way to open a seam is to cut the threads. "Sewing Companion" sets were sold under the labels of Ideal or Globe. The patent holder was the Unsinger Razorblade Company of Fremont, Ohio. The boxes were covered in leather-simulated paper lined in velvet. The sets contained a straight-edge razor held in a textured metal handle for cutting open seams. Another tool in the set had a matching handle with a sharp pointed tip for opening sewn seams. In addition to these two tools there is a velvet lined section in the box for spare razor blades.

Sarah DeMerrirt and Eugene Leighton received a patent for a seam ripper in 1900. The scissor-like handled tool was used for removing stitches, or removing threads for drawn work. The lower tip was used to pull threads up from the fabric. Once the threads were raised the upper edge was brought down by the handle to cut the threads.

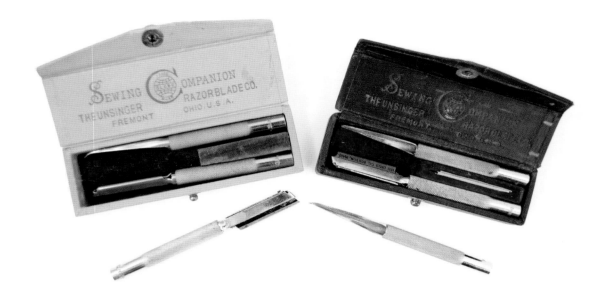

Seam ripper set, sold as a "Sewing Companion" set. The textured handles added safety to the grip. One tool securely holds a straight edge razor for cutting open stitches in seams. The second tool is a sharp curved blade to open stitches. Extra blades are wrapped in brown paper and stored in the velvet lined case. 6" case. *Collection of the author.*

Wooden-handled seam rippers. The loop is for the thumb, and the painted wooden handle is held in the hand. The top blade is sharp and the lower blade is wider and flat. 7" long. *Collection of the author.*

Blade detail showing the difference in the upper and lower blades. 1.25" blade. *Collection of the author.*

# 6 Sewing Rolls, Reticules, Bags, and Waist Pockets

## Sewing Rolls

A sewing roll is a small portable rolled sewing set made to conveniently hold sewing supplies like needles, thread, and thimbles for hand sewing. When unrolled these sets are generally rectangular in shape, made of soft materials like cloth and leather. They are rolled or folded and tied with a ribbon or closed with a button, snap, or clasp. The oblong-shaped sewing rolls were made of scraps of fabric, elegant silk or ribbon that could be rolled up and put into a pocket or left out for show during fancy parlor stitching. The rolls typically had smaller inside pockets and wool pages for needle storage. Sometimes initials, names, or dates were embroidered on the interior of the roll.

Sewing rolls are sometimes referred to as a "huswif" or housewife. Shakespeare used the word "huswif" in *Othello*, 1604, during a time when the meaning of words was undergoing change. At this time it meant a woman who managed a house; but could also mean a bold, shameless woman now known as a "hussy."[1]

The rolls, in many variations, have been used for two centuries by women and men alike. Sewing rolls were often part of men's travel sets. Soldiers carried them off to war and sailors took them out to sea. There is little difference between the supplies found in men's and women's sewing rolls.[2]

Early fabrics used in the sewing rolls included rare block- and roller-printed glazed cottons, making them highly collectible today. Frequently they were made without a pattern so the rolls show great variation, limited only by the maker's imagination. The makers creatively designed the shape, placement, and size of the sewing roll to suit their needs. The most basic style is a cotton roll with a few flat pockets. *The Workwoman's Guide* of 1838 offers a basic drawing and a few sentences of instruction to make a housewife. The suggested materials are leather, satin, velvet, or any other common print fabric.

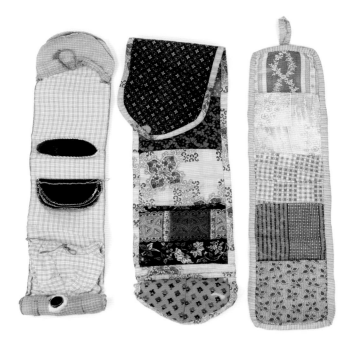

Inside view of cotton sewing rolls from the nineteenth century. Left to right: The orange plaid example has an outer fabric colored with unstable purple dye. There is a velvet-covered pincushion in the center above the embroidered black wool needle pages. A thimble holder and bodkin strap is built into the bottom roll. Two gathered pockets complete both ends. 4.5" × 18". The entire roll is finished off with narrow lilac cord. The center indigo blue roll is lined with five pockets made in five different prints. A wool needle page was added at the bottom of the roll. The binding is the same print as one of the pockets. 5.5" × 24". The roll on the right is lined in four pockets in four cotton prints. The outer fabric is the same yellow stripe used for the binding. A small loop is used to close the roll with a glass shoe button. 4.5" × 18". *Collection of the author.*

Examples of closed sewing rolls, compact and secured. 4.5" × 2". *Collection of the author.*

Variety of sewing rolls in linen, silk, and cotton. 4.5" × 18". *Collection of Kathryn G. Lesieur.*

Leather sewing roll closed with wool braided tape. Possibly a repurposed man's wallet. 6" × 3.75" × 2.5". *Chester County Historical Society, West Chester, Pennsylvania.*

Interior wool needle pages of leather sewing roll. The red wool pages and braid ties are possible later additions to what used to be a wallet. 6" × 3.75" × 2.5". *Chester County Historical Society, West Chester, Pennsylvania.*

Embossed eagle motif on the interior. *Chester County Historical Society, West Chester, Pennsylvania.*

Leather sewing roll that wraps around a box. The box is made from leather-covered pasteboard. The end of the box has a red-velvet-covered pincushion. The roll is lined in silk. There are two sets of colored-wool needle pages with embroidered edges. 5" × 2.5" × 15". *Collection of the author.*

Leather box–style sewing roll with glass button and loop closure. Bound in brown silk ribbon. 2.5" × 2.5" × 5". *Collection of the author.*

Leather box–style sewing roll molded over time to fit in the hand. Worn brown silk ribbon binding. Missing closure. 5" 2.5" × 2.5". *Collection of the author.*

Leather box–style sewing roll interior view. Lined in silk, one end is a pincushion; the other is a small compartment for storage. The underside of the lid has a leather strap to hold bodkins and small tools. 5" × 2.5" × 2.5". *Collection of the author.*

Sewing roll made from at least six different block-printed cottons and linen. There are five interior pockets. Separate binding applied on each pocket and outer edge. 5" × 21". *Collection of Tex Johnson.*

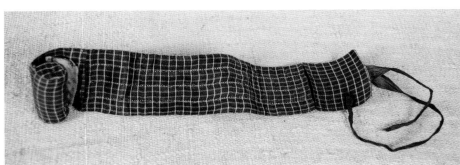

Hand-stitched sewing roll with channels for thread. The end roll has a wool needle page. There is a pocket at the top. Green ribbon tie closure. 3" × 21". *Collection of Tex Johnson.*

Sewing roll made of five glazed cotton print pockets bound in silk ribbon. Spade-shaped wool needle page at the bottom of the roll. Hand sewn in brown and red thread. Possibly from Montgomery or eastern Berks County, Pennsylvania, 4.25" × 16". *Schwenkfelder Library & Heritage Center, Pennsburg, Pennsylvania.*

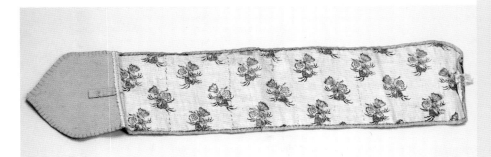

Sewing roll made of glazed cotton bound in silk ribbon. Spade-shaped wool needle page at the bottom of the roll. Hand sewn in brown and red thread. Possibly from Montgomery or eastern Berks County, Pennsylvania, 4.25" × 16". *Schwenkfelder Library & Heritage Center, Pennsburg, Pennsylvania.*

Outside cotton print fabric of a sewing roll. 6" × 18". *Chester County Historical Society, West Chester, Pennsylvania.*

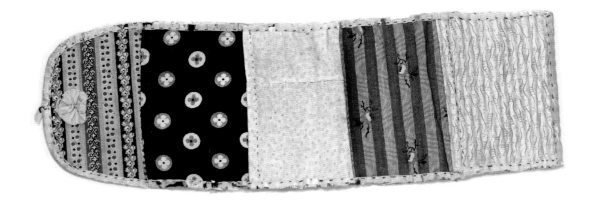

Inside four pockets of cotton print fabric sewing roll. 6" × 18". *Chester County Historical Society, West Chester, Pennsylvania.*

Cotton sewing roll with three interior pockets. The bottom has six pinked-edge wool needle pages made of brown, rust, and navy wool. Half-inch-wide binding edges. Closes with a hook and eye. 3" × 19". *Collection of Tex Johnson.*

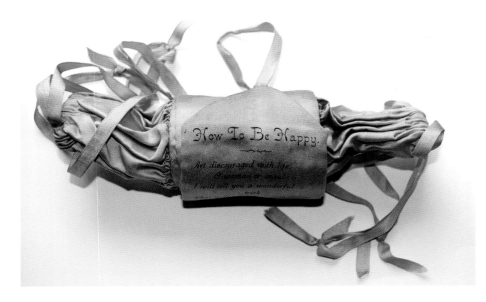

Yellow silk sewing roll printed "How To Be Happy. Art discourage with life, O woman or man? I will tell you a wonderful trick that will bring you contentment if anything can. Do something for somebody quick! Do something for somebody quick. Are you awfully tired with what is called 'Gay' Weary, discouraged and sick? I'll tell you the loveliest game in the world. Do something for somebody quick! Do something for somebody quick!" Author unknown. 4" × 20". *Collection of Kathryn G. Lesieur.*

Pink silk sewing roll printed "O Women! Do what you can! Not what you cannot, not what you think 'might be done,' not what you 'would like to do,' not what you 'would do if you had more time,' not what 'somebody else thinks you ought to do,' —but what you can.—" Author unknown. 2.25" × 7.5". *Chester County Historical Society, West Chester, Pennsylvania.*

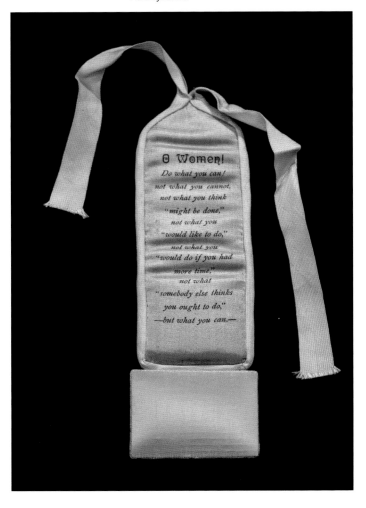

Gold and pink silk sewing roll printed "I am wishing for you today, and wishes are prayers they say. What wealth of joy, if this prove true, will surely Dear Heart come to you. If half the wishes I have said Descend in blessings on your head." 2.25" × 7.5". *Collection of Kathryn G. Lesieur.*

Hand-pieced cotton sewing roll of assorted cotton prints. Three pockets made of twenty-five patch blocks bordered in strips of fabric. Multiple prints used in the binding. 7" × 26". *Collection of Kathryn G. Lesieur.*

Details of cotton prints used in a quilt block pocket for a sewing roll. Twenty-five 0.75" squares for the block. The block is bordered in 1" strips of fabric. *Collection of Kathryn G. Lesieur.*

Six cotton pockets form the interior of this toile print sewing roll. Probably linen applied binding. All hand sewn. 4.5" × 24". *Chester County Historical Society, West Chester, Pennsylvania.*

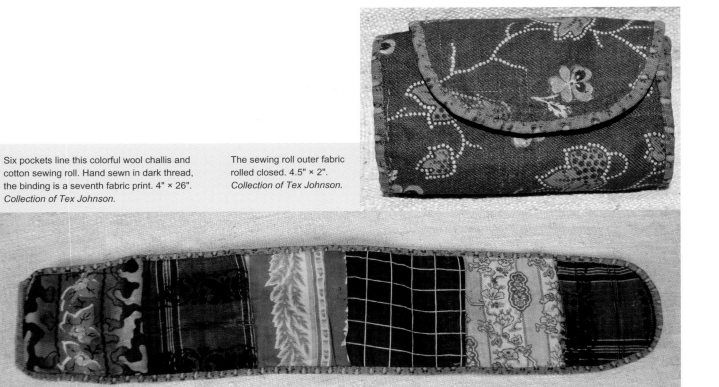

Six pockets line this colorful wool challis and cotton sewing roll. Hand sewn in dark thread, the binding is a seventh fabric print. 4" × 26". *Collection of Tex Johnson.*

The sewing roll outer fabric rolled closed. 4.5" × 2". *Collection of Tex Johnson.*

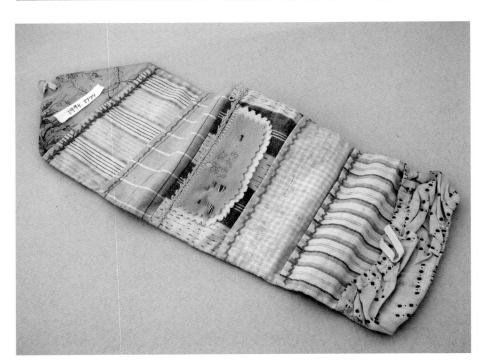

Interior pockets inside of printed cotton, gingham, and stripes in blues, browns, and pinks. The pocket edges embroidered in decorative stitches. Bottom pocket gathered at top with white grosgrain ribbon loop. The white and blue wool needle pages are embroidered with "1893." 5" × 14". *Chester County Historical Society, West Chester, Pennsylvania.*

More-creative rolls include interior gathered pouches, draw-string bags, and thimble holders. Some very complex styles may have been made in girls' sewing schools. These styles are inge-niously designed with several buttoning and folding components. The end result could include details for a thimble holder, thread winders, needle packets, and embroidery storage.

Embroidered roll-ups include queen stitch, needlepoint, and other decorative embroidery stitches. They are often bound in silk ribbon or woven tape. Linings include colorful silks and cottons. Interior pockets are varied from flat to drawstring gathered styles. Some trim yardage was used to simulate embroidery in these roll ups.

Military sewing rolls were made in support of numerous American war efforts. It was general practice for enlisted men to attend to their own uniforms.[3] The soldiers needed something compact for their needles, thread, and any other sewing supplies. In the nineteenth century, soldiers were often sent off to service equipped with a sewing roll made by their mothers, sisters, or sweethearts. During the American Civil War, sewing roll styles were diverse and homemade. Some rolls were constructed in patriotic red, white, and blue—they were made of fabric scraps perhaps remind-ing soldiers of loved ones at home. Answering a newspaper request during the Civil War, young ladies in Sunday school classes were taught to make sewing rolls and provided suggested wording for a letter to be included with the sewing roll. Suggested supplies to include with the roll included buttons, needles, thread, pins, and yarn. The Reformed Presbyterian of 1864 reports that thousands of "housewives" were forwarded to the United States Christian Commission for distribution to the soldiers. "I suppose you all know what a housewife is? It is a long piece of cloth with a number of small pockets sewed along one side, and made to fold up like a pocket-book, having separate places for buttons, thread, needles, pins, &c., such as some of you may have seen your mothers or grandmothers use."[4]

Cotton sewing roll made primarily from a single print. One flat pocket and two gathered interior pockets. Two sets of wool needle pages with different edge finishes. Two small drawstring bags are stored inside the lower pocket. 6" × 24". *Collection of Kathryn G. Lesieur.*

Cotton sewing roll with three gathered pockets. Each pocket is made from a different brown print. A stripe print was used for the outer side of the roll. 4" × 17". *Collection of Kathryn G. Lesieur.*

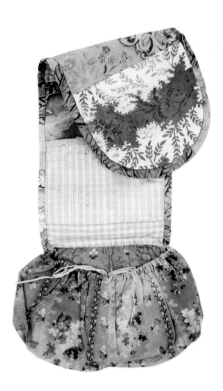

Sewing roll with three flat pockets and one gathered bottom pocket. The drawstring in the lower pocket is a 1/8" narrow tape. Bound in a glazed chintz print. Nine different prints make up the roll. 5" × 25". *Collection of the author.*

Sewing pillow with flaps that roll over the top and tie closed. Under the right flap are wool needle pages with glass-headed pins. Under the left flap is a ribbon holding scissors in place, in addition to wool needle pages holding pins and needles. 6" square. *Collection of the author.*

Small sewing roll made from pieced cottons. The roll closes with a small thread-knotted loop on the curved edge. 6" × 8". *Collection of Tex Johnson.*

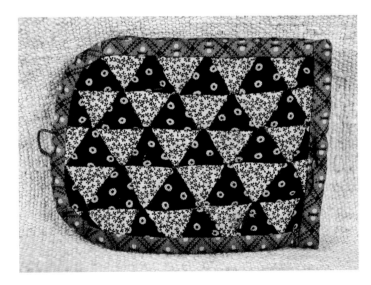

Queen stitch sewing roll with strawberry and heart motifs and the initials "A.Y." Bound in brown silk ribbon with matching ribbon ties. Probably from Chestnut Hill, Philadelphia County, Pennsylvania. 8" × 14". *Schwenkfelder Library & Heritage Center, Pennsburg, Pennsylvania.*

Inside of the queen stitch sewing roll has pink and blue silk pockets. The inside of the pockets is lined in a bleached plain-weave linen. Probably from Chestnut Hill, Philadelphia County, Pennsylvania. 8" × 14". *Schwenkfelder Library & Heritage Center, Pennsburg, Pennsylvania.*

Silk sewing roll made from six different silks. The two interior pockets are gathered. The lower pincushion has a cream wool needle page. The curved top has three colorful wool needle pages edged in embroidery. The binding is blue silk ribbon. 3.5" × 18". *Collection of the author.*

This sewing roll is an Irish stitch embroidery worked on canvas in wool and silk. The letters "LP" and the year 1763 are cross stitched at the top of the roll. The interior has five pockets made with a brocaded silk with a leaf-and-vine pattern on a striped ground. The bottom interior pocket is a loose pouch with a gathered drawstring top. The drawstring is made from dark-green tape, and all of the edges of the sewing roll are bound by the same silk tape. *Courtesy Winterthur Museum, Sewing Roll (Huswif) by Lydia Parker, 1763, Chester County, Pennsylvania, Wool, Silk, Canvas, Gift of Jeanne L. Asplundh, 2011.45.*

Sewing roll and pocket pair attributed to Sabra Gallup. The sewing roll has five pockets. 4" × 16". The patchwork pocket is embroidered in cross stitch, "Sabra Gallup Her Pocket." 16" × 14". *Collection of Tex Johnson.*

Close-up of the cross stitch embroidery on the linen square of the Sabra Gallup pocket. At least three thread colors were used. *Collection of Tex Johnson.*

Close-up of Sabra Gallup pocket opening where the pocket slit joins the waistband. The cotton pieces were possibly taken from a garment. *Collection of Tex Johnson.*

*The Child at Home* published a story in their August 1864 issue encouraging support of war efforts. It tells of a "nice little girl" who made her papa a "housewife" because soldiers had to care for their own clothing. Her mother filled it with sewing supplies. It was sent to her father in the battlefield with a note pinned inside. The authenticity of rolls containing soldier-themed notes, and that are in good condition, should be suspect. If the roll was used by a solider, the roll should show wear and use.

Formed in 1881, the American Red Cross provided suggested patterns and accessories for supplies to add to sewing rolls that would support soldiers. The solider rolls are sometimes also referred to as "Comforts" in later Red Cross publications.[5] Eventually, military service members could buy factory-made, mass-produced sewing rolls in a variety of styles.

Some sewing roll styles were designed to hold skeins of thread. The early examples are all hand sewn, including a small buttonhole-stitched loop used to close the roll. Long channels were sewn the length of the roll. Each channel held a skein of thread secure, clean, and tangle free. Occasionally, the thread sizes were embroidered at the top of each channel. Roll ups in this style were also popular into the twentieth century. The more recent styles fold rather than roll and hold embroidery floss. They sometimes contain pincushions.

A sewing roll was not just for use in the parlor or by soldiers. On July 12, 1871, the *Green Mountain Freeman* of Montpelier, Vermont, advised male travelers to carry a "huswife full of pins, needles, thread and buttons." Of equal importance, the suggested list of contents included calling cards, an umbrella, and a revolver. They suggested the revolver not be talked about.

Silk rolls were made of ribbon, or pieces of ribbon, and dress silk. The linings and pockets are also made of silk. The needle pages are made of wool; often embellished with embroidery. The fine silk fabrics rolls could become very small and compact but were not as durable as cotton, linen or velvet.

American Red Cross label from the interior of a military sewing roll. Probably made by an American Red Cross volunteer in the Topeka, Kansas, chapter. Includes the notation "Not to Be Sold." The sewing rolls were made to be given to the soldiers. 0.5" × 2". *Collection of the author.*

Brown wool sewing roll with two gathered interior pockets. One set of wool needle pages. Found inside the bottom pocket was a spool of silk thread wrapped in paper. The roll ties closed with narrow brown tape. 5" × 17". The blue and brown wool sewing roll has three pockets and red wool needle pages. 3" × 12". *Collection of the author.*

Sewing rolls with long channels to hold skeins of thread or floss. The two examples with monograms are made with linen on the outside and silk on the interior. 7" × 18" closed. The example with red binding is shown unfolded with the thread skeins showing at the tops of the channels. There is one pocket at the bottom. It is all hand sewn. 4" × 23" open. The example on top has 32 channels for thread. It is all machine sewn. 4.5" × 20". *Collection of the author.*

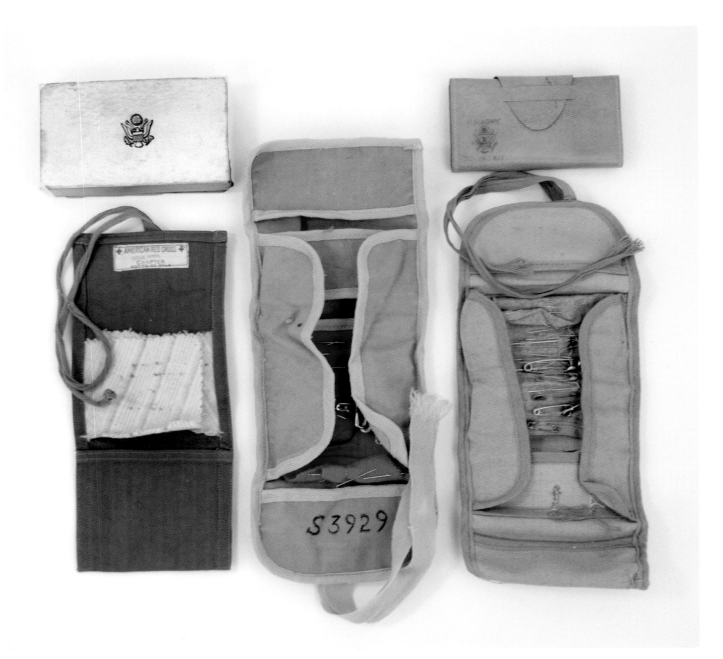

Assortment of military sewing rolls. The leather roll came in the white box. The dark-green khaki roll has one pocket and two flannel needle pages. It has a Red Cross label. 5" × 15". The other two rolls have folding flaps, two pockets, and tie closed. 6" × 18". *Collection of the author.*

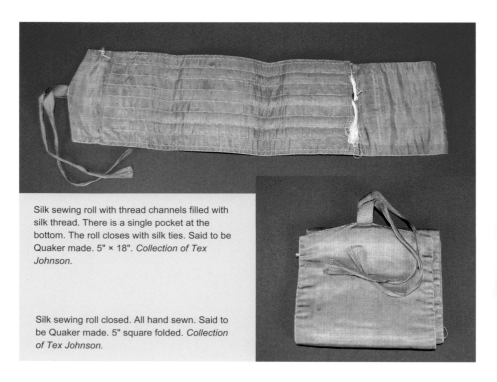

Silk sewing roll with thread channels filled with silk thread. There is a single pocket at the bottom. The roll closes with silk ties. Said to be Quaker made. 5" × 18". *Collection of Tex Johnson.*

Silk sewing roll closed. All hand sewn. Said to be Quaker made. 5" square folded. *Collection of Tex Johnson.*

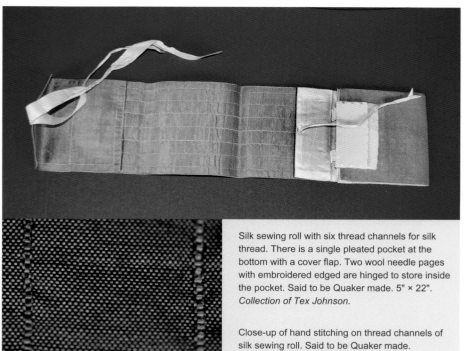

Silk sewing roll with six thread channels for silk thread. There is a single pleated pocket at the bottom with a cover flap. Two wool needle pages with embroidered edged are hinged to store inside the pocket. Said to be Quaker made. 5" × 22". *Collection of Tex Johnson.*

Close-up of hand stitching on thread channels of silk sewing roll. Said to be Quaker made. *Collection of Tex Johnson.*

The all-red silk sewing roll has three embroidered wool needle pages. The lower pocket is monogrammed in chain stitch. Above the lower pocket is a purple velvet pincushion. It is all hand stitched in purple thread. 6" × 18". The cream silk–lined dot roll has two spools of thread tied on a ribbon. A piece of wool is included in the binding. It has four needles wrapped in thread. There is one internal gathered top pocket. The roll ties closed in red silk ribbon. 4.5" × 21". *Collection of the author.*

Interior view of a linen sewing roll for thread. There is a pincushion in the center and loops for accessories sewn into the bound edge. 21" × 18" open. *Collection of the author.*

Cotton sewing roll with long channels to hold skeins of thread. The flap to cover the end of the channels is embroidered "M. Garrett." The hand sewing is so precise, it could be mistaken for machine stitching. 6" × 20". *Chester County Historical Society, West Chester, Pennsylvania.*

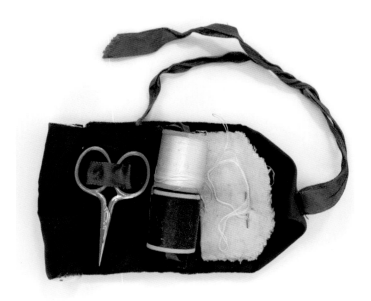

Navy-blue silk sewing roll that includes two spools of thread, scissors, and wool needle pages. The tube at the bottom is a thimble holder on one end and a pincushion on the other. The roll ties closed with a silk ribbon. 4" × 7". *Collection of the author.*

Silk-lined sewing rolls with a variety of embellishing embroidery, gathered pockets, and beading. Closures include a ribbon loop, thread ties, and silk cording. 2.5" × 12". *Collection of the author.*

Petite silk sewing rolls with small sewing accessories. The pink silk roll is bordered in cream feather stitching. The pincushion is filled with wool. The wool needle pages have pinked edges. 2" × 10". Mother-of-pearl bodkin and thread winder are lying on top. 0.25" × 2.5". The blue roll has silk-covered discs at the end of the roll. It is wool lined and is shown with a child's thimble. 1" × 6". The wooden spool of thread is 0.5" × 0.75". *Collection of the author.*

Silk-lined examples shown closed. Feather stitching was a popular stitch on the edges of sewing rolls. 2.5" – 3.5". *Collection of the author.*

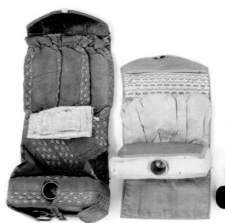

Silk-lined sewing rolls in a variety of styles. Included with the silk are some trims, ribbon, and embroidery. 5" – 18". *Collection of the author.*

Velvet sewing roll with a box for storage attached at the end. Two small latches made of velvet secure the top. The inside of the roll is lined in multiple colored strips of velvet. There are three pockets. It is bound in wool braid, with matching ties. 6.5" × 21". *Collection of the author.*

Velvet sewing rolls were also made. The thicker velvet does not roll up as small as cotton or silk. The examples found to date are all dark velvet colors like black, possibly made for mourning customs. Some included embroidery embellishment. The needle pages sometimes include a velvet page mixed with wool pages. Like other sewing rolls, the velvet rolls include pockets, pincushions, and holders for sewing tools.

Sewing rolls made of leather are frequently lined in silk. The edges are sometimes bound in silk ribbon. Leather finishes include brown, bronze, red, suede, and leather embossed with gold. Certain styles are attributed to Shakers and Quakers. While they may have made some, or used them, there is no primary evidence they produced them in large quantities for sale to the outside world.

In addition to roll styles, some leather rolls wrap around a firm box. The box was built from sturdy pasteboard. The pasteboard was padded with wadding on one side and then covered with silk. The silk was laced over the pasteboard. The covered board pieces were hand sewn into a box. Corresponding leather pieces are bound in dark silk ribbon and hand sewn to the silk lining the box. The interior of the box is often fitted with matching silk and leather sewing accessories like thimble holders, scissor sheaths, and needle books. The closures could be made of ribbon ties, snaps, or latches.

Other leather styles incorporate leather covering, and silk lining with a metal roll at the base. The roll has leather-covered metal ends that secure a rod for holding spools of thread. The entire roll is silk lined and includes leather pockets, and two areas of needle pages, one hidden under a buttoned silk flap. Other leather attachments to the silk lining include a thimble holder embellished with a brown silk bow, three loops for sewing accessories, and a scissor sheath. An identical example is shown in the March 1940 issue of *The Magazine Antiques*, described as an 1840 housewife of heavy brocade and fine leather.

Dark-blue velvet sewing roll bound in silk ribbon. The closure is a small round pin securing a bow and tiny flower. *Collection of the author.*

The interior is lined in colorful silks with contrasting embroidery. A poem was enclosed in the lower pocket, "For something to wear, to make or repair, from cradle to grave one must plan. Though the brain may get dizzy we must keep the hands busy and use all the helps that we can." The note is signed Sarah E. Allcock. 8" × 20". *Collection of the author.*

Interior view of velvet sewing rolls. The large dark-red roll on the left includes a single pocket, four needle pages, and an accent fabric band for bodkins and other small tools. Two small snaps are used to securely close the roll. 6" × 21". The center green velvet roll is lined in cream wool challis and embellished with white feather stitching; the needle pages have scalloped edges. 4.5" × 15". The red lace edged roll on the right has six channels for skeins of thread. Two small pockets close with pearl buttons. There is a pocket at the bottom with two embellished wool needle pages. 6.5" × 18". *Collection of the author.*

Closed view of velvet sewing rolls. *Collection of the author.*

Detail view of closures on the end of a sewing roll. The hollow ends of the roll can hold thimbles or thread spools. To close the ends, a length of fine cord is wrapped around buttons. 4" long. *Collection of the author.*

Leather sewing roll with dark-brown silk lining. The wool needle pages are lobe shaped with a pinked edge trimmed with chain-stitched edging. 7" × 12". *Collection of Tex Johnson.*

End view of closed sewing rolls. Creative designs include thimble compartments, pinned initials, embroidery, and openings for spools or thimbles. 2" – 3". *Collection of the author.*

A variety of leather sewing rolls shown tied closed beside an unfinished interior roll. 12" – 1". *Collection of the author.*

Light-brown leather sewing roll with dark-gold silk lining. The lower roll has two velvet ends and a center impression to hold a thimble. There is a gathered pocket in the center. The needle pages are embroidered and the scissor sheath holds a small pair of embroidery scissors. 5.5" × 16". *Collection of Tex Johnson.*

Light-brown sewing roll closed for storage. 5.5" × 2". *Collection of Tex Johnson.*

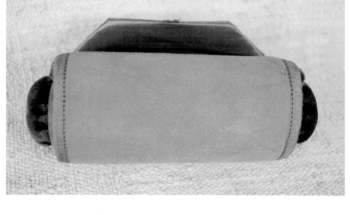

Light-brown box-style sewing roll shown with the original marbleized paper box. The yellow silk lining includes a scissor sheath, gathered pocket, snap closure box, wool embroidered needle pages, and section leather pocket for storing packets of needles. 5.5" × 18". *Collection of Tex Johnson.*

Interior of a leather sewing box lined in orange silk. A leather pinking tool similar to the one shown would have been used to cut the scallop shape, used to create the tool holder in the lid. Box: 6" square. Tool: 5" × 0.5". *Collection of the author.*

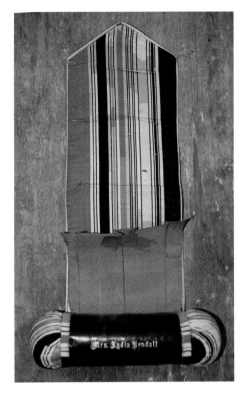

Black leather sewing roll lined in striped silk ribbon. The roll is embossed in gold letters, "Mrs. Lydia Kendall." There is a single interior pocket. 7" × 18". *Collection of Kathryn G. Lesieur.*

Red leather sewing roll with red velvet ends and silk binding. The red leather letter "B" and square pin keeps complement the red of the sewing roll. 5" – 2". *Collection of Kathryn G. Lesieur.*

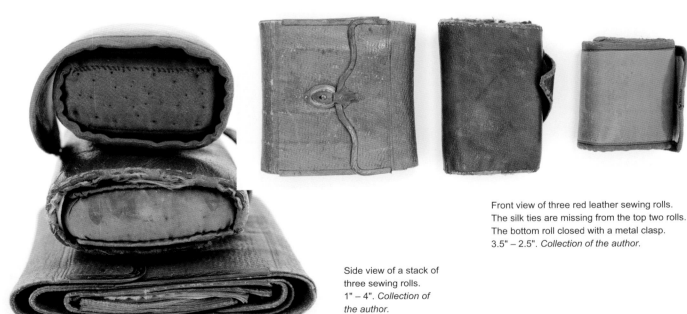

Side view of a stack of three sewing rolls. 1" – 4". *Collection of the author.*

Front view of three red leather sewing rolls. The silk ties are missing from the top two rolls. The bottom roll closed with a metal clasp. 3.5" – 2.5". *Collection of the author.*

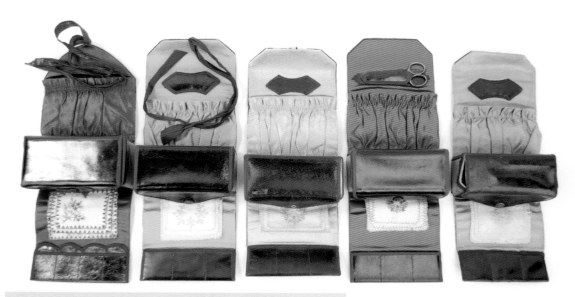

Box-style leather sewing rolls with silk linings. No two are exactly the same. Variations include the finish on the leather, number of wool needle pages, scissor sheath shape, snap on the box closure, and the edge treatment. 6" × 18". *Collection of the author.*

Side view of a closed box-style leather sewing roll. 6" × 2.5" × 2.5". *Collection of the author.*

Examples of snaps and a latch on the box-style leather sewing rolls. 0.25" – 0.375. *Collection of the author.*

Leather sewing rolls, embossed in gold metallic designs, lined in silk. Similar techniques were used by book binders to embellish the leather covers of books. 6" × 12". *Collection of the author.*

Silk-lined leather sewing roll with numerous pockets and compartments. The lower roll has leather-covered metal ends with a rod for holding thread reels or spools. There is a silk pincushion at the end and an emery suspended in the center. There is storage in the leather middle section for a thimble, scissors, small hand tools, and two pockets for small items like buttons. Under the button top flap are concealed wool needle pages. It ties closed with brown silk ribbon. 12" × 16". *Collection of the author.*

Silk-lined leather sewing roll with numerous pockets and compartments. The lower roll has leather-covered metal ends. The hollow roll has a rod for holding thread reels or spools. There is storage in the leather middle section for a thimble, scissors, small hand tools, and two pockets for small items like buttons. Under the top flap are concealed wool needle pages. 12" × 16". *Chester County Historical Society, West Chester, Pennsylvania.*

Red sewing rolls with words on the fronts. The top roll is embossed in metallic gold, "Forget Me Not" in gold ink. 3.5" × 2.5". The center sewing roll is bound in green silk and has the name "Lydia Bissell" stamped in black ink. 3.5" × 4.5". The bottom roll has a metal closure with the name "L. M. Stoddard" stamped in black ink. 5.5" × 5". *Collection of the author.*

Housewife of seal and fish skin acquired by the museum in 1869. *Unalakleet, Norton Sound, Alaska. Catalog Number - E7601 Department of Anthropology, Smithsonian Institution. Photo by Donald E. Hurlbert.*

Red suede sewing roll with green velvet pincushion roll ends. The gathered pocket and bands on the roll end are silk. The wool needle pages have embroidered edges. 6" × 16". *Collection of the author.*

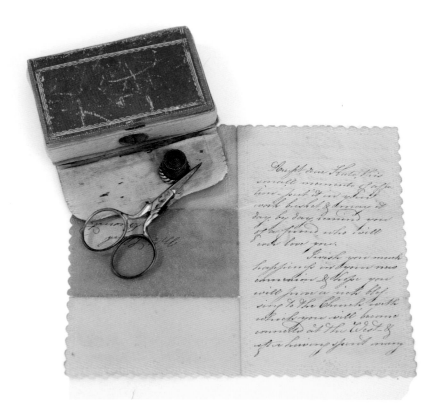

Red leather sewing roll with thimble holder, thimble, scissors, and enclosed letter. The green silk lining of the roll is in high contrast to the red leather gold embossed exterior. The stationery has a scalloped edge and a female silhouette at the top of each page. *Collection of the author.*

The interior of the sewing roll is fitted with an impression for holding the thimble. 4" × 5". *Collection of the author.*

Oil cloth, sometimes called enameled cloth, was used to simulate leather. Using tinted linseed oil, canvas was coated to create a waterproof surface to simulate leather. It could be made at home and was also produced commercially. As it ages, the oil cloth sometimes cracks. The *New York Observer* published a story on September 29, 1898, written by Julia Darrow Cowles of Minneapolis, about a newly formed Junior Red Cross Chapter to support the Spanish-American War. The young girls worked under the supervision of their mothers who had made soldiers sewing rolls for the American Civil War. The girls gathered with their workbags filled with needles, threads, and scissors. An uncle supplied twelve yards of oil cloth for the exterior of the rolls; the girls brought silk scraps for lining the rolls. Needle pages were made of black flannel. The edges were bound with black silk. The style of sewing rolls they made were described as "housewifes." These cases folded up for storage in a small spaces like pockets. This style roll contained three interior pockets that were filled with needles, black and white thread, straight pins, large safety pins, and court plaster. The larger safety pins were used as clothes pins for outdoor laundry. Court plaster was specially treated fabric for wound care.

Sewing rolls were also given as gifts to loved ones. As people headed west to the American frontier, sewing rolls were often given along with other mementos for the journey.

One letter found inside a sewing roll reads:

*Accept, Miss Kate, this small memento of affection – put it in your work basket & may it day to day remind you of a friend who will ever love you.*

*I wish you much happiness in your new commission & hope you will prove a rich blessing to the church with which you will become connected at The West & after having spent many happy & useful years may an abundant entrance be ministered unto you into the everlasting kingdom of our Lord & Savior Jesus Christ.*

*Yours Affectionately*
*J H M'D*
*March 13, 1857*

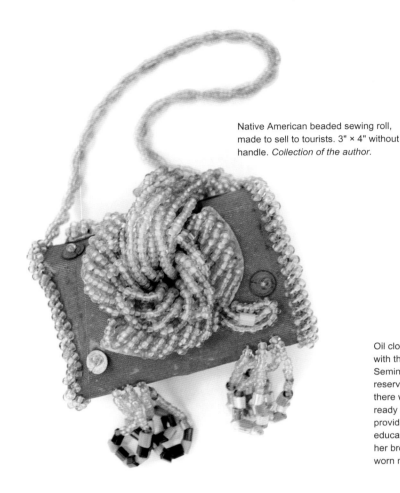

Native American beaded sewing roll, made to sell to tourists. 3" × 4" without handle. *Collection of the author.*

Oil cloth sewing roll examples that simulate black leather. One is marked with the name "Mary Van Alstyne." Mary attended the Troy Female Seminary in 1862. A teacher, Emma Willard, wrote of Mary: "She was a reserved and quiet girl, but in every respect one of the best of pupils. If there was a knotty question in arithmetic or algebra, Mary was always ready to answer it." The Troy Female Seminary was the first in America to provide young women with an education comparable to that of college-educated young men. Thirty-five years later Mary is recorded as living with her brother in Valatie, New York. 3" × 5". The example on the bottom has worn metallic trim for binding. 7" × 5". *Collection of the author.*

Eskimos and Native Americans also needed places to keep sewing supplies close at hand. Eskimos used seal gut and skin to fashion sewing and tool rolls. While some were practical, others were ornately embroidered. Similar items used include moose skin sewing bags and pouches.

Native Americans beaded souvenir sewing rolls. These rolls were sold at popular vacation destinations like Niagara Falls. They are three to four inches wide and about seven inches long unrolled. The base material is thin paper board covered in brightly colored wool. Wool colors include orange, blue, red, and black. Since the base fabric didn't wear well, finding undamaged examples is difficult. Beading includes raised work, loops, and handles completed in sparking clear and brightly colored glass beads. The interiors were lined in glazed cotton that extends around the sides to form binding. The interior includes a pincushion filled with wool and a pocket for storage. The rolls close with a hook and eye.

Native American beaded sewing roll, made to sell to tourists. This example was sold at the entrance to Niagara Falls in New York. 2.5" × 4.5". *Collection of Tex Johnson.*

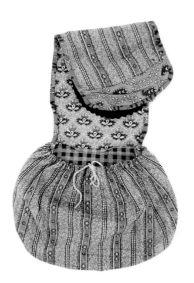

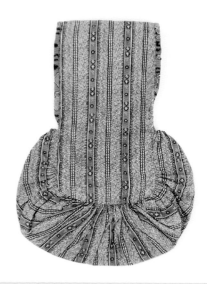

Linen sewing roll with wool braid binding and feather stitch embroidery. A linen strap wraps around the sewing roll and buttons to secure it closed. 8" × 16". *Collection of the author.*

Cotton sewing roll with a lower pocket that gathers closed with thread. Behind the gathered pocket is a flat pocket with partitions for needle packages. Five cotton prints were used in the roll. There are four red and black wool needle pages with pinked edges. 8" × 23". *Collection of the author.*

Back view of a cotton sewing roll showing the fullness of the lower pocket. Applied binding finishes the long edge of the sewing roll. 8" × 23". *Collection of the author.*

Highly contrasting color of silk-lined sewing rolls. Materials include silk, leather, brocade, wool, and velvet. 6" – 17". *Collection of the author.*

Sewing roll from Elmira Thomas (1840–1914), daughter of Sarah (1815–1885) and John Thomas. No evidence was found that Elmira ever married. The padded end of the roll is made of layers of the same wool used for the needle pages. 3.5" × 10". *Collection of the author.*

Green silk bag made from 4" wide silk ribbon. The bag is lined in pink silk ribbon. The drawstring top gathers closed with 3/8" silk ribbons. All hand sewn. 4" × 4" × 8". *Collection of the author.*

## Reticules and Bags

When visiting family, friends, or places of interest, needlework supplies were sometimes carried in a bag. These bags were sometimes called reticules. A reticule was decorative in nature and meant for show as much as for practical purposes. Geoffrey Warren in the book *A Stitch in Time* writes of decorative embroidered bags hung on the arms of furniture in Victorian times. Their decorative nature offered further embellishment to the room. Inside the bags were discreetly hidden small dusting cloths.

In the eighteenth and nineteenth centuries small bags could be carried in pockets worn at the waist under the dress skirt. Small silk or embroidered bags suspended from a waistband were shown in some early-nineteenth-century fashion plates. Silk drawstring bags made of ribbon or silk yardage were carried on the wrist. Brightly colored shimmering silk, sometime embellished with additional ribbons, was very noticeable and intended for admiration. Beautiful silk ribbons were available from milliners and dry goods stores in most metropolitan areas. Some bags were further finished with beads, tassels, and fringe. Sophisticated reticules include interior pockets, concealing needle books in the bottom, and pin discs in the covers. The details of each bag are cleverly designed and sewn.

The March 1834 issue of *Godey's Lady's Book* includes instructions for a basket reticule. The reader is instructed to line a basket with silk stitching directly to the basket. A ribbon is used in the drawstring top.

Storage bags for mending and plain sewing at home were often called work bags. The bags were made in a variety of shapes and are typically larger than reticules. Work bags were made of durable fabrics like linen and bark cloth. The bags were functional and durable to stand up to heavy use. Interior pockets provided necessary storage for threads, thimbles, and other small sewing supplies. Some styles include built in needle books. Drawstring styles are generally closed with linen tapes, wool braid, or other long-lasting narrow goods threaded through rings around the top of the bag.

Bags were also used to hold balls of thread and were hung on the left wrist (for right-handed sewers). The thread flowed freely from the top or a special opening without rolling away during crochet, knitting, and tatting sessions. Some of the wrist thread bags are crocheted, to hold the very thread they are made from.

Hoop bags were made by sewing fabric around embroidery hoops. The size of the bag was defined by the size of the hoop. Fabrics used included cotton, silk, or rayon. Thinner fabrics gathered fuller and more easily around the hoop. Lids and bottoms were made by covering circles of cardboard with fabric. The interiors sometimes included needle books, pockets, and loops for holding small tools. The bag handles were also made of fabric. The bags were somewhat delicate and used for holding light mending, small projects, and kerchiefs.

Silk sewing bags made with gathered silk attached to hard-sided needle books. The gathered silk closes with silk ribbon drawstrings. The black bag has an added small bag for a thimble and a matching emery. 3" – 5". *Collection of the author.*

Collection of silk reticules made in an assortment of silks and brocades. Lightweight and colorful, they were often worn on the wrist. 3" – 8". *Collection of Kathryn G. Lesieur.*

Needle book bottom of the pink bag. Needles and glass-headed pins were conveniently stored away when the needle book was tied closed with the ribbon. 5" diameter. *Collection of Kathryn G. Lesieur.*

Hand-embroidered bargello bag with matching tassels and corded handle. At least ten colors of wool were used to create the pattern. 12" × 12". *Collection of Kathryn G. Lesieur.*

Hand-embroidered Irish stitch or bargello stitch bag with silk ribbon accents. The embroidery is worked in at least eleven colors of thread. 8" × 10". *Collection of Kathryn G. Lesieur.*

Silk reticule bags with silk ribbon handles. The blue bag has black feather stitch accent embroidery. Black-glass-headed pins are inserted all around the base. 4" tall. The khaki green silk bag has a needle book base that is secured closed with a pearl-headed pin. The circular base is kid leather. 6" tall. *Collection of the author.*

Interior view of a silk reticule lined with pockets. Each pocket has a paper thread winder with assorted colors of silk thread. The drawstring top closes with black ribbon. 3" circular base. *Collection of the author.*

Green silk reticule with gathered sides and needle book sides. The edge of the needle book is made of pink silk ribbon and is filled with pins inserted vertically. The needle book has wool needle pages. The bag came filled with several small items and notes. The note with the handkerchief reads, "The Handkerchief was one of mother's wedding presents from dear old Mrs. Miner (I do remember her). Jan. 29, 1852." The note with the silk remnant reads, "Silk from one of mother's wedding outfits." Also enclosed was the small heart-shaped emery. 1.75" emery. *Collection of the author.*

Sewing rolls with drawstring tops and compartmental bases. The base of each bag unfolds and unbuttons to reveal numerous functions and compartments. Note paper, thimble holders, needle pages, and storage are all hidden away when the base unit is closed. 10.25" × 2.5" × 3.5". *Chester County Historical Society, West Chester, Pennsylvania.*

Handmade button detail from drawstring top sewing roll. 0.375". *Collection of Tex Johnson.*

Detail on one interior compartment showing leather bodkin holder band, thimble bucket, emery holder, and button flaps. *Collection of Tex Johnson.*

Interior notebook page with the name "Rachel Fell" and the date 1804. Possibly the Rachel Fell born March 9, 1804. She married Isaac Chambers on November 15, 1821, at the age of 17. The marriage took place at the West Grove Meeting, West Grove, Pennsylvania. She died September, 8, 1826, at the age of 22 and is buried in West Nottingham Township, Chester County, Pennsylvania. *Collection of Tex Johnson.*

Sewing roll with drawstring top and embroidered edge base. 10.25" × 2.5" × 3.5". *Collection of Tex Johnson.*

Yellow silk bag with pleated sides and a needle book base. Matching silk ribbon is used for the drawstring closure, end pleats, and needle book closure. 2.5" × 13". *Collection of Tex Johnson.*

Drawstring top sewing bag with spade-shaped needle book base. There are accent bows where the bag meets the needle book. The same blue silk ribbon is used for the drawstring handles, side of the pin keep insert, and bows and ties on the needle book. 5" × 15". *Collection of Tex Johnson.*

Sewing bag with a woven basket base and silk drawstring top. Gathered with a purple cord. 8" × 7". *Collection of the author.*

Linen drawstring bag, all hand sewn. 6" diameter. *Collection of the author.*

Silk sewing bag possibly made from a man's tie. The bottom of the bag is a two-layered pocket. The top layer is divided into compartments with feather stitching. The sections are the size of needle packages. The pocket below is one large pocket. The middle section is a padded pin keep with embroidered wool needle pages on top. An additional pocket is stitched halfway up the drawstring bag top closed with a brown silk ribbon. 7" × 17". The small leather box fits inside the drawstring bag. 4.5" × 2.5". The penny was wrapped inside the note that reads, "1 Penny for being good Fred." 2" note. *Collection of the author.*

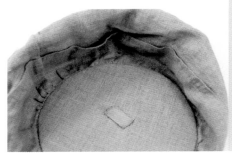

The interior of the linen bag is unlined and has pockets stitched around the base. A small loop of twill tape is attached to the base to secure the tip of scissors in the center of the base, away from the side of the bag. 6" base. *Collection of the author.*

Lined cotton sewing bag with matching sewing accessories. All hand sewn, the accessories include a thimble holder, scissor sheath, and needle book with a pin keep side. 3" base. *Collection of the author.*

Interior label from the cotton sewing bag set. The label reads, "Friends Meeting, Wilmington, Delaware." The Wilmington Monthly Meeting of Friends was founded in 1738. Possibly sold for Quaker fund-raising, the Wilmington Meeting now has approximately 400 members. 0.66" × 2.25". *Collection of the author.*

Double-layer cotton work bag sewn over the bottom of a milk carton. The tall inner layer forms the lining. The outside layer forms the binding-topped pockets. Small pearl buttons close the top of the pockets. Feather stitching attaches the casing with a hand-stitched buttonhole for threading a ribbon drawstring. Below the embroidered dragonflies, around all four sides, is the verse "It is never too late to mend but a man should not expect a button sewed on much after midnight." 4.25" square base. *Collection of the author.*

Hand-stitched linen bag with a twill tape drawstring (left). 1.75" × 2". The patchwork bag on the right is lined in plain cotton. The seams in the patchwork appear to be overcast stitched and not done in a running stitch. The bag closes with hand-loomed tape. 6" × 8". *Collection of the author.*

View of the bag with the top gathered and closed with the hand-woven tape ties. With the tape permanently attached to the bag, the tie cannot be lost and is readily available. *Collection of the author.*

Homespun linen storage bag with embroidered cross stitch initials and tape loom–woven ties. All of the seams are hand sewn. The top edge of the bag is selvedge. 11.5" × 18". *Collection of the author.*

Work bag made by gathering fabric around the edge of a needle book. Wool braid is threaded through rings along the top edge of the bag to gather it closed. The amount of fullness in the gathers allows for many pieces of mending to fit in the bag. The edge of the needle book cover is embellished with pleated wool braid. 15" × 10.5". *Collection of the author.*

Work bag made by gathering fabric around the edge of a needle book. Wool braid is threaded through a casing at the top edge of the bag to gather it closed. The amount of fullness in the gathers allows for many pieces of mending to fit in the bag. The wool pages of the needle book have pinked edges. There is an interior pocket on the back of the needle book. 17" × 18.5". *Collection of the author.*

Cotton storage bag with drawstring top that closes with machine-made tape. The hand-sewn bag is unlined. 9" × 12". *Collection of the author.*

Detail of velvet needle book cover. The flat edge is hinged to cover the enclosed wool needle pages. 4" × 6". *Collection of Pat L. Nickols.*

Detail of the needle book edge finish. The gathered trim is hand sewn to the velvet edge. The braid is the drawstring closure. 0.5" trim. *Collection of Pat L. Nickols.*

Double-ended needle book work bag with a brass ring drawstring top. Each of the two needle books has wool needle pages. 24" × 18". *Collection of Pat L. Nickols.*

Embroidered linen mending bag. The edges are finished with satin stitching. The drawstring top is closed with a red cording. 14" × 18". *Collection of the author.*

Embroidered cotton mending bag with tape drawstring closure. Machine seams and hand embroidery. 12" × 18". *Collection of the author.*

Bag made from gathering fabric to fabric-covered pieces of pasteboard. The bag is lined in solid-green cotton. The drawstring top closes with black ribbon. The bag is all hand stitched. Each square side is 8". *Collection of the author.*

Hanging bags in the shape of clothing. The bottom of the pant legs are stuffed for pincushions. The pockets are sized to hold thimbles. The neck opening is also the bag opening for small mending or soiled handkerchiefs. 8" × 10". *Collection of the author.*

Silk bag made from gathering wide ribbon around a needle book. The finished edge of the ribbon is hand stitched to the finished side of the needle book. The needle pages are buttonhole-edged wool. The needle book and casing edge of the bag close with dark-blue silk ribbon. 5" × 3". *Collection of the author.*

Silk and leather pieced together for a reticule shaped like a blimp. A navy flap bound in matching leather covers the opening and is secured by two tiny black snaps. The bag is lined in matching blue silk. The handle is brown silk ribbon with a bow. 7" × 3.5". *Collection of the author.*

Reticules made from silk ribbon gathered in a circle. The red-handled example is gathered onto a small ring. The narrow ends of the ribbon are hemmed but not joined to create the opening for the bag. The striped example is made from silk velvet ribbon that has shattered. The finished edge of the ribbon is gathered and secured with a knot. The bags could be used for balls of knitting yarn or crochet thread, with the ends extended through the round openings. 6" diameter. *Collection of the author.*

Bags made from crochet bands attached to silk. The top of the bags close with a ribbon drawstring pulled through the crochet edging. The blue bag is unlined; the pink bag is lined in light, delicate silk fabric. 8" diameter closed. *Collection of the author.*

Bags made by gathering fabric around the rings from embroidery hoops. Oval and round hoops were used. Fabrics include cotton and silk. The lids were made by covering pasteboard with fabric. When empty the bags store flat. 6" – 12". *Collection of the author.*

Cotton hoop bag with a sixteen-patch block on the lid. The handles and body of the bag are made from pieced cotton like a quilt. 5" diameter. *Collection of Pat L. Nickols.*

Detailed photo showing the hand stitching used to cover the lid. A thread loop over a button secures the lid to the top hoop. 0.375" button. *Collection of Pat L. Nickols.*

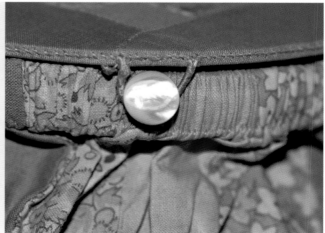

Pocket pair said to have belonged to Thomazine Downing Thomas, wife of Colonel Richard Thomas. They were married in 1774. The same cotton print is used on both fronts. Different cotton prints are used for the bindings, and the lining. A separate piece of cotton was added behind the pocket opening; the hand stitching can be seen on the light-colored linen back. The linen tape ties are hand sewn to the binding at the waist. 16.5" × 11.66". *Chester County Historical Society, West Chester, Pennsylvania.*

## Waist Pockets

When garment pockets are discussed today, we envision pockets sewn into and onto garments. This was not always the case. In centuries past, pockets were often independent of the garment. Women's clothing in the eighteenth and nineteenth centuries did not include pockets incorporated into the seams of the dress. Following past trends and techniques in fashion, women's antique waist pockets are found in a variety of shapes and styles. Women's independent waist pockets were tied at the waist with a fabric, tape, or braid band and were worn underneath petticoats; openings in the layers of fabric were needed for access.[6]

The convenient location gave quick access to the contents; personal articles, sewing supplies, snuff, and small household supplies.[7] Pouches could also be sewn into a garment. While not the exclusive way for a woman to carry her possessions, pockets were certainly the most personal, lying hidden under the clothing layers.

Women's pockets carried an air of mystery by their private nature, worn against the body. There is speculation ones most private and treasured possessions were inaccessible by any other person when carried in a pocket. Because there was very little personal private space in the eighteenth and nineteenth centuries, carrying personal and valuable possessions on the body for safe keeping was common practice. Women had a diverse set of responsibilities in the home, and the waist pocket helped her manage her possessions. She needed a secure place for personal items like eye glasses, fans, and keys, as well as sewing items and other household supplies. A small sewing wallet or roll was a common way to keep sewing tools together in the waist pocket.[8] The ability of women to legally own property varied by state law and was changing during the nineteenth century. What women carried on their person was private and generally not included in estate lists.[9] In order to know what was in a woman's pockets, someone would have been in rather intimate contact.

Pair of pieced patchwork pockets illustrating what contents might have been inside. There was ample space for a sewing roll, letters, smaller bags with jewelry and keys, small household linens, and plenty of room for more. One pocket measures 12" × 18". *Collection of the author.*

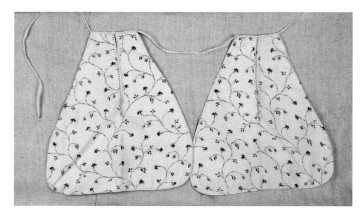

Pair of matched pockets on a tape tie waist. Printed linen fronts and solid backings, possibly linen. The openings are bound in the same print as the pocket fronts. 18" × 22". *Collection of Tex Johnson.*

There was a risk of theft, especially when the pocket was worn on the outside of a skirt. Thieves would look for an exposed waist tie and cut it with a knife while grabbing the freed pockets. The ties were frequently made of woven cotton, wool, or linen tape. Newspaper accounts document both the reported thefts and the prosecution of "cut-pocket thieves." The alternative, a reticule, was hand carried and was even more prone to loss by misplacement or theft. In some regions, wearing the pocket(s) under a skirt or apron was more desirable. Tie-on waist pockets were sometimes part of a young girls possessions. The age at which a girl would begin to wear pockets is unknown. Dolls of the period were occasionally fitted with tie-on waist pockets.

Women's waist pockets are found in singles and pairs. The pockets are attached to narrow fabric bands of woven tape or braid that is tied at the waist. Occasionally they were made with a button at the narrow waistband. They tend to be longer than they are wide and generally widened at the bottom. They have been represented in eighteenth- and nineteenth-century art worn under the outer skirt and over the petticoat as well as over the outer skirt. Some were worn over the outer skirt, but under an apron. The variation in placement could depend on local custom, station in life, and personal preference.

Unlike other women's textile accessories and garments, some pockets are found with embroidered initials, dates, and numbers marked in cross stich on the back of the pocket. Some are embroidered with only initials. If the pocket is marked with a low-value two-digit number, it is unknown if this is for inventory or dating purposes.

There is variation in pocket construction. Some are fully lined; others are partially lined on the back fabric piece where the hand could cause excess wear entering the pocket. The basic pocket shape is narrower at the top and wider at the bottom. Fabrics include chintz, cotton roller prints, homespun linen, and silk. Textured linen fabrics like Manchester cloth are also found.

Pockets decorated with embroidery are found as singles and pairs. Embroidery patterns were sometimes designed and arranged specifically for pockets. The embroidery design was symmetrical and centered on the pocket opening, often including floral motifs connected with curving vines.[10] Florentine stitch embroidered pieces were stitched in the areas in and around Philadelphia. Some needlework teachers in nineteenth-century girls' schools came from Europe. They were skilled in sewing and embroidery. Teaching sewing and embroidery provided a way of living for women. The pair of Florentine pockets shown in this chapter are beautiful examples of the embroidery technique. While some embroidery was clearly designed to fit the pocket shape, other pocket examples are constructed of recycled embroidery, which may have been recycled from the better portions of worn bed hangings or gowns. In the recycled examples, the embroidery design may not be symmetrical to the pocket shape or opening. The Winterthur Museum has a 1781 example from Lancaster County, Pennsylvania, with symmetrically arranged cross-stitched scattered motifs.

Pockets made of printed cotton demonstrate the wide variety of cotton prints available to American women, with examples spanning one hundred years. The pockets sometimes mix cotton and linen fabrics. Some use one cotton print on the front and linen on the back. Some are lined or partially lined, using neutral or contrasting fabrics in the lining. Another variation reinforces the pocket opening with a facing fabric.

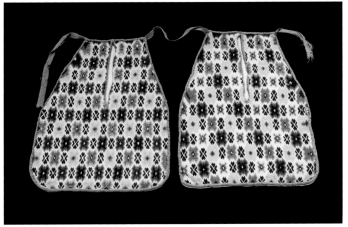

Florentine stitched pair of pockets bound in green wool twill weave tape. The pockets are backed in white fabric and the front embroidery panels are lined in white linen. 10.125" × 13.25". *Chester County Historical Society, West Chester, Pennsylvania.*

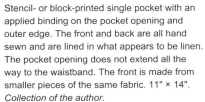

Stencil- or block-printed single pocket with an applied binding on the pocket opening and outer edge. The front and back are all hand sewn and are lined in what appears to be linen. The pocket opening does not extend all the way to the waistband. The front is made from smaller pieces of the same fabric. 11" × 14". *Collection of the author.*

Pair of matching pockets with a cotton print on the front and white linen backing. Two separate machine-made tapes are used for the waist and pocket openings. The pocket opening does not extend all the way to the waistband. 11.5" × 19". *Chester County Historical Society, West Chester, Pennsylvania.*

Pair of white pockets, possibly made of homespun linen and cotton. The fronts and backs are pieced from multiple pieces of matching fabrics. The waistband and ties are made from linen tape. 12" × 21". *Collection of the author.*

Back of pocket showing cross stitch used to mark linens. The letters stood for the owner; the number could be a linen rotation number, an inventory number, or possibly a year. The letters are fourteen threads high, hand stitched one cross stitch over two linen threads. 0.66" high. *Collection of the author.*

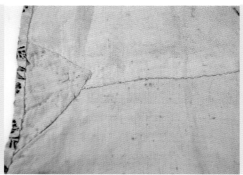

Single pocket, unlined with no binding. Possibly made for use by a child. The pocket opening is a hand-sewn rolled edge. The machine-made tape is hand sewn to the pocket, creating the waistband and ties. 6" × 14". *Collection of the author*

Back of pocket showing the reuse of textiles. The backing could have come from a garment or household linen. The seams are all hand sewn. 2" triangle. *Collection of the author*

Patchwork pocket examples are found in quilted and unquilted variations. Possibly constructed of old quilts, the unworn quilt sections were recycled for pockets. The piecework could also be pieced specifically for the pocket front. Variations include patchwork that is not quilted, but lined to provide a smooth interior and protect the patchwork seams. Some of the unquilted patchwork examples do include a soft interlining like batting. Patchwork examples sometimes include applique motifs.

While the fabric composition of pockets varied greatly, women exercised variations in other ways when constructing their pockets. The basic construction was fairly simple, making pockets affordable to all women of the eighteenth and nineteenth centuries. *The Workwoman's Guide* of 1840 encouraged enforced seams and folded-over tape waistbands to increase durability. The seams are sometimes bound with tape, including the pocket opening. The tapes don't always match each other or the pocket's color aesthetic. Another seam option recommended was a French seam that left the inside secure and smooth. More-complex pocket designs included an inner pocket or two placed in the back fabric that rested against the body.

The waistband and ties varied on pockets. To minimize the amount of tape needed, it was sometimes started and stopped at the pocket fabric, not extending across the entire top. In some styles the tape is a single long length extending the full waistband and ties. The earliest tapes on pockets were hand loomed, probably in the home. Later in the nineteenth century tapes were manufactured and machine-made tapes replaced hand-loomed tapes. Some pocket styles used fabric sewn in narrow strips to create the ties. Other variations are cords and wool braids. Tapes wore out with frequent use and were mended or replaced as needed.

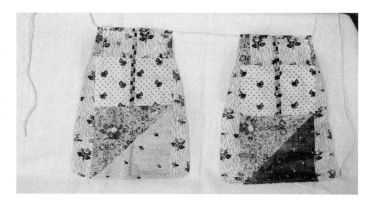

Pair of pieced patchwork pockets with tape ties. Similar prints can be seen in each pocket. Hand-sewn top stitching covers the outer seams. 12" × 20" each pocket. *Collection of Tex Johnson.*

Single pocket of pieced cottons and applique accents. The entire pocket is bound on all sides in the same linen used for the backing. Separate tape ties with red accent threads are hand sewn to the corners of the top pocket edge. The pocket is lined with additional cotton prints. 10.25" × 14.66". *Chester County Historical Society, West Chester, Pennsylvania.*

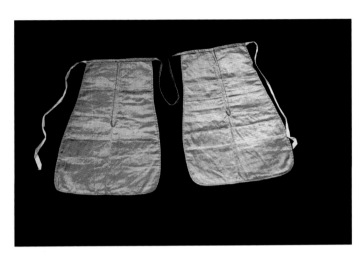

Pair of pockets said to have belonged to Phebe Ann Sharpless (?–1898), daughter of Abigail Garrett Ashbridge, (1808–1857) and Samuel Sharpless (?–1872). In the 1850 federal census records, Phebe lived with her parents in East Goshen, Pennsylvania. There is no record Phebe ever married. In the 1880 federal census Phebe was living with her Aunt Eliza H. Ashbridge. The family was Quaker and is buried in the Goshen Friends Burial Ground in Pennsylvania. The pockets are joined in the center with matching fabric. The attached tape ties are white. 9.75" × 15" each pocket. *Chester County Historical Society, West Chester, Pennsylvania.*

Single pocket with layers of repairs over the original patchwork front. Lined and backed in linen. Later hand-stitched patches were partially removed to expose seams to examine the original stitching techniques. The top patchwork was laid over the linen lining with no batting or quilting. The ties are braided cotton. 8" × 16". *Collection of the author.*

Exposed inner seam in the linen lining. 0.125" seam allowance. *Collection of the author.*

Back side of the pocket shows the hand-stitched top stitching around the outer edge of the pocket. 0.25" from edge. *Collection of the author.*

Single cotton pocket with a horizontal opening. The outer edge is bound in two separate plaids. There is no evidence the pocket had ties. This style may have tucked into the apron waistband. 8" × 14". *Collection of the author.*

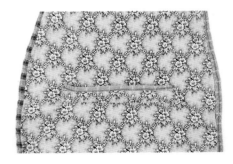

Detail of the horizontal pocket opening with a bound top and insert bottom. The attached placket is 1" × 5". *Collection of the author.*

Tabletop-size nineteenth-century tape loom. The looms were used before machine-made tapes were readily available. Tape in the home was used for clothing, drawstring in bags, and a multitude of other uses. 6" × 18". *Collection of the author.*

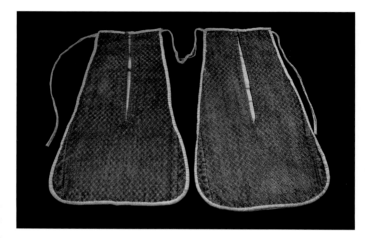

Matching pair of hand-sewn green plush wool pockets. The pockets are backed in tan linen. A different weave linen is used for the binding for all of the outer edges of the pockets. The pocket openings are bound in brown linen. Red and tan tape is used for the ties. 11" × 16.5". *Chester County Historical Society, West Chester, Pennsylvania.*

The opening in the pockets were also varied. Most openings were vertical to the waist; however, horizontal openings are also found. The opening in pockets received heavy wear from repeated abrasion from the hands. The dominant-hand (right or left) pocket will usually show the most wear. The openings are finished with fabric binding, tape, fabric facing or plackets, and buttonhole-stitched embroidery. Some openings are reinforced at the bottom with stitching.

The 1838 book *The Workwoman's Guide* provides instructions for apron pockets hidden in the gathers of a ladies apron. A slit was placed in the apron fabric, and the opening edge was hemmed or finished with binding. The pocket was placed behind the opening.

Multiple pockets could be worn under or over the skirt, in many combinations with singles or doubles. For example, valuables could be kept in a pocket or pockets under the skirts and a single or double worn on top. Less valuable items that needed quick access could be kept in the top pocket. Some top pockets were tucked into the waistband of an apron. A shop keeper could keep a few small coins in the top pocket, moving larger amounts to the under pockets as needed for security.

Travel waist pockets were worn by men and women in the late nineteenth century. *Godey's Lady's Book* published a pattern for a "Gold Pocket With Belt." They suggest cutting two pieces of linen eight by sixteen inches, square top and rounded bottom. The opening is cut in the upper piece three inches from the top and six inches long. The edges are to be finished in buttonhole-stitched red cotton. The same stitching is added around the outer right side of the seam. A security slide ring is added at the top of the pocket to secure the opening. The waist belt that is attached to the pocket is also made of the linen fabric.

This pocket is made from linen, wool, and cotton. The edges are bound with wool twill weave tape. Symmetrically designed crewel embroidery on the front includes chain, Romanian couching, and satin stitches creating trailing flowers in shades of rose, green, blue, and tan. The waist tie is made of hand-woven tape. The exposed edges under the worn binding provide a view of the basted edge and hand-sewn seam. 9" × 7.8". *Courtesy Winterthur Museum, Lady's pocket, 1740-1775, United States, Linen, Wool, Cotton, Bequest of Henry Francis du Pont, 1958.1758.*

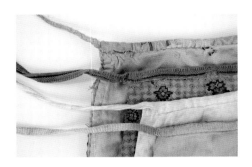

An assortment of waist pockets showing the variety of tape ties and the various ways they are attached. *Collection of the author.*

Back side of packet edge with an applied binding hand sewn down. The maker cut the fabric the length of the cotton stripe. 0.25" binding. *Collection of the author.*

Inset pocket opening that does not extend to the waistband. This caused stress to the inset seam, causing it to tear. *Collection of the author.*

Bottom of a pocket opening showing the bias binding piece curve around the inset opening. 0.25" binding. *Collection of the author.*

Pockets showing the openings extending through the waistband with no applied binding used on the pockets. *Collection of the author.*

Non-bias binding applied to a pocket opening. *Collection of the author.*

Hand-stitched buttonhole stitches reinforce the stress point at the base of the pocket opening. *Chester County Historical Society, West Chester, Pennsylvania.*

BERK'S
REPLACEMENT
POCKET

HIP

FRONT

PRICE **5**¢ EACH

DOUBLE-STITCHED

HIP POCKET

Factory made twentieth-century pre-sewn pockets sold for ready-made garments. 4" – 7". *Collection of the author.*

# *Sewing Sets*

## Sets

Attractive matched sets of sewing tools have long been favored by women. They were popular gifts, and women often owned more than one set. The inventory of Margaret of Austria, Duchess of Savoy, in 1524, mentions a small needle case covered with green velour, in which were tweezers, little scissors, a stiletto, and other little instruments with handles of tortoiseshell, mother-of-pearl, and "the rest gilded."[1]

Sewing sets were used for practical as well as social needs. In 1836, Hans Christian Anderson, in his novel *O.T.*, wrote this of his character Sophie: "You will see her work-box with all the curiosities. That little plays a great part: it is always taken with her when she pays a visit—for the sake of conversation it is brought out; all is then looked through, and every article goes round of the company. Yes, there are beautiful things to be seen: a little wheelbarrow with a pincushion, a silver fish, and the little yard measure of silk ribbon." While the author and character are Danish, one can imagine a similar social interaction in many nineteenth-century women's social circles in America.

### Metal Companion Sets

Inexpensive metals like aluminum and brass were used to mass produce sewing sets in the twentieth century. The inexpensive sets were popular with American advertisers. The set is so small that the thimble is the lid. Inside the body of the set is a hollow wooden spindle with two colors of thread. Inside the wooden spindle are sewing needles, safety pins, and straight pins topped with a wooden cap. The advertising was applied with a sticker around the center of the outer case.

In 1896, Huebel and Manger of Brooklyn, New York, invented a combination pincushion, spool holder, and thimble holder that slid onto the edge of a table.[2] The device was advertised as attractive, durable, useful, and not easily lost. In the center of the velour-covered pincushion is an acorn-shaped metal finial for holding a thimble. There are four thread spool posts surrounding the pincushion.

### Leather Sets

Some of the sewing sets are enclosed in silk-lined leather folders like wallets. Contents can include small thread spools, needle cases, scissors, thread winders, needle packages, and pincushions. When opened flat on a table they provide everything needed for mending and small sewing projects within easy reach.

### Homemade Sets

Ladies' magazines in the nineteenth and twentieth centuries published numerous patterns for sewing sets. The instructions were general and gave the maker plenty of room for creative interpretation. Examples from *Godey's Lady's Book* includes instructions like, "Cut to desired size, cover the rings with crochet and sew them together or cover the entire piece with silk." It is rare that instructions were more than a couple of paragraphs for a complete project.

### Advertising Sets

Paper sets for mending often included advertising. The sets may have included scissors, threads, needles, and straight and safety pins, as well as a needle threader and sometimes shirt buttons. The product advertising was sometimes incorporated into the sewing set and directed toward a target audience. For example, bourbon bottle–shaped paper kits were targeted toward men.

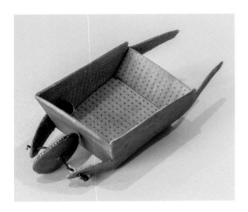

Wheelbarrow sewing set includes a front-wheel pin disc. The interior of the wheelbarrow has a thimble holder and room for a small sewing project or additional sewing tools. 7" × 2.5". *Chester County Historical Society, West Chester, Pennsylvania.*

The lid of the blue bird house sewing set lifts for storing sewing tools. Contents include a small sewing ball, scissors, and thread (not shown). 2.5" base. *Collection of Kathryn G. Lesieur.*

Leather sewing sets in the form of shoes. The shoe sets include thimble holders, emeries, thread spools, needle books, and pins. 1" – 5". *Collection of the author.*

The heel of this leather shoe sewing set is made of silk ribbon stuck with pins. The needle book ties closed with a silk ribbon. 1" × 2". *Collection of the author.*

Needle books below the bottom sole of shoe sewing sets. 1" – 5". *Collection of the author.*

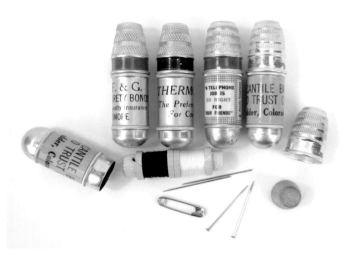

Aluminum advertising sewing sets were often given away. The thimble lifts off the top to access the contents. Inside is a cylinder wrapped in black and white thread. Inside are needles, straight pins, and safety pins. 0.75" × 2". *Collection of the author.*

Leather shoe sewing set with three spools of thread placed in the interior. The red berry emery is stored in an opening in the top of the shoe. The interior heel has a thimble holder with an American sterling thimble. 1.25" × 5". *Collection of Kathryn G. Lesieur.*

Slide-on sewing set that includes pincushion, thread spindles, and acorn-shaped thimble holder on top. 5" × 5". *Collection of the author.*

### The Sewing Companion

Made in (Patent Pending) U. S. A.

One of the most useful articles for users of needle and thread ever made. A combined holder for Spooled Thread, Thimbles, Pins, Needles, Scissors, Buttonhooks and Keys.

Saves steps as "a place for everything and everything in its place." The Companion is made of select material, substantially formed and firmly riveted. New process "Everwear" finish.

The velvet cushion is filled with non-rust dust, the only secure place for hand and machine needle. The holders between glass and cushion are adjustable to large or small thimbles. Select the most convenient place and hang on wall with small nail or screw through hole at top.

If you like the Companion kindly tell your friends.

The Sewing Companion was sold to hang on the wall and hold sewing supplies. It was designed to hold spooled thread, thimbles, pins, needles, scissors, buttonhooks, and keys. The finish on the metal was called "Everwear" but was probably an inexpensive alloy. 4" × 8". *Collection of the author.*

Paper back of the Sewing Companion with an illustration showing how the sewing tools can be stored on the various spindles and hooks. 4" × 8". *Collection of the author.*

Assorted leather sewing boxes with hinged lids. They are silk lined and include small accessories in interior holders. 10" – 1.5". *Collection of the author.*

Interior view of silk-lined leather sewing boxes. Interiors include sewn-in needle books, thimble holders, pincushions, emeries, and straps for holding small hand tools. 10" – 3". *Collection of the author.*

Red leather sewing sets with thimble holders, pincushions, and wool needle pages. The previous owners made improvised thread winders from matchbook covers. Red ribbon is used to tie the sets closed. 1.5" × 6". *Collection of the author.*

Suede leather sewing boxes with cotton fabric lining. The gray suede box has interior flaps under the lid for the needle book and small hand tools. The box section has a pincushion, thimble holder, and room for other sewing supplies. 4" × 5". The light-brown box has sectioned areas for small sewing supplies like buttons. 3.5" × 4". *Collection of the author.*

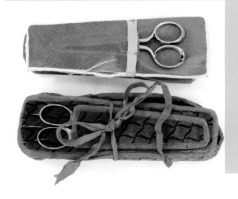

Closed view of red sewing sets showing scissors stored on the tops. 1.5" × 6". *Collection of the author.*

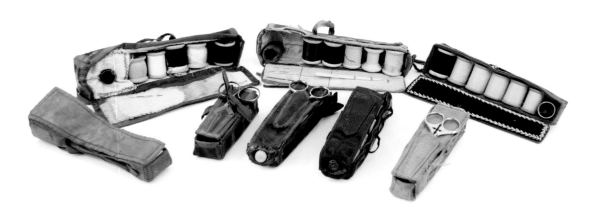

Leather sewing sets with thread spools laced in place with ribbon. Some snap closed; others tie with ribbons. Thimbles holders vary in style as do the wool needle pages. 1.5" × 6". *Collection of the author.*

Small leather sewing set with pins and scissors stored on the cover. 1" × 3.75". *Collection of the author.*

Small leather sewing set in original box. Included in the set is a bodkin, thimble, straight pins, gold eye needles, emery, thread wax, three thread colors, and a scissor sheath. 1" × 3.75". *Collection of the author.*

Paper-covered sewing set holder tied closed with a silk ribbon. Another ribbon is on the top to tie it into the interior of a sewing basket. Four pointed ovals are hand sewn together with one seam left open to add contents. 3" × 3". *Chester County Historical Society, West Chester, Pennsylvania.*

Leather work box with original paper box. "Christmas 1881 From Grandmother" is written on the bottom of the paper box. The box is lined in red silk and includes a child-sized sterling thimble. 4" × 6". *Collection of the author.*

Every edge of the five-sided decorative paper box is hand bound in fabric. Once bound, the panels were hand sewn together. A four-sectioned black wool pincushion is mounted along the upper edge. 8" × 8". *Collection of Kathryn G. Lesieur.*

Decorative paper-covered oval box lined in newsprint and finished with a triangular pincushion. The top edge is bound in double pink cotton fabric hand stitched through the paper. The newsprint includes German-language articles and an ad from the National Bank of Kutztown, Pennsylvania. 9" × 6.5". *Collection of Kathryn G. Lesieur.*

Interior of newsprint lining of the oval box showing the ad from the National Bank of Kutztown, Pennsylvania. *Collection of Kathryn G. Lesieur.*

Fabric-covered pasteboard sewing sets. The two rectangular sets include pincushions, wool needle pages, waxers, and interior pockets. The center example is shaped like a purse with four small beads as the base. 2" × 6". *Collection of the author.*

Kentucky Gentleman paper advertising mending kit. The kit opens like a book and holds threads, needles, pins, and a needle threader. 1.25" × 4.5". *Collection of the author.*

# Chatelaines

A chatelaine is a collection of objects connected to a loop that is worn on the body. One style is worn at the waist and consists of a series of tools on chains suspended from a central waist hook or clip. The second style is a ribbon or a band of fabric worn around the neck, with tools attached at the ends.

The word *chatelaine* is derived from the French word, which means "wife of the lord of the castle." In the sixteenth century, the castle keys were worn on a hook at the waist by the lady of the castle. Over time the style changed to include more chains and commonly used implements hanging from the waist clip.

Men used chatelaines in the eighteenth century, which hung at the waist. They held watches, seals, and other small tools. Like the chatelaines used by women, they were available in several metals. Not all tools on a woman's chatelaine were related to sewing. Examples of non-sewing tools include watches, perfume vessels, aide memoires, and skirt lifters.

From 1811 to 1820, chatelaines fell out of favor due to the high-waist, slim dresses of the Regency period. Once the Victorian fashions became popular, women once again adopted the use of chatelaines. By about 1840, chatelaines were basic in design with utilitarian tools, usually made of steel. The waist clip was often sold separately, and the decorative features of the implements didn't necessarily match the clip. Later in the nineteenth century, the preferred styles were more specific in their function as well as highly decorative.[3]

Silk ribbon styles had the needlework tools suspended from lengths of ribbon. They were made to pin to a waistband or blouse. There were also styles that draped around the neck. To reinforce the ribbon, it was often woven between small rings, thus creating a chain. The ribbon was about one half inch wide and the tools are tied onto the ribbon ends. The ribbon style is sometimes attributed to Shakers. While they may have had some examples, no primary evidence has been found to support the Shaker attribution.

The waist clip on this chatelaine is ornamented with a scene of birds, flowers, and leaves made of applied silver, copper, and gold. The back is marked TIFFANY & Co. Sterling. The three chains hold a pin disc, penknife, and ivory-leaved book. The cover of the book is engraved "MPF." The previous owner was Mary Pauline Foster. The first owner was Mrs. Henry A. du Pont (Mary Apuline Foster, 1849–1902). 9.3" × 3.1". *Courtesy Winterthur Museum, Chatelaine by Tiffany & Company, 1870-1875, New York, NY, Silver, Gold, Copper, Iron, Velvet, Ivory, Bequest of Henry Francis du Pont, 1970.1441.*

Chatelaine clips were also used to suspend small purses or a single object at the waist. The decorative front is hinged to the back piece. The hook is hidden behind the front piece. The front is similar in size and styled similar to the handles of American silverware. It is possible the same molds were used.

Sweetgrass needlework tool holders were also sometimes suspended with silk ribbon. These were designed to promote sales to tourists and not part of any historical practice. The ribbon set could be stored in a larger sweetgrass basket, or used alone. Sweetgrass needlework tools included woven scissor sheaths, thimble holders, and needle books.

Silver chatelaine with six accessories: perfume bottle, pin disc, bent ivory pad, pencil, comb, and scissors with sheath. Hook 2.75" × 1". *Chester County Historical Society, West Chester, Pennsylvania.*

Dated 1784, this chatelaine has a pin ball, scissors, and awl. 17" chain. *Chester County Historical Society, West Chester, Pennsylvania.*

Silk ribbon chatelaines in shades of blue. The styles with rings were worn around the neck. The style without rings was pinned on the bodice. Accessories include sock and glove darners, awls, scissors, needle books, pincushions, emeries, pin discs, thimble holders, and fruit-shaped waxers. 0.5" rings. *Collection of the author.*

Silk ribbon chatelaines in shades of pink. The styles with rings were worn around the neck. The styles without rings were pinned on the bodice. Accessories include sock and glove darners, awls, scissors, needle books, pincushions, emeries, pin discs, thimble holders, and fruit-shaped waxers. 0.5" rings. *Collection of the author.*

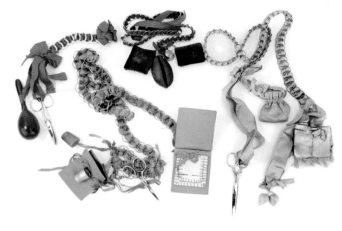

Silk ribbon chatelaines in a variety of colors. The styles with rings were worn around the neck. The style without rings was pinned on the bodice. Accessories include sock and glove darners, awls, scissors, needle books, pincushions, emeries, pin discs, thimble holders, and fruit-shaped waxers. 0.5" rings. *Collection of the author.*

Sweetgrass chatelaine set attached with ribbon. Accessories include a needle book, covered thimble holder, and thimble as well as a scissor sheath. All of the components fit in the round basket. The interior of the round basket has a small ink label with the name "Emeline Scanlon" hand-stitched in place. *Collection of the author.*

Front view of a sterling chatelaine waist clip and mesh reticule bag. Only the decorative front of the clip would show, with the bag hanging down the side of the skirt. 3" × 6" bag. *Collection of the author.*

Side view of a silver chatelaine waist clip. The small hook catches in the waistband. The long hook is used to suspend bags, reticules, and other small necessities at the waist. 2.5" clip. *Collection of the author.*

## Sewing Baskets

The oldest American sewing baskets are Native American baskets. Woven initially for storage, the styles varied by region and tribe. Eventually, due to economic hardship the baskets were sold to tourists to generate income. Styles changed to cater to their customers' needs. Sewing baskets and accessories were popular.

Sweetgrass is considered a sacred plant by many Native American tribes. The plant is used for prayer and special ceremonies. The grass is braided, dried, and burned. Sweetgrass baskets were woven in multiple parts of the country.[4] During the 1860s the Mohawk developed decorative weaves and experimented with a wide variety of baskets.[5] In the 1920s, the Seminole Indians of Florida began to make sweetgrass baskets.[6] Sweetgrass needlework baskets were woven in large quantities for tourists. They are unmarked by the makers and difficult to identify to specific tribes and makers.

Pine needle baskets were made using the coil method of weaving from fallen dried needles with the fascicles (sheaths) removed. The rounds of coils are joined to the previous coil with a wheat stitch, using a raffia-threaded needle. The raffia is sometimes used to create detailed patterned motifs in pine needle weaving. The baskets woven for sewing were often lined with fabric. Sometimes ornamented woven lids were included with sewing baskets.[7]

Splint baskets for sewing are usually woven of wood splint from the brown or black ash tree. Oak splint is for other basket types that are less finely woven and that require strength.[8] The style of the baskets vary by region and maker. Some of the earliest known wood splint baskets were made in the mid-1600s by the Iroquois in what is now western New York.[9] The Oneidas of New York began to weave splints when they lost their old way of living in the late 1700s. Their main customers were white locals and later tourists.[10] The interior details of splint sewing baskets also varies. Some have multiple interior baskets attached to the rim to hold sewing tools like pincushions, thimbles, and scissors. The larger center portion of the basket was free to hold mending or sewing projects.

The assortment of sewing accessories includes sewing baskets, pincushions, thimble holders, and wax. The largest sewing basket has four accessories mounted to the interior rim: scissor sheath, wax cake holder, thimble holder, and a pincushion. By mounting the pieces at the rim, sewing projects could rest in the bottom of the basket. 1" – 15". *Collection of the author.*

Baskets were also made of bone pieces. Working with whale bone was an appealing and harmless pastime that occupied hours of a sailor's time on long journeys. An estimated 200,000 whalers created one-of-a-kind scrimshaw pieces in the nineteenth century. Carving gifts may have served as a balm for their long separations from home. America had more than three times as many whaling vessels as any other country. Objects made at sea were small to fit within the tiny confines sailors were assigned at sea.[11]

After World War I, imported sewing baskets gained favor over fitted wooden sewing boxes. Most of these baskets were inexpensive and readily available. They were sized to hold basic mending supplies and hand sewing for small projects. Ladies' uncovered workbaskets sold in mail order catalogs for about one dollar. Willow work basket styles on legs stood about thirty inches tall to stand beside a chair. The floor standing basket sold for under $2, the equivalent of 5 gallons of milk.[12]

The pink-silk-lined sewing basket set has the sewing tools mounted to the underside of the lid. The lid is unattached to the silk-lined base. 12" diameter. *Collection of Kathryn G. Lesieur.*

These round baskets are hinged and have woven handles. They are lined in blue silk and have the sewing tools mounted to the inside lids. 12" diameter. *Collection of the author.*

These pink-accented sweetgrass sewing accessories include pincushions, thimble holders, and small storage baskets. 3" × 5" rectangular box. *Collection of the author.*

This hinged-lid sewing basket is made of pine needles. The top is embellished with the end of pine cones. The interior is lined in a cotton print. 16" × 6". *Collection of the author.*

This is the woven pattern created on the base of the pine needle basket. 0.25" per needle round. *Collection of the author.*

Woven basket with six smaller woven baskets mounted around the interior rim. There are two handles on each side of the basket. 20" × 8". *Collection of Kathryn G. Lesieur.*

This willow sewing basket has a wooden base and six posts for spools of thread. The 18" × 12" base has 3" sides. *Collection of the author.*

This oval basket is made from carved ivory, wood, and brass. The wooden base of the basket is incised on the bottom as follows: "A MARION HORNET 1852 With fondest regard all to my aunt SARAH." The interior is lined in red velvet. The dowel between the handle is possibly for holding thread. 4" × 3.8" × 3.7". *Courtesy Winterthur Museum, Basket by Marion A. Hornet, 1852, Probably United States, Whale bone, Ivory, Wood, Brass, Cotton, Gift of Mr. & Mrs. Davison B. Hawthorne, 2011.0051.113.*

## Sewing Boxes

Sewing boxes are sometimes referred to as work boxes. In the early nineteenth century the sewing box was a social symbol and used as much for show as it was for sewing. During this period, women often carried their sewing boxes with them when visiting. The ladies would do needlework together, displaying their implements and supplies. In their home parlors they often had larger work tables and boxes for needlework. The larger tables and boxes were also for making social statements.

The most basic implements in a fitted work box include scissors, thread, pins, needle holders, a thimble, and bodkin. Larger boxes have fittings for an awl, thread winders/barrels, fragrance bottles, knitting and crochet needles, and occasionally a hidden compartment. Many lids when raised display a mirror for reflecting candlelight into the work area. Fitted boxes were appropriate gifts to celebrate important occasions in a young girl's life.[13]

The 1838 book *The Workwoman's Guide* provides suggested sewing supplies for a work box for the lady, as well as outfitted boxes for hired help. They provide several suggestions for each servant's work box. Each servant should have a box or basket in a unique shape, making them easily identifiable. The scissor in a sheath should be tied to the basket with a string. The pincushion should be a brick placed in a bag filled with bran padded in flannel then covered in calico. Also included should be a large needle book, a bag of tapes and darning cottons, a small tin of buttons, hooks and eyes, and bodkins. It is also suggested the supplies be marked with the title of the servant's position. For example, the marking HB would indicate "housemaid basket."

The exterior of wooden boxes were decorative, including inlays of various materials and handles. Their makers followed the decorative trends of furniture makers. Some sewing boxes have locks and hidden compartments.[14] The interiors have trays with compartments that lift out to expose small spaces for additional needlework.

This sewing box is designed to resemble a clothing dresser. There is a mirrored back and three drawers each with a pair of small mirrors on each side of the drawer knob. Decorative strips of wood were applied to the sides of the box with brass tacks. 16" × 10" × 20". *Collection of the author.*

Each drawer of the dresser-styled sewing box is fitted with specialized compartments. There are thimble holders, spool posts, and small trays. 16" × 10" × 20". *Collection of the author.*

The paper-covered storage box is labeled "Edgings and Insertions." When the box was on a shelf the label was positioned to face out. A small latch secures the lid in place. 12" × 6" × 4". *Collection of Kathryn G. Lesieur.*

Detail of the latch and label on the box. *Collection of Kathryn G. Lesieur.*

The interior of the "Edgings and Insertions" box is colorfully painted. In the center of the underside of the lid is an etching of the Female Collegiate Institute, Buckingham, Virginia. Possibly the box was used at the school for storing sewing supplies. 6" × 4" image. *Collection of Kathryn G. Lesieur.*

NEEDLE CASE OF REBECCA BUDD WHO
ENTERED WESTTOWN 1799 AS GIRL
#16.   BRINTON COLLECTION.

This wooden sewing box was owned by Rebecca Budd when she attended the Westtown School in 1799. The school is a Quaker school located in West Chester, Pennsylvania. The sewing set is similar in design to some leather sets. The spools are laced in place, and the thimble holder is at the wide end of the box. 7" × 2" × 1". *Chester County Historical Society, West Chester, Pennsylvania.*

The sewing box with doors is rimmed in adhesive tape painted gold to look gilded. Two brass knobs are centered on the front of the doors. 14" × 14" × 8". *Collection of the author.*

The interior of the sewing box has two wooden pockets on each door to stand up scissors, pointed ends down. There are four drawers and two pullout shelves. The center shelf has spool posts for thread. The lower shelf has a velvet pincushion and a small post for a thimble. 14" × 14" × 8". *Collection of the author.*

The plaid top sewing box is stamped "BROWN" on the end. 4.5" × 7" × 5". *Collection of the author.*

The interior of the sewing box is lined in flocked paper with a small mirror in the lid. The newsprint on the interior of the box has a story about General Hancock, infantry troops, and yellow fever in New Bern, North Carolina. The paper is possibly a Civil War edition. 4.5" × 7". *Collection of the author.*

The double-layered sewing box has two hinged layers. The locking top lid is lined in red silk bordered in narrow gold paper trim. There are eighteen wooden thread winders in slots around the outer edge of the tray. Each corner of the tray has a lidded compartment. There are two circular openings for thimbles. The lower compartment also locks and has two side compartments. 14" × 9" × 5.5". *Collection of the author.*

The sewing box with an open center box has a single drawer at the base. It is assembled with square-head nails. Four pins are missing across the top of the box; the center pin and thread spool remain. There are two cups on posts at each end of the box. There is no evidence pincushions were ever attached. Possibly they are small pin cups. 12" × 12" × 10". *Collection of the author.*

This locking sewing box has several compartments in the upper tray. In the center of the tray, under the pincushion, is a hidden drawer. When the drawer is closed, a thin strip of wood slides over the opening, covering it completely. A two-knobbed lid covers the compartment. 10" × 7" × 6". *Collection of the author.*

This sewing box has a false bottom under the tray. The tray lifts out with red ribbon handles. A red velvet pincushion flips up to make the pins more accessible. 12" × 10" × 5". *Collection of the author.*

This sewing box sits on a central leg that fans out at the bottom with four brass tipped legs. The lid is hinged and flips up. The interior is fitted with a sliding try, spool posts, and a large compartment for storage. The lower handle pulls out a drawer. 16" × 12" × 24". *Collection of the author.*

The interior of this sewing box has a mirror on the underside of the lid. Decorative paper strips are glued over the edge of the mirror to hold it in place. The lower box and edge are brightly painted. The removable tray has two removable lids and a pincushion covered in cotton fabric. 11" × 7" × 3.5". *Collection of the author.*

The outside of the sewing box has a slightly domed lid with multiple veneered woods. The box locks and has inlay strips. 11" × 7" × 3.5". *Collection of the author.*

The interior of the black-painted sewing box is brightly colored in blue velvet and green paper. The mirror is glued in place under gold embossed paper strips. The interior is painted in bright-blue paint. The tray has velvet lid covers and two pincushions. 11" × 7" × 3.5". *Collection of the author.*

The black-painted box is stenciled in gold paint. 11" × 7" × 3.5". *Collection of the author.*

Three-tier wooden sewing box built with dovetail construction. The top is covered with a red velvet pincushion with a cut pile motif of a leaf. The bottom two tiers are drawers. Decorative shapes are mounted behind the drawer pulls. An inlaid ivory strip is set into the top tier with the writing "J.M. Tubbs." *Courtesy Winterthur Museum, Sewing Box, possibly made in Ohio, US, 1800-1940, Wood, Ivory, Iron, Velvet, Gift of Mr. and Mrs. Davison B. Hawthorne, 2011.51.118.*

These Shaker sewing boxes were made in East Canterbury, New Hampshire, and Sabbathday Lake, Maine. They were boxed and sold in gift shops to raise funds for the Shaker community. They are lined in silk and often outfitted with matching small sewing tools. The tools include needle books, emeries, waxers, and pincushions. 5" × 2.5" box. *Collection of the author.*

The "Trade Mark" ink stamp from the bottom of a poplar sewing box from Sabbathday Lake Shakers, Maine. 1.75" diameter. *Collection of the author.*

The United Society of Believers in Christ's Second Appearing is a religious sect known as the Shakers. The Shakers referred to themselves as sisters and brothers. At their peak in the mid-nineteenth century, there were 6,000 believers in the United States. Before the Civil War the Brothers sold practical items to "the world," but could not compete with reduced prices of the Industrial Revolution. At about the same time the Sisters began making small, colorful, easy-to-carry items to sell to "the world." Referred to as fancy goods, the items sold to tourists were often related to sewing. The fancy goods were distributed at resort and vacation destinations, first by horse and wagon then later by car. Keeping with their belief in the practical nature of possessions, the fancy goods included many sewing accessories. Examples include pincushions, emeries, thread waxers, spool holders, disc clamps, and needle books.[15]

Fancy goods were also sold in Shaker community gift shops. Woven poplar straw sewing baskets made by the Sisters were bought by tourists. The poplar ware process took the entire Shaker community. The Brothers selected the poplar trees and processed them into two-inch by two-inch by twenty-inch sticks at the sawmill. The sticks were then frozen and further processed into thin strips. The Sisters then dried gauged the strips. The looms for weaving the poplar strips were warped with 216 threads on no. 30 cotton sewing thread. Yards of the poplar was woven daily, then cut off the loom. For stabilization, the poplar was glued to white paper before cutting the pattern shapes.[16] The poplar sheets were cut in a variety of patterns and placed around reusable wooden forms. The seams and outer edges were bound in kid leather. The interiors were fabric lined and ornamented in ribbons to attract buyers. The sewing boxes sometimes included matching sewing accessories. The Sabbath Day Lake community sold 2,500 to 5,000 pieces annually until 1965 when production stopped.[17]

The Shakers also designed and built sewing boxes based on the style of their oval carriers and boxes. Built of cherry, oak, apple, or quarter-sawn oak wood, the "finger" sides wrap around a pine base. Each carrier had a swing handle. The wood carriers were built by the Brothers. The interiors were lined in silk by the Sisters and completed with four sewing supplies: emery, needle book, pincushion, and thread waxer. Each of the four accessories was tied through the sides of the box with ribbon. Thousands of the oval sewing boxes were sold between 1897 and 1955.[18] Shapes other than oval are rare and highly prized by collectors.

173

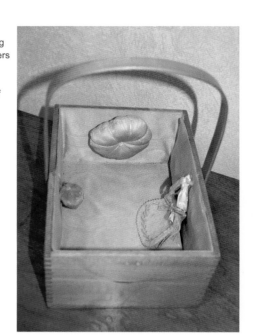

Rectangular wooden Shaker sewing boxes were made in smaller numbers than round and oval shapes. The corners are finely dovetailed. The sewing tools are tied to the sides of the box through small holes in the wood. 10" × 6" × 4". *Collection of Kathryn G. Lesieur.*

This oval bent-wood Shaker sewing box is lined in replacement silk. The accessory ribbons are tied through sides of the original box holes. 11" × 9" × 6". *Collection of the author.*

The ink marking on the bottom of the oval sewing box identifies it as Sabbathday Lake Shakers, Maine. 2" diameter. *Collection of the author.*

Boxes made from recycled cigar boxes are commonly referred to as tramp art. Tramp art is a misleading term probably coined in 1958 in Frances Lichten's book *Tramp Work: Penknife Plus Cigar Boxes*. It is possible the early edge carvers and itinerant artists were mistaken or appeared to some people as tramps.[19] Less common earlier references include the term "wood applique," used in 1891 by John Jacob Holtzapffel in the book *A Manual of Wood Carving*.[20]

The technique utilizes thin pieces of wood that have been notched and cut with a basic penknife. The pieces are stacked in multiple progressive layers then applied on all kinds of objects to create a decorative surface. The pieces were made for decorative and practical uses. The layers are sometimes painted and further embellished with knobs and metal tacks. The interiors were sometimes painted or lined in colorful papers. They were given as gifts and also sold. The sewing boxes usually incorporate at least one velvet pincushion on the top.

The exterior of this tramp art sewing box is embellished with green and gold paint. There are red velvet accents, including a red velvet pincushion on the top of the hinged lid. There is a decorative brass tack in each corner of the lid. 11" × 8" × 6". *Collection of the author.*

The interior view of the tramp art sewing box shows the oval mirror mounted on the underside of the lid. The interior is lined in a variety of decorative papers. This box had probably been fitted with an interior tray since the partitions start 1.125" down from the top edge. 11" × 8" × 6". *Collection of the author.*

The tramp art sewing box locks. The front of the lock was also embellished with paint accents contrasting with the red velvet that surrounds it. 0.75" × 1". *Collection of the author.*

A detail of the interior paper under the lid of the box. The mirror edge is decorated with a serrated-edge silver paper. 3" × 4" mirror. *Collection of the author.*

Tramp art box with red velvet accents. There are five levels that are chipped wood. A single tack is used as a knob to lift off the lid. The seller said the box was sold to her father in Wisconsin from a man who would just appear from the woods into the yard, selling items for cash. 6.5" × 6.5" × 6.5". *Collection of the author.*

The interior of the square box is painted green with a light coat of gold paint washed over the top. 6.5" × 6.5" × 6.5". *Collection of the author.*

The painted paper box is embellished with a watercolor oval labeled "Friendship Offering." The box has a hinged lid. On the top of the lid is a silk pincushion and matching needle book. 4.5" × 3" × 2.75". *Chester County Historical Society, West Chester, Pennsylvania.*

## Paper Boxes

Brightly painted polychrome paper boxes were also used for sewing boxes in the nineteenth century. Made of plain paper, they were assembled then painted in gradations of rainbow colors. The edges are sometimes embellished with gold paper bands for an elegant finished appearance. Pieces of wallpaper were also used over pasteboard to create sewing boxes. Some of the paper pieces were joined together with narrow fabric bindings. Some had hinged or loose lids also made of paper that sometimes included a mirror for reflecting light. Other styles were without lids and were intended to be left open. Many styles include built in pincushions and personalized art work.

Paper boxes covered in fabric gave the maker unlimited options to create shapes and forms. Some creative makers designed interesting shapes like wheelbarrows and hearts. Dates and initials were incorporated into the embellishment for personalized boxes. The lids were sometimes hinged with thread. Open-top styles sometimes have sewing accessories and pockets attached to the sides.

By the end of the nineteenth century the sewing work box became solely a functional item. Very few women were carrying needlework as social norms shifted and embroidery became less valued. The popularity of sewing machines for plain sewing created a need for storage of machine attachments and accessories. The mass production of garments decreased the need for heavy home sewing and large work boxes. Socially, there was no need to "pass around" sewing tools to make polite conversation.

Travel cases and boxes often included sewing tools. Part of the grooming process was keeping clothing in optimal condition while away from home. Included with sewing tools were writing instruments, toilet articles, and personal tableware. Many high-end travel sets were custom made to the owner's specifications.

These paper boxes are colorfully decorated with paint and trim. Each top has a velvet pincushion top. 4" × 7" × 5". *Collection of the author.*

Each of these fabric-covered pasteboard boxes has four lift top compartments. Each lid is padded for pins and needles. The center compartment is open for hand sewing projects. 12" square and 6" high. *Collection of the author.*

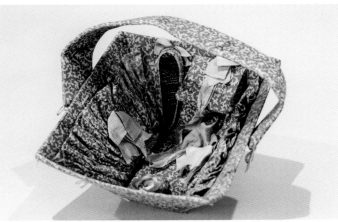

This four-compartment sewing container does not have padded lids. Each corner has a silk ribbon tie. 6" square and 3.5" high. *Chester County Historical Society, West Chester, Pennsylvania.*

This fabric-covered pasteboard basket is lined on two sides with pockets. It is accented with blue bows. The sewing tools are tied to the sides with blue ribbons. Included in the set is a scissor sheath, needle book, and thimble holder. 5.25" square × 2.25" sides. *Chester County Historical Society, West Chester, Pennsylvania.*

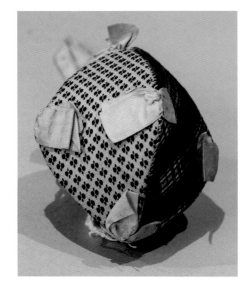

This fabric-covered paper holder is made of four pointed ovals accented with silk ribbons. One seam is left open to add contents to the container. All hand sewn. 3". *Chester County Historical Society, West Chester, Pennsylvania.*

The seat of this silk-fabric-covered chair lifts up for storage of small sewing supplies. The edges are trimmed in gimp. Light-blue glass-headed pins hold small fabric florets in place. 5" × 4" × 12". *Collection of the author.*

This plaid silk-covered pasteboard basket is lined on two sides with pockets. It is accented with red bows. The sewing tools are tied to the sides with red ribbons. Included in the set is a scissor sheath, needle book, and pincushion. 5.25" square × 2.25" sides. *Collection of Kathryn G. Lesieur.*

The interior view of the sewing basket shows how compact all of the supplies fit together. 5.25" square. *Collection of Kathryn G. Lesieur.*

This fabric-covered box is dated 1848 in the embroidery. Made by a member of the Reverend Christopher Schultz Junior family, Hereford Township, Berks County, Pennsylvania. 8.75" × 5.5" × 4". *Schwenkfelder Library & Heritage Center, Pennsburg, Pennsylvania.*

The side view of the embroidered box shows some of the hand-sewn stitches. Made by a member of the Reverend Christopher Schultz Jr. family, Hereford Township, Berks County, Pennsylvania. 8.75" × 5.5" × 4". *Schwenkfelder Library & Heritage Center, Pennsburg, Pennsylvania.*

The interior view of the embroidered box shows embroidery work. The heart reads, "All by love and not by force." Made by a member of the Reverend Christopher Schultz Jr. family, Hereford Township, Berks County, Pennsylvania. 8.75" × 5.5" × 4". *Schwenkfelder Library & Heritage Center, Pennsburg, Pennsylvania.*

This round sewing basket is made from enameled cloth bound in wool braid. The green lining is wool, as is the attached needle book. Pearl-embellished emeries fill a leaf made of green wool. The small velvet pumpkin is filled with emery. Basket 5" diameter. *Collection of Kathryn G. Lesieur.*

Velvet oval box hinged with silk ribbon bows. The lid is made of multiple velvet oval layers tacked together. 5" × 2.5" × 2.5". *Collection of Kathryn G. Lesieur.*

An assortment of colorful pinch pouches for storing small objects like thimbles and sewing tools. The green example has a crochet handle. The tasseled example has all of the edges bound in green cotton. The blue brocade example on top has a matching pin disc. 1" – 5". *Collection of the author.*

Crazy-quilt-covered paper sewing box with a decorative trim edge. Three pointed oval shapes are joined together with one seam left open. Lined in red silk. 10" × 5" × 5". *Sewing Case – 2012-35-388, Mingei International Museum, Gift of Pat L. Nickols.*

Another view of the crazy-quilt-covered paper sewing box with a decorative trim edge. Three pointed oval shapes are joined together with one seam left open. Lined in red silk. 10" × 5" × 5". *Sewing Case – 2012-35-388, Mingei International Museum, Gift of Pat L. Nickols.*

Top view of the crazy-quilt-covered paper sewing box with a decorative trim edge. Three pointed oval shapes are joined together with one seam left open. Lined in red silk. 10" × 5" × 5". *Sewing Case – 2012-35-388, Mingei International Museum, Gift of Pat L. Nickols.*

This black metal sewing basket was designed to look like a lantern. The label reads, "Ye Lantern Sewing Baskette." Thread spools can be stacked on the wooden posts. There are two swing handles. One side has a wool page for needles and pins. The center compartment holds a standing pair of scissors. 4.5" base. *Collection of the author.*

The original paper card advertises "Stuffy" as a saver of needles and pins. His hat holds a thimble and the ribbon at the top of his hat allows him to be conveniently hung. 3" × 8". *Collection of the author.*

Bakelite sewing box manufactured by Domart was designed to simulate tortoiseshell. The lift-out internal tray has compartments for spools of thread. Under the tray are larger compartments for other supplies. US Patent 1454639 issued May 8, 1923. 10" × 3.25". *Collection of the author.*

# 8 Clamps

A clamp is used to hold a sewing tool or workpiece such as a piece of fabric to a tabletop. Most styles of clamps are secured to the stable surface with a thumbscrew turned by the hand. The opening of the clamp does not move like a vise; rather, the tension between the thumbscrew and the table holds the tool in place.

Clamps are made in a wide variety of styles. American clamps are generally found in wood or metal but can be made of other materials. Many clamps include pincushions; some include thread winders and other sewing aids. Most clamps were designed to hold fabric secure when the clamp was mounted on the edge of a table. Other common clamps feature pincushions that kept pins close and from spilling from an open container. Winding clamps were used before threads were sold on spools. Larger spool clamps remained in use for skeins of yarn. An alternate tool for a pair of winding clamps is a swift. Yarn swifts are still made and used today.

## Metal Clamps

In America, metal clamps in the shape of birds were sometimes called grippers, third hands, or hemming birds. Once clamped to the table, the bird's tail is pressed, and through a spring hinge mechanism, the beak opens. Fabric is placed in the open beak and the beak closes on the fabric through spring tension. The closed beak holds the fabric firmly while the seamstress has free hands for needlework.

The first sewing bird was patented by Charles Waterman of Meridian, Connecticut. The design is in the shape of a song bird and carries the patent marked on one wing, "Feb.15th 1853." In the patent application Waterman wrote, "The highest degree of beauty is attained where the useful and ornamental are properly blended or combined."[1] The year of manufacture can sometimes be determined by the specific design features of the sewing bird. From the 1853 Waterman design, thirty-two variations could be made by changing four molds.[2]

The *Hartford Times* of June 5, 1852, has an ad showing two women on opposite sides of a table. The one without a sewing bird is bent over her work in an unhealthy posture, while the woman using a sewing bird is upright, showing the clamp's "health preserving property." According to Waterman's daughter, "he wanted to make sewing a little easier for the ladies."[3] The Waterman bird was produced well into the twentieth century, and variations in the design, as well as painted and plated versions, came and went. The sewing bird clamp style is so popular collectors should be wary of reproductions.[4]

Thirdhand devices were required for other work that required that both hands be free. Rugs made by braiding strips of wool used a bird-style clamp for holding the wool ends secure. The rug bird tail clamp has a serrated edge that clamps the wool to the perch frame. The clamps were boxed and sold in the twentieth century under the brand Fern Carter. The company sold rug-related patterns, kits, and accessories.

Some clamp styles were made by local blacksmiths. These are usually one of a kind and often have artistic additions like creative thumb screw shapes and attachments. Clarke Hess, in the book *Mennonite Arts*, shows a pincushion clamp presented to Harriet Long.[5] The clamp is engraved with her name and was given to her prior to her 1845 marriage. A similar clamp is shown in this chapter with a wool thread woven pincushion top.

Other metal clamp designs to help with needlework were used in sets of four for some styles of quilt frames. The clamps held the corners of the frames secure during hand quilting. They were sometimes made by blacksmiths and adorned with decorative thumb screws like heart shapes. Maker's marks are sometimes seen on the clamp frame.

A metal table clamp to hold an embroidery hoop was patented in 1902. The clamp adjusts in height and also swivels on a ball and socket. The top most latch has a thumb screw that loosens a latch against the upper loop. An embroidery frame or hoop can be clamped in the upper loop. Having a hoop clamp freed the hands of the embroiderer for complex stitching.

Metal sewing birds in assorted styles. The serrated tail bird clamp on the left was sold by the Fern Carter Company for use in braiding rugs. 7" × 2.5" × 2". The pincushion bird is a Waterman bird and is dated 1853 on the wing. 6" × 4" × 3". The smooth iron bird second from the right has a heart shape in the thumb screw. 6" × 4" × 3". The goose head clamp has a spring loaded mechanism for grasping fabric. 5" × 2.5" × 0.38". *Collection of the author.*

Metal pincushion clamps. The orange pincushion clamp has a deep clamp that allows it to be mounted several inches onto a table top. 7" × 4" × 3". The red pincushion in the middle swivels on the top of the chrome plated clamp. 4.5" × 4.5" × 1.25". The beige example on the right holds spools of thread, and a thimble on the acorn finial. 4" × 4". *Collection of the author.*

Cotton and wool thread woven and crochet pincushion top attached to a clamp. 3" diameter. *Collection of the author.*

Side view of clamp showing holes in the pincushion cup for directly securing the pincushion to the metal. *Collection of the author.*

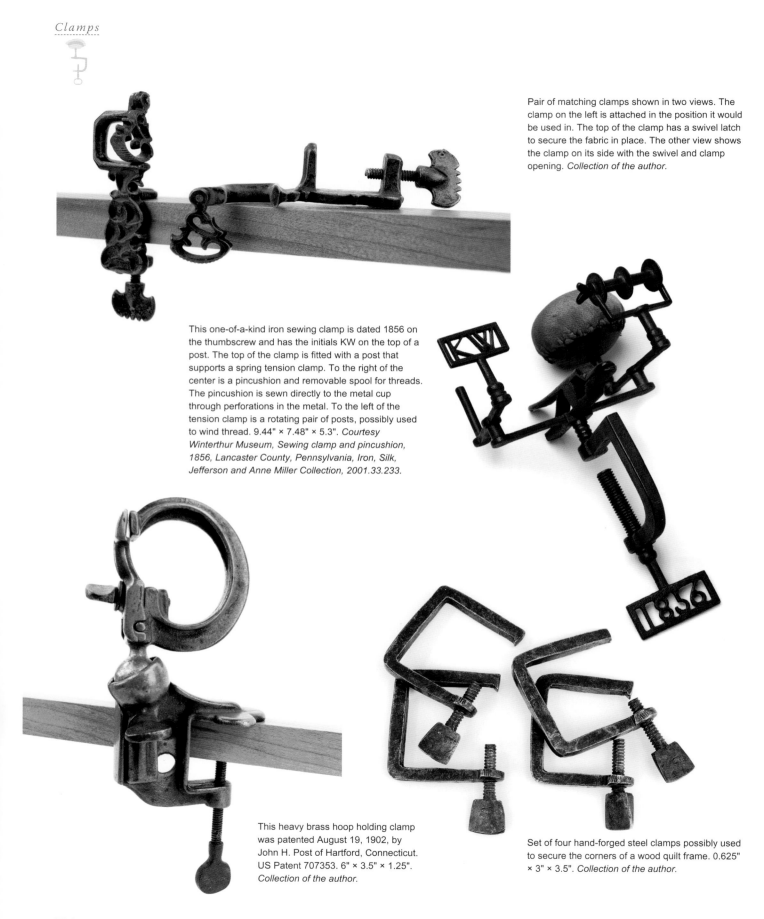

Pair of matching clamps shown in two views. The clamp on the left is attached in the position it would be used in. The top of the clamp has a swivel latch to secure the fabric in place. The other view shows the clamp on its side with the swivel and clamp opening. *Collection of the author.*

This one-of-a-kind iron sewing clamp is dated 1856 on the thumbscrew and has the initials KW on the top of a post. The top of the clamp is fitted with a post that supports a spring tension clamp. To the right of the center is a pincushion and removable spool for threads. The pincushion is sewn directly to the metal cup through perforations in the metal. To the left of the tension clamp is a rotating pair of posts, possibly used to wind thread. 9.44" × 7.48" × 5.3". *Courtesy Winterthur Museum, Sewing clamp and pincushion, 1856, Lancaster County, Pennsylvania, Iron, Silk, Jefferson and Anne Miller Collection, 2001.33.233.*

This heavy brass hoop holding clamp was patented August 19, 1902, by John H. Post of Hartford, Connecticut. US Patent 707353. 6" × 3.5" × 1.25". *Collection of the author.*

Set of four hand-forged steel clamps possibly used to secure the corners of a wood quilt frame. 0.625" × 3" × 3.5". *Collection of the author.*

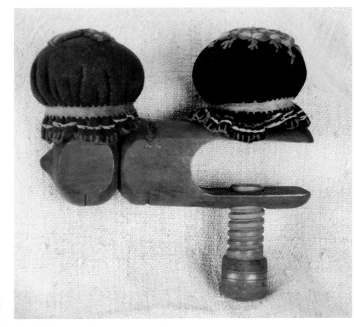

Nineteenth-century double-headed pincushion clamp made of wood and wool. 5.5" × 1.5" × 4.5". *Collection of Tex Johnson.*

## Wooden Clamps

Turned-wood clamps were made on wood lathes. Some makers marked their work; some examples from Lancaster County, Pennsylvania, are stamped "JNB" for Jacob N. Brubacher (1838–1913).[6] His clamps are rectangular in shape and have an elongated pincushion on top, often trimmed in woven tape or braid.

A wooden double-headed pincushion-style clamp is said to have been made for quilters. The cushion head farthest from the quilter was used to hold pre-threaded needles. Children would thread the needles in advance so as the quilter finished one thread, another was ready for use. This would keep the children occupied while the adults quilted.

Pincushion tops from double-headed clamp, showing wool-embroidered flowers. 1.5" diameter each. *Collection of Tex Johnson.*

Turned-wood pincushion clamp with painted accent stripes. The knitted pincushion top is mounted to the clamp with woven tape. 6" × 2" × 2". *Collection of Tex Johnson.*

Clamp side of a turned and painted wood pincushion clamp. 8" × 2.75". *Collection of Tex Johnson.*

Pincushion top with a repair layer of fabric added to the turned and painted wood pincushion clamp. 8" × 2.75". *Collection of Tex Johnson.*

Decorative side of a turned and painted wood pincushion clamp. The initials are possibly that of the original owner. 8" × 2.75". *Collection of Tex Johnson.*

Painted clamp with pincushion top and light reflecting mirror side. The pincushion has an accent band of gold paper covering where it attaches to the clamp. 7" × 2.75" × 1.25". *Collection of the author.*

Veneer wood sewing box clamp with a green wool pincushion top. 10" × 4.5" × 6". *Collection of the author.*

Worn silk pincushion box mounted to a walnut wood clamp. The shattered silk top is bordered in metallic trim. 7.5" × 3" × 2.5". *Collection of the author.*

Marbleized painted interior of the pincushion box clamp top. The interior of the lid has a receptacle for holding a thimble. 3" × 2.5" box. *Collection of the author.*

Turned wooden clamp with black silk pincushion top. A wide fabric tape band is attached where the pincushion meets the clamp for a finished look. There is a brass tack accent in the center of the circular clamp end. 5" × 5" × 2.5". *Collection of the author.*

Turned-wood pincushion clamps with velvet and printed faux patchwork tops. The example on the table does not have tape trim between the fabric cushion and the clamp. 2.5" – 6.5". *Collection of the author.*

Pincushion clamp with light-reflecting side mirror. 3" × 1.5" × 8". *Collection of the author.*

187

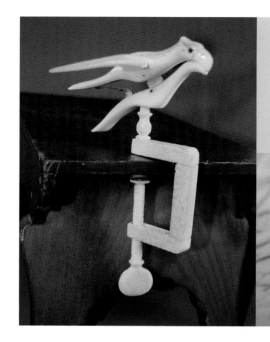

Ivory or bone clamp with metal fittings supporting an ivory parrot. 6.5" × 4" × 2.5". *Collection of Tex Johnson.*

Carved feather texture on the ivory parrot clamp. 0.0625". *Collection of Tex Johnson.*

## Ivory and Bone Clamps

Ivory clamps were made by carvers who had access to the materials in medium to large pieces. American materials were primarily whale bone. Sailors and woodworkers had the skills and supplies necessary to create the clamps. The designs are original and usually not duplicated. There are currently strict legal restrictions to buying and selling ivory, even historical pieces.

Sewing clamps continued to be used into the twentieth century. Notions catalogs listed sewing birds through the 1940s. Even home seamstresses with sewing machines had to hand-stitch hems, which was made easier using a sewing bird. Some women continue to enjoy hand sewing even when they own sewing machines, and a sewing bird makes this all the more pleasurable.

Ivory and tortoiseshell whale clamp with metal spring fitting. 7" × 4.5" × 1.75". *Collection of Tex Johnson.*

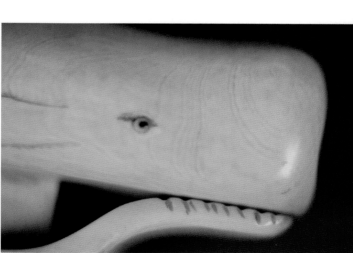

Detail of whale ivory grain pattern, eye and mouth. 0.125 eye. *Collection of Tex Johnson.*

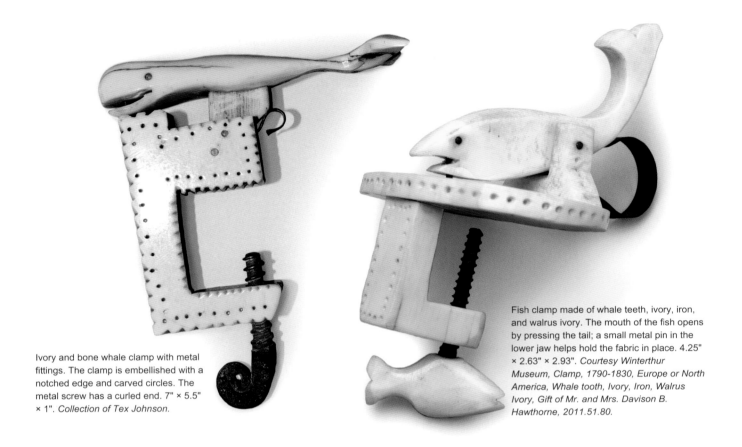

Ivory and bone whale clamp with metal fittings. The clamp is embellished with a notched edge and carved circles. The metal screw has a curled end. 7" × 5.5" × 1". *Collection of Tex Johnson.*

Fish clamp made of whale teeth, ivory, iron, and walrus ivory. The mouth of the fish opens by pressing the tail; a small metal pin in the lower jaw helps hold the fabric in place. 4.25" × 2.63" × 2.93". *Courtesy Winterthur Museum, Clamp, 1790-1830, Europe or North America, Whale tooth, Ivory, Iron, Walrus Ivory, Gift of Mr. and Mrs. Davison B. Hawthorne, 2011.51.80.*

Wooden and ivory clamp with ivory holders for spools of thread, ivory thread cutter, ivory fabric-holding vise, and a fabric-covered pincushion. The body of the table clamp is made of wood and is secured to the table with a metal screw. Behind the clamp is a triangular blade with ivory support for cutting thread. 3.3" × 3.1" × 3.1". *Courtesy Winterthur Museum, Clamp. 1850-1900, Wood, Bone, Ivory, Europe or North America, Gift of Mr. and Mrs. Davison B. Hawthorne, 2011.51.28.*

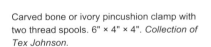

Carved bone or ivory pincushion clamp with two thread spools. 6" × 4" × 4". *Collection of Tex Johnson.*

# 9

## Threadwork: Crochet, Tambour, Knitting, Tatting, and Cording

## Crochet

*Crochet* is a French word meaning "hook." In France it was a common threadwork activity where loops and knots were formed with a hook to create a pattern during the Renaissance. Some researchers believe it derived from tambour work as it is similar to tambour without the ground fabric. It gained popularity in America beginning in the second quarter of the nineteenth century.[1]

Crochet hooks are about the length of a hand. They are thin like a pencil with a hook at one end. Crochet hooks are made of wood, plastic, metal, bone, and ivory. Some styles had handles with interchangeable hooks of various sizes. Some handles are elaborately carved or inlaid. The hooks vary in size to adjust the size of the loops in the crochet stitch. This creates the gauge of the crochet work. Some crochet hooks are so fine and delicate they were sold with caps to protect the hook end. Another design for fine hooks has a retractable feature that slides or folds the hook down into the handle for protection and ease of storage.

Larger hooks were made for wool work. This early wool work was initially referred to as knitting. Another hybrid between knitting and crochet is Tunisian crochet. The Tunisian hook is thicker and longer than a regular crochet hook. It also has a knob at the end of the hook. Tunisian crochet is worked on a long crochet hook. Stitches are worked across the width of a strip, stitched off, and repeated, forming long strips that are joined to form larger widths.

In America, crochet gained popularity in the mid-nineteenth century with the distribution of printed patterns in magazines. Many popular crochet patterns have been in use for more than a century.

In their 1929 catalog, Butler Brothers lists nickeled, steel-plated crochet hooks for thirty-nine cents a dozen. They also offered bone hooks six inches in length in a set of two dozen. Eight of the set are double pointed. The set, mounted on a display card, retailed for thirty-nine cents a dozen.

Metal retractable crochet hook shown with a spool of crochet thread. The hand-crocheted bodice includes a row of insertion trim. The bodice would have been attached to a gathered cotton bottom. 10" × 20". *Collection of the author.*

Another variation of crochet is called hairpin work. Hairpin work holds loops wrapped around the frame and secured with a crochet stitch. It is worked in strips, which are then joined together with additional crochet stitches. In its finest form, the work is done on actual ladies hair pins.

One of many characteristics of crochet that keeps it popular is that like knitting, once learned, long stints of stitching can be performed without looking at the work. Women can watch children or food on the stove, or they can just relax. A multitude of new materials and patterns was available to maintain consumer interest.

Set of chrome-finish crochet hook heads and threaded handle. Any of the five sizes of hooks can be screwed into the handle for use. 0.25" × 7". *Collection of the author.*

Set of Boye Company crochet hooks in the original velvet lined box. Any of the graduated-size hooks can be attached to the handle with the metal screw collar. The set is lying on an ecru crochet edging. 3.25" × 6". *Collection of the author.*

Bone and metal crochet hooks shown on white crochet edging. 5.5" – 7" hooks. *Collection of the author.*

Fine-gauge steel crochet hooks used for thread crochet work. To protect the fine hooked ends, the hooks were sometimes stored in wooden cylinder cases. Shown lying on a white band of crochet edging. 7" hooks. *Collection of the author.*

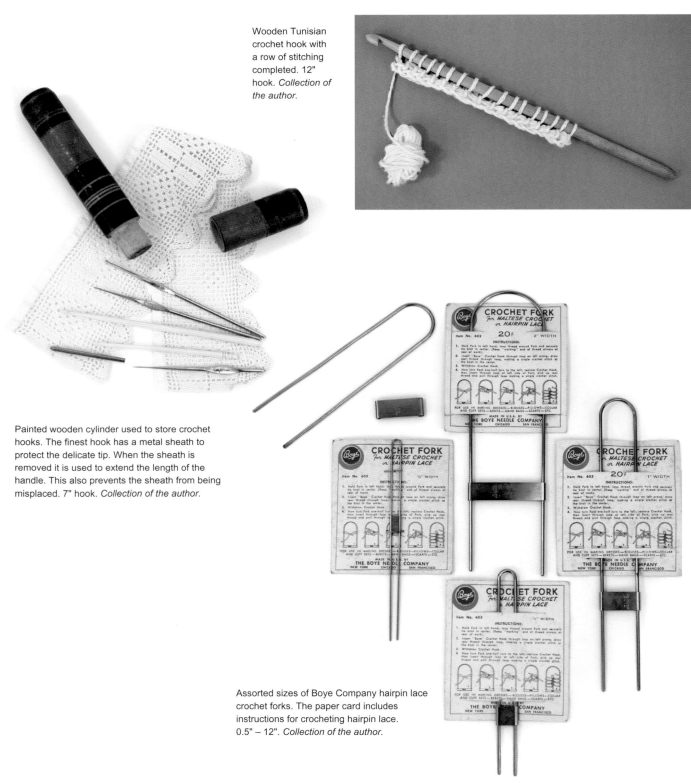

Wooden Tunisian crochet hook with a row of stitching completed. 12" hook. *Collection of the author.*

Painted wooden cylinder used to store crochet hooks. The finest hook has a metal sheath to protect the delicate tip. When the sheath is removed it is used to extend the length of the handle. This also prevents the sheath from being misplaced. 7" hook. *Collection of the author.*

Assorted sizes of Boye Company hairpin lace crochet forks. The paper card includes instructions for crocheting hairpin lace. 0.5" – 12". *Collection of the author.*

Cotton hairpin lace made on a metal hairpin. 0.25" × 3". *Collection of Tex Johnson.*

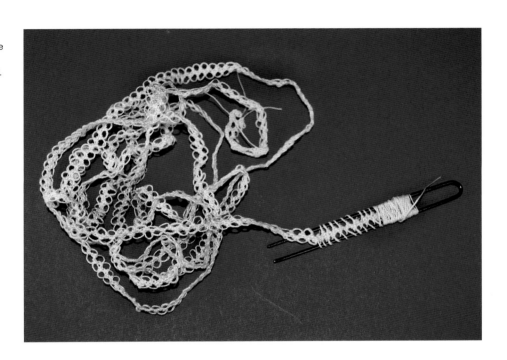

Woven baskets to hold rolls of thread or yarn on the wrist. This kept the balls close, clean, and safely stored. 10" – 3". *Collection of the author.*

Thread or yarn ball holders made of cotton fabric or thread worn on the wrist. This kept the balls close, clean, and safely stored. 5" – 13". *Collection of the author.*

Tambour hooks can be mistaken for crochet hooks. Tambour hooks tend to have a sharper tip at the end of the hook. The sharp tip pierced the ground fabric to hook the thread held underneath. The fine-gauge hooks were often made to be removable. 5". *Collection of the author.*

## Tambour

Tambour embroidery is a chain stitch variation done in a frame or hoop with a fabric base. The embroidery is done with a handled tambour hook and thread on the underside of the ground fabric. The end of the hook is small and sharp in order to pierce the ground fabric then loop the thread hook to pull it up on the top of the ground fabric. The hook is usually affixed to a handle and held in place with a small retention screw. The handles were made of a variety of decorative materials: carved bone, tortoiseshell, wood, or ivory. Extra hooks were sometimes stored in hollowed cavities of the handle.[2] So similar are crochet and tambour hooks that they are sometimes used interchangeably. The main difference is the sharper point on a tambour hook. As chain stitching could also be created with a needle and thread, it soon replaced tambour work.

Another tool used in tambour work is the spool knave, which was worn at the waist. The spool was attached to a bar held in place with a semicircle metal frame, which kept the thread close and easy to unroll. The thread unwound as it was pulled under the ground fabric for the tambour work. Changing the thread to the top of the ground fabric during the tambour process allowed the use of heavier fabrics and threads. The process options allow for a diverse array of tambour work, from sheer bridal veils to heavy fabrics and metallic threads.

## Knitting

The earliest knitting needles were probably long pieces of bone or wood. Eventually some knitting needles had small ivory or wooden balls added at the ends to prevent stitches from slipping off the needle ends.

One theory is that knitting started as a male occupation and gradually became the work primarily of women. It was a source of income for many people.[3] Knitted items could also be bartered for labor or household supplies. Efforts to introduce knitting machines were delayed out of fear of unemployment for knitters. Knitting is possible to perform while multitasking, since the work can be performed without directly looking at the threads. For example, sheep herders could knit while tending sheep. Letters and inventories list that slaves owned by George and Martha Washington were trained in knitting for the household.[4]

In colonial America stockings were either pieced from fabric or hand knit. Fabric stockings were inelastic and had uncomfortable seams. Garters were needed to keep the stockings in place. Knitted stockings became preferred because of their superior comfort. In 1759 the women of Germantown, Pennsylvania, sold 60,000 pairs of knitting frame stockings.[5] It has been reported that a framework knitter produced ten pair of stockings per week. An experienced hand knitter could produce six pair of high-quality stockings per week. In the early nineteenth century, knitting machines made it to American shores.[6]

Knitting had many social references over the years, and some not so flattering. On August 20, 1920, the Nineteenth Amendment to the American Constitution was ratified, granting all women the rights and responsibilities of citizenship.[7] Prior to its passing, women were often accused of being too hysterical, foolish, and nervous to exercise citizenship rights like voting. Knitting magazines like *Stitches* used wording like "loud mouthed girls ... mannish attire," encouraging readers to relax with a simple piece of knitting that would not tax the brain. Knitting, they suggested, "provided a more rational view of life in hectic times."[8]

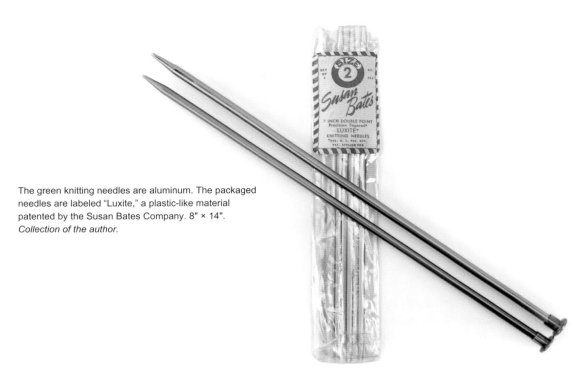

The green knitting needles are aluminum. The packaged needles are labeled "Luxite," a plastic-like material patented by the Susan Bates Company. 8" × 14". *Collection of the author.*

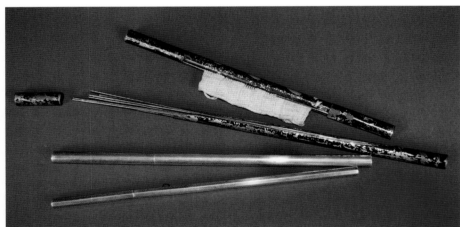

Sterling silver and aluminum knitting sheaths holding fine knitting needles called knitting pins. 12" – 15". *Collection of Tex Johnson.*

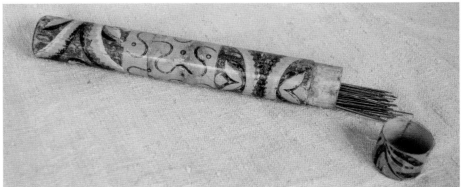

Painted knitting needle sheath with removable cap. Filled with multiple sizes of knitting pins. 12". *Collection of Tex Johnson.*

Knitting lace is done with very fine thread and needles. The needles are sometimes called knitting pins due to their pin-like fineness. Knitted lace is less common than crochet lace. *Collection of the author.*

Detail of knitted lace and knitting pins. *Collection of the author.*

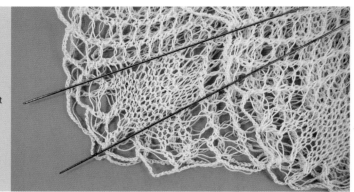

Knitting needles include many sizes and styles. Large, heavy wooden needles about a yard long were used for knitting wool strips into rugs. The wool strips came from recycling worn clothing and blankets. Even larger needles were made that were the size of broomsticks. The twentieth-century popularity of broomstick needles advertised knitting a garment in a day. On the other end of the spectrum are lace knitting needles or knitting pins, barely thicker than sewing needles.[9] Knitting pins, both sharp and blunt tip, were used for knitting gloves, mittens, and stockings in the eighteenth and nineteenth centuries.[10]

The highly successful Boye Needle Company of Chicago held seventy-five percent of the knitting needle market in 1934. They only hired sale representatives with knowledge of knitting—including men. They had patents on circular knitting needles, which were popular for knitting skirts and sweaters. During the American Depression years, the company recommended women unravel yarn from old sweaters and knit new styles.

Knitting to support war efforts continued from the Revolutionary War through modern times. Wives of Civil War veterans contributed more than 600,000 knit items. During World War I knitters used more than 250,000 knitting pamphlets and produced 6.5 million refugee and 24 million military garments. Knitting to support World War II started as soon as reserves were sent to training camps. Pattern books included titles like *Hand Knits for the Boys in the Service* and showed soldiers on the cover. Knit items from home provided warmth and memories of home. Soldiers also took up knitting when recuperating from injuries.[11]

Knitting needle guards were used for knitting needle tips so no stitches slipped off the needles. They were often homemade and reflective of the supplies and styles their owners preferred.

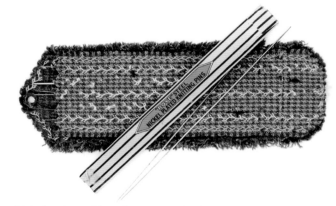

Original package of Boye Company steel knitting pins lying on a homemade wool knitting pin holder. Each channel of the wool holder was embroidered with a feather stitch. The bottom of the holder is a needle book with wool needle pages. *Collection of the author.*

Miniature leather boot knitting needle guards. 0.5" × 2.25" boot. *Collection of Tex Johnson.*

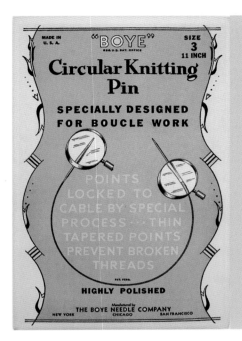

This package of Boye circular knitting needles is sealed like an envelope with no preview window. Smooth, highly polished points were required so the needle tips do not snag the yarns. The needles were sold in numerous sizes and lengths between the needle points. 5" × 7". *Collection of the author.*

The back of the circular knitting needle package has advertising for other Boye Company products. Customers are also encouraged to use a magnifying glass to see the quality of their products. 5" × 7". *Collection of the author.*

Crochet mitten knitting needle guards. 0.5" × 1". *Collection of Kathryn G. Lesieur.*

Embroidered blue felt bonnet-shaped knitting needle guards accented with red bows. The bonnets are connected with an 8" ribbon threaded through eyelets in the bonnet. The bonnets were placed over the pointed tips of the knitting needles to prevent stitches from slipping off. 1" × 1.25" bonnet. *Collection of the author.*

Abalone shell tatting accessories were popular gifts and tourist souvenirs. The interior of the shell was used to get the beautiful iridescent colors. The bottom of the square box says, "To Martha, September 24th, 1915." 2.5" approximate shuttle sizes. *Collection of the author.*

## Tatting

Tatting is a knotted thread art in which a shuttle and thread are used to form knots in a pattern, making lace. Each stitch becomes an individual knot, making it very strong while retaining a delicate appearance. Tatting shuttle materials include bone, shell, metal, celluloid, and plastic. Some tatting uses two shuttles. The tatting shuttle consists of two ovals pointed at each end and joined in the center with a post or bobbin. The thread is wrapped around the center post or bobbin of the shuttle. Some tatting methods use two shuttles.

Some American shuttles have hooks at the end to assist in pulling the thread through loops. The hooks are used to connect rings in tatting patterns. A separate tatting ring is used if the shuttle does not have a hooked end. The ring has a small hook attached by a short chain connected to a ring. The ring is worn on the left thumb while tatting. Purling pins are used to gauge the size of loops.[12]

Example of basic tatting rings with picot loops at each top. 0.375" loop. *Collection of the author.*

## Cording

Lucets are simple tools used for making cord in the eighteenth and nineteenth centuries. Sometimes called chain forks or knitting forks, making lucet cord was essential to fasten clothing when laced closures were the norm on most garments. Lucets are shaped similar to a two-pronged fork with a dip in between the tines. They were made of bone, wood, or ivory, with rare examples of mother-of-pearl. Some styles have handles; however, most do not. The diameter of the cord made depended on the size of the thread used. The process creates a square, tightly knotted cord. The cord is made with the use of a hook or with the fingers. Some lucets have an opening below the fork where the finished cord is threaded as it is worked.[13] By the mid-nineteenth century, homemade lucet cords were replaced with inexpensive machine-made cords.

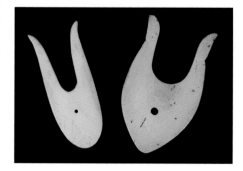

Carved-bone lucets used for making cord. Making lucet cord was so simple, it was often made by the children in the household. 1.5" – 5.5". *Collection of Tex Johnson.*

Assorted tatting shuttles arranged in a circle centered on a ball of J & P Coats tatting thread. Shuttle materials include sterling silver, Bakelite, aluminum, plastic, and shell. 2.5" approximate shuttle size. *Collection of the author.*

The size 70 cotton and original box were from Wieboldt's Department Store. The store's price sticker is for 2 cents a ball. The handkerchief has a tatted edge made with variegated thread. 3.5" × 4.5" box. *Collection of the author.*

Sterling silver tatting shuttle engraved with an uppercase R. The shuttle is resting on a small coaster with a tatted edging made with variegated thread. 3.25" shuttle. *Collection of the author.*

This brass ring was worn as a tension gauge as the thread is pulled through while tatting. 1" × 1.5". *Collection of the author.*

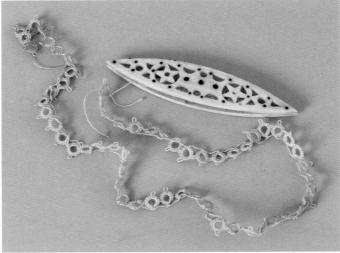

Bone tatting shuttle with stars carved through the surface. There are colored circular inlay dots in red and blue. 2.875" × 0.625" × 0.25". *Chester County Historical Society, West Chester, Pennsylvania.*

# 10 *Hoops and Darning*

## Hoops

Hoops are used to hold fabric so it is taut, uniform, and comfortable for needlework. Embroidery hoops are also sometimes referred to as rings. An embroidery hoop is actually two smooth rings, one slightly smaller than the other so that they nest firmly together. When fabric is placed between the two rings, enough tension is placed on the fabric for it to be pulled taut for embroidery. Hoops are made in round and oval shapes. They are made of materials including tortoiseshell, bamboo, wood, rubber, metal, and plastic. There are also wood and metal combination styles.

Early models sometimes required light fabric to be wrapped around the inside ring to provide additional tension for the upper ring. Another option for added tension was a strip of wool glued to the inner ring. Sometimes the inner ring had smooth grooves carved in it to grip the fabric. The rings for embroidery hoops have to be smooth so fabric doesn't snag.

A rubber alternative to wooden hoops was invented by Isaac Q. Gurnee in 1897. Isaac was granted US Patent 28301 on February 15, 1898, and he assigned his patent to the Butler Rubber Company of Butler, New Jersey. The design featured smooth-surfaced corrugations or serrations parallel with the side of the ring. A second ring, smooth on both sides, fits loosely over the textured inner ring to allow for fabric between the two rings.

In 1903, Helen A. Harmes was awarded a patent for an adjustable embroidery hoop. In her design, both the inner and outer hoop were adjustable by several inches to accommodate a variety of embroidery sizes. An added feature was legs to support the hoop, leaving one hand free.[1] In 1913, Lewis Gibbs was issued a patent for an adjustable hoop where one ring was cut and a mechanism was added for adjusting the fabric tension.[2]

Wood hoop sets include floor standing and table clamp styles, which leave both hands free to stitch. Some of the table clamp styles include sets of rings in nested sizes. The hoops were not always made in the adjustable style. Hoops could be used independent of the clamp, but the attachment post was not removable.

Assortment of wooden embroidery hoops with various tensioning methods. 6" – 10". *Collection of the author.*

Hard black rubber hoop from the Butler Hard Rubber Company of New Jersey. US Patent 28301, February 15, 1898. The inner hoop has a textured surface. 6.5" × 0.5". *Collection of the author.*

Detail of the imprint on the outer hoop. The Butler Rubber Company was located in New Jersey. *Collection of the author.*

Vintage knit stocking with completed darning repair to the heel. 2" area. *Collection of Kathryn G. Lesieur.*

## Darning

Darning was a critical household task to keep clothing in repair. Before mass-produced, ready-made clothing, garments were expensive and were used for several years. Darning materials were part of most every household's essential sewing supplies. Darners were made in a variety of shapes and numerous materials.

It was important that people knew the correct way to darn so that the repair was secure and caused no irritation to the wearer. Lumpy socks could cause blisters and discomfort. Having lumpy stitches, crude knots, or gaps would cause discomfort when the garment was worn again. Items frequently darned include high-wear areas in garments like sweater elbows and socks, and household items like bedding and towels. The item is stretched over the top of the darning form—right side out. By having the right side out, sewers could ensure the "invisibility" of their work. The darning stitch is reweaving thread or yarn to re-create the appearance of the original fabric. An argument to wrong side out is that a smooth finish could be assured against the skin. Less desirable techniques include pulling the sides of a hole together over the darner and overcasting it closed. This technique creates a raised seam or ridge. Another technique is a running stitch around the circumference of the hole and gathering it closed, which tends to create an uncomfortable lump or ball. Both of the latter techniques can cause irritations like blisters since the repaired area is no longer smooth against the skin.

Anna Green Winslow, while boarding at Madame Smith's Sewing School in Boston, wrote in her March 9, 1722, diary entry, "mended two pairs of gloves, mended for the wash two handkerchiefs."[3] Darning skills were taught to boys and girls, sometimes at home and sometimes in school. Even in wealthy households it was considered the right thing to do—but was probably done by household help. Some darning was done as a preventive measure in places a new item was most likely to wear, like the heel area of socks. Former first lady Eleanor Roosevelt learned to darn as a child of six and continued to sew throughout her life.[4] Even into the twentieth century, darning garments was an essential activity in all households. Darning was so mainstream, it was depicted by Norman Rockwell on the April 8, 1922, cover of the *Saturday Evening Post*. The illustrator chose to show the sock laid across the man's lap as he threads a needle. Through the hole in the toe of the sock, the viewer can see the tip of a red-colored darner. Darning was also depicted on greeting cards, children's books, and even dishware.

Darning forms are found in wood, glass, rubber, and plastic. Their primary purpose was to hold the fabric in place during the stitching process. The shape variations are based on two primary approaches. The first is a shape something like a light bulb, where the fabric is stretched over the firm convex surface. The second style floats the textile over an opening so the darning needle does not touch a hard, concave surface. Wood darners were made in many shapes, including mushroom, egg, and dome tops. Some wooden darners have hollow handles that provide storage for needles. Some have hollow caps for storing thimbles and thread. Darners were available commercially in the last quarter of the nineteenth century. Substitutes prior to the availability of commercial darners were plaster-filled eggs, rocks, pottery, bars of soap, and egg cups.

The darner style that is particularly American is the late nineteenth-century silver-handle darner, marked sterling, with a wooden ebony egg-shaped top. The silver handles can be sterling or silver plate. The exact manufacturers are difficult to identify due to the lack of maker's marks. Some examples sold are repurposed handles, made from old sterling flatware. Another modification of this style of darner features a sterling silver cartouche mounted on a painted wooden handle, which provides a hint of silver elegance at a fraction of the cost of a full silver handle.

The foot-form darner, small double-ended glove darner, hoop end, and colored-ended darner illustrate some of the wide variety found in darners. 3" – 10". *Collection of the author.*

A sterling cartouche is attached to the handle of this darner. The owners initial could be engraved on the silver. 7.5". *Collection of the author.*

This lathe-turned double-ended darner is made of a single piece of wood. The card of mending wool was made in Boston, Massachusetts. 3" × 5" card. *Collection of the author.*

CYNTHIA

MENDING WOOL

FOR A GENERATION

*Cynthia*

DISCRIMINATING KNITTERS

ASK FOR THEM AT THE YARN COUNTER.

100% WOOL **24** YDS. ART. 330

CYNTHIA MILLS, Inc.
BOSTON, MASS.

MADE IN U.S.A.

YARN PREPARED FOR DARNING

MAKERS

WE DO NOT GUARANTEE OUR GOODS UNLESS THEY CARRY OUR TRADE MARKS.

MADE BY AMERICAN GIRLS.

TRADE MARK REGISTERED

TRADE MARK REGISTERED.

This package of darning yarn proudly states, "Made by American Girls." The combination of sheep and people working in cotton fields implies they sell wool and cotton threads. 2" × 4". *Collection of the author.*

This square darning bag has pockets on each side. A darner and thread easily fit inside. The embroidered verse reads, "It is never too late to mend but a man should not expect a button sewed on much after midnight." 4.25" square. *Collection of the author.*

202

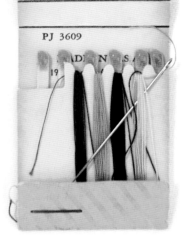

Folder containing darning thread and needles. The cutout in the front cover on the model's legs allows the buyer to see the color of thread. Open the cover and the skeins of thread can be removed. A package of needles is glued inside. 3" × 5". *Collection of the author.*

Colorful packaging for darning and mending supplies. The blue box contains ten small two-ply spools of darning silk in assorted colors. 2.5" × 7.5". The small packages are referred to as matchbook mending kits because they use the same style of packaging. This style was popular for advertising. 1.5" × 2.5". *Collection of the author.*

Matchbook mending kit for ladies' stockings. The sticks are not match sticks; they are tipped with adhesive. When moistened and applied to a stocking snag, the adhesive would prevent a run. The thread is for darning tears. 1.5" × 5.25" × 0.25". *Collection of the author.*

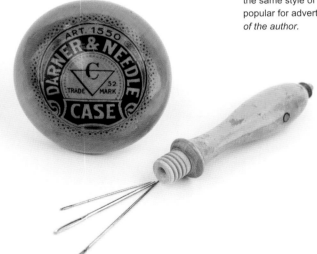

This mushroom-shaped darner has a removable handle. The threaded handle is hollow for needle storage. 3.5" × 5". *Collection of the author.*

Patented in 1874, the Harley Darner has a concave top, thread storage under the cap, and needle storage in the handle. There is a thread portal in the storage area for feeding thread out. 6" long. The stockings have their original price sticker of thirty-nine cents. *Collection of the author.*

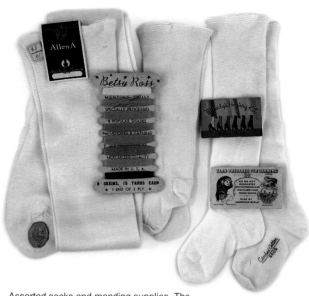

Assorted socks and mending supplies. The patriotic Betsy Ross card has stars and proudly claims, "Made in U.S.A." 3.25" × 7.5". *Collection of the author.*

Darners were made in various sizes for mending gloves and socks. 0.5" – 7". *Collection of the author.*

Wood darners could become rough with use. The surface imperfections caused by darning needles scratching the surface could snag delicate silks and knits. Hard, smooth surfaces like glass and ceramic were popular for darning any delicate textiles that would easily snag.

Cleminsons Pottery, of California, made ceramic darners in the shape of a bowling pin. The darners were hand painted to look like girls and were lettered "Darn It" on their apron fronts. In business from 1941 to 1965, they produced dinnerware, pie birds, and other ceramic pieces for the home. Darners were a small part of their business.

Glass darners were also made in a variety of shapes and colors, many being one of a kind. Some are nicknamed "end of day" darners, the theory being the glass blower had bits to use up at the end of the day, and a darner was a way to end the day's work using the last of the molten glass. Very few glass companies made darners as part of their regular lines. Some foot-formed glass darners that were mass produced in molds came from outside the United States.

Owning darners of multiple colors was thought to be an efficient approach. Darners with heads in high contrast to the item being darned made the work in covering the hole easier to see. Multiple sizes were also helpful in a household with diverse mending needs.[5]

Gloves needed a small darner that could fit down into the tips of the glove finger. Glove darners were narrow with oval-shaped tips similar in size to a fingertip. They are usually found in wood or silver. Some styles have a removable end for storing needles in the shaft of the darner, like some general-purpose darners. There were eras in fashion when girls or women wouldn't leave the house without covering their hands with gloves. Keeping the gloves in full repair was a fashion necessity.

The price of darners varied by the decade, material, and quantity purchased. Egg darners are listed in the 1895 Montgomery Ward mail order catalog. They are painted black wood with a handle, priced at four cents each or a dozen matching for thirty-five cents. In the same catalog, a single pair of men's heavy seamless ribbed cotton socks sold for ten cents a pair. The 1897 Sears catalog listed a darner with a solid-silver handle. The listing reads, "Solid sterling silver mounted hose darner. The ball is made of enameled wood while the handle is made of sterling silver with raised ornamentation. The handle is detachable, and has a receptacle on the inside for needles, a very desirable present for an elderly lady or anyone who has such work to do." This model was priced at $1.75.

There were numerous patents issued for inventions related to darning. At least ten women were awarded patents for darning equipment from 1865 to 1979. Inventions to support improved darning included changing the shape of the darner, using new materials, and added clamps, battery, and electric light attachments. Sewing machine attachments for darning were also patented to replace hand darning in an effort to streamline household work.

Glass darners are hollow and are not scarred by the sharp tip of a needle. They don't snag delicate silk stockings but are breakable. Women often owned multiple darners for different types of mending needs. 6" long. *Collection of the author.*

Darning hoop for use with a sewing machine claimed to make darning quick and easy. 3" × 4.25" box. *Collection of the author.*

Numerous darners in all kinds of shapes and sizes. *Collection of the author.*

Darning hoop for use with a sewing machine includes a tension spring. The package encourages the consumer to do darning the new modern way, which is ten times faster. 3.5" × 4". *Collection of the author.*

The darner on top is painted wood. The black-and-white darner is made of molded plastic and was used to darn light and dark socks. The contrasting color was placed under the hole of the sock for better visibility. 7.5". *Collection of the author.*

# 11 Closures and Fasteners

## Buttons

Prior to the use of buttons, common methods of fastening clothing were lacing, hooks and eyes, and temporary stitching. While buttons are not directly needlework tools, very few needlework projects would exist without the use of a button. Buttons hold sewing rolls closed, require multiple stitching processes to incorporate button use in garments, and are common contents in sewing baskets. Buttons can serve functional and decorative purposes. In their highest form they exude social standing and prestige. Buttons made of precious metals were kept and reused, and were often included in estate inventories.[1]

Bee's Universal Button Fasteners were designed to replace using thread to sew on buttons. They can be used for any style of button. 2" × 4.5". *Collection of the author.*

### Bone Buttons

In the seventeenth and eighteenth centuries, buttons were often made of horn or bone in the home for basic purposes. This style of "utilitarian" button was preferably used on underwear, where it was not generally seen. More-decorative styles incorporating carving or inlays were preferred for outer wear. Horn was sliced crosswise with holes drilled through the center. Bone and horn made sturdy buttons and were readily available American materials. In the twentieth century, bone underwear buttons were decoratively painted and used as embellishments. The painting design used the stitching holes as eyes.[2]

### Metal Buttons

In eighteenth- and nineteenth-century America, buttons either were imported or were made in small workshops. Metal buttons included brass, pewter, and alloys like pinchbeck. Efforts to be independent from imports led entrepreneurs to build button-manufacturing equipment. In the nineteenth century, two Northfield, Connecticut, inventors and machinists, Maltby and Fowler, teamed up to process metal into numerous household items, including buttons. Machine-stamped buttons were produced in 1812 and were popular with the military. In 1830 Maltby Fowler (named for his two grandfathers, Maltby and Fowler), harnessing the power of the Farm River, used his power press to mass produce buttons. He produced enough buttons to keep four peddlers' carts busy.[3] The Waterbury Button Company of Connecticut, started in 1812, is still manufacturing buttons today. Over 200 years they have created more than 40,000 button dies. They produce buttons for the fashion industry, professional sports, and every branch of the American military.[4]

The mother of the button family carries a large sewing needle. She wears a Dutch-style hat and shoes. 4" square base. *Collection of the author.*

Square button bag with a pocket on each side. Button-faced family members are represented on each pocket. Bone buttons are painted for each face. The red binding at the top of the drawstring bag is worn away. This pocket has tinted embroidered twin girls. 4" square base. *Collection of the author.*

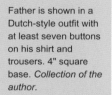

Father is shown in a Dutch-style outfit with at least seven buttons on his shirt and trousers. 4" square base. *Collection of the author.*

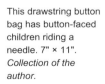

This drawstring button bag has button-faced children riding a needle. 7" × 11". *Collection of the author.*

Even the cat is included in the button family. 4" square base. *Collection of the author.*

Calico buttons, made of porcelain, are colorful and found in a variety of sizes, patterns, and colors. 0.375" × 0.5".
*Collection of the author.*

### Calico China Buttons

Ceramic buttons were handmade as early as the 1700s. In 1840 a mechanical process was invented to produce porcelain buttons from china-clay powder. Porcelain is fired at a higher temperature than china. These colorful, mass-produced porcelain calico buttons were popular in the mid-nineteenth century. Calico buttons were transfer printed with designs similar to calico fabric. This style was preferred for women's clothing, coordinating with cotton prints popular for dress wear. The first calico buttons were probably made in Minton, England. In France, Jean-Felix Babtrosse combined technical expertise with marketing skills that rivaled all calico button producers in the world. A single circa 1850 calico button sample card has one hundred different choices. It has been reported more than 300 calico button styles were produced.[5] Some of the buttons can also be dated by the color and motif or shape. The buttons were initially stamped with country of origin or registry marks.

Charles Cartlidge & Co., an American soft-paste porcelain factory in Greenpoint, New York, began making calico buttons in the United States. The factory at Greenpoint opened in 1848 and closed in 1856. The company started with making porcelain buttons and later moved into china tableware, knobs, and jewelry cameos.[6]

Calico buttons were mass produced without registry in the twentieth century in response to demand from history reenactors. There was also a resurgence in reproduction of calico china buttons when designer Ralph Lauren used them in clothing lines in the late 1900s.

### Pearl or Shell Buttons

Abalone shells from the Pacific coast were made into buttons as early as 1750. In 1855 mussels from the Mississippi River were used to make buttons. The industry flourished, with special machines punching out millions of buttons a year. By 1899 sixty button factories were located in the Mississippi River valley. Mussel shell harvesting reached 21,000 tons of shell from the Mississippi River near Muscatine, Iowa. The area was also popular with treasure hunters looking for freshwater pearls. In some locations entire mussel beds disappeared due to overharvesting as shell hunters could earn ten times what an average laborer earned.[7]

In *The Story of My Life by Billie Button*, published by the Wisconsin Pearl Button Company, ten chapters detail the "Descriptive Story of a Purely American Industry." In 1900 almost fifty percent of buttons manufactured in America came from the pearl, iridescent interior of freshwater mussels. By 1922, freshwater mussel fishery was one of the largest and most profitable inland fisheries in America. The shell population quickly decreased and harvested shells became smaller as older shells were depleted.[8] In 1925, the industry declined due to pressure on available raw-material harvests, as well as foreign markets, the economy, and labor issues. It can be challenging to date shell buttons. Several types of holes, shanks, shapes, and decoration were used to make shell buttons. Smooth backs are generally thought to be from after 1880.[9] Shell buttons were eventually replaced with less expensive synthetic pearl-looking buttons.

Carded shell buttons. The buttons are sewn to the cards with cotton thread. Approximately 2.5" × 4" cards. *Collection of the author.*

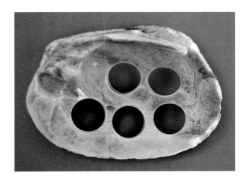

Shell with holes from where buttons were cut out. 6" × 4". *Collection of the author.*

## Vegetable Ivory Buttons

Vegetable ivory or tagua palm nut became an acceptable replacement for ivory buttons. In the early twentieth century, the Rochester Button Company of New York had as many as 500 workers processing imported tagua palm nuts into buttons. Small machines were used to carve, shape, color, and polish tagua palm nut buttons. Rochester Button Company was making half of all the buttons manufactured in America in 1910. By the 1940s, button production transitioned to plastics.[10]

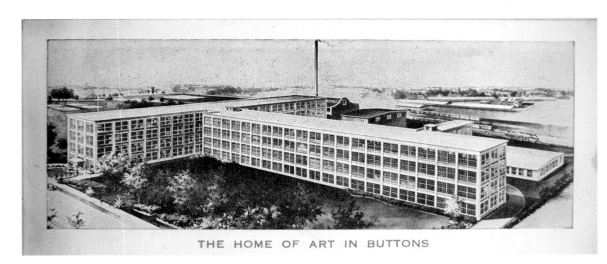

THE HOME OF ART IN BUTTONS

Etching of the Rochester Button Company, Rochester, New York. The four-story multi-wing factory produced up to 3.6 billion buttons per year. 5.5" × 2.25". *Collection of the author.*

A partially carved tagua nut is mounted on a paperweight base to advertise the Rochester Button Company. The buttons on the table show the variety of buttons made from the nut. On the right is another partially carved nut, showing the versatility of the material. 2" metal base. *Collection of the author.*

The bottom of the tagua nut paperweight has a label with advertising and company contact information. 2" metal base. *Collection of the author.*

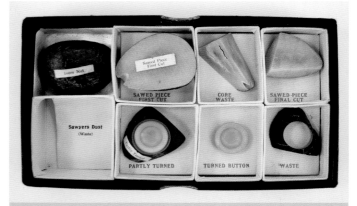

The boxed set was possibly an aid for sale representatives. It includes the nut in every step of the button-manufacturing process. 7" × 4". *Collection of the author.*

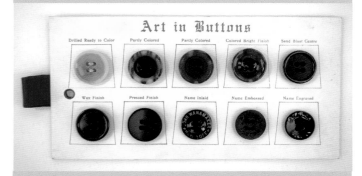

This sample card rests on top of the nut samples in the Art in Buttons box. The purple ribbon is a tab to lift the card from the box. Each button is sewn to the card. The buttons represent various finishes and custom features the company offered. 7" × 4". *Collection of the author.*

## Rubber Buttons

Rubber, in a hard form, was patented with improvements between 1849 and 1851 by Charles Goodyear. In the manufacture of buttons, the name "Goodyear" and the dates 1849 to 1851 were often molded into the back of buttons. Charles Goodyear required evidence of his rubber-hardening patent to be on the product during the life of his patent. The buttons ranged in size from one-quarter inch to two inches in diameter. Designs and rings were sometimes molded on the button surface. Other manufacturers' marks included the N.R. Co. mold from the Novelty Rubber Company (1855–1870) and then the Indian Rubber Company (1880–1890).[11]

## Thread Buttons

Buttons were also made of thread. The most basic style, shown in *Godey's Lady's Book*, advises readers they need never be without a button if they have linen thread and a needle. This style is not recommended for long-term wear; rather, it works as an emergency fix. Thread is wound around a pencil to make a sturdy circle of thread. The thick ring of thread is slid off and knotted around the circumference with the needle and thread. Spokes of thread are added in the center. The last sentence of the Godey's directions states, "it will be far better than no button at all."[12]

Needle lace buttons were worked over the top of fabric-covered buttons for over 200 years in cottage industries. There were also many styles of homemade thread buttons that were popular beginning in the mid-nineteenth century. The thread industry

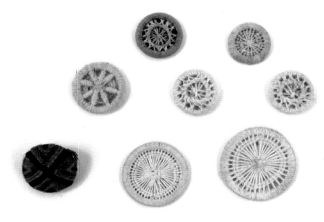

Thread-woven buttons are made over metal and plastic rings. 0.5" × 1". *Collection of the author.*

Crochet buttons are made with thread crocheted over the top of shanked buttons. 0.38" × 1". *Collection of the author.*

promoted the art in an effort to boost sales. With the invention of mass machine-made linen-covered buttons, the foundations of thread-covered buttons were readily available for home sewers. An English-style needle lace button called Dorset wheel buttons was made using a bone or metal ring for the outer rim. Instructions for buttons similar to Dorset ring buttons were published in American magazines under the name of Victorian woven buttons.

Other styles of needle lace buttons are shirtwaist, teneriffe, and darned net buttons. Shirtwaist buttons are dainty yet durable enough to stand up to twentieth-century laundry methods. Button patterns were distributed for free by thread companies. Braids like soutache were also used as decorative button covers.[13]

Crochet covers for buttons were also popular. Beautiful lace textures were crocheted over the top of fabric-covered smooth button blanks. They varied from tiny, closely placed buttons on women's blouses, to large elaborate black designs. Some crochet patterns incorporated bead and metallic-thread embellishments.

## Snap Fasteners

One of the leading manufacturers of snap fasteners in America was the Scovill Company of Waterbury, Connecticut. They began business in the early nineteenth century, making buttons. With vast growth during World War I, they were able to purchase many businesses prior to the Great Depression.[14] In 1929 they were assigned a patent for a design by inventor Paul E. Fenton for a Resilient Snap Fastener.[15]

This empty card for two-part snaps illustrates how to sew the snaps on a garment. 3.5" × 5". *Collection of the author.*

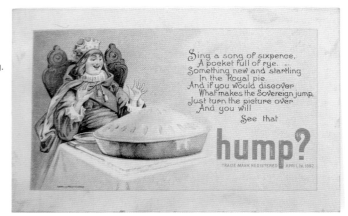

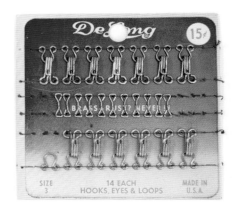

De Long hook, eye, and loops feature a hump that prevented accidental unfastening. The company made extensive use of the hump feature in advertising. 3.5" × 5" card. *Collection of the author.*

## Hook-and-Eye Fasteners

Hook-and-eye fasteners have been around for a couple of hundred years. They were manufactured in America after the 1889 United States patent was issued to Richardson and Delong of Philadelphia. Their design had a raised elevation, called a hump, in the wire hook that prevented the eye from slipping out of the hook until the wearer unhooked them.[16] Additional variations on the hook and eye received US patents in the early 1900s. Hook-and-eye tapes followed and are still used on bras and corsets today.

## Zippers

Elias Howe received a patent in 1851 for an "Automatic Continuous Clothing Closure." His design consisted of "a series of clasps united by a connecting cord, the said clasps running or sliding down ribs formed of any suitable material."[17] His patent was not marketed; perhaps he was too busy with his other patents for the sewing machine. In 1893 Whitcomb Judson patented a design he called the "Clasp Locker." He partnered with Lewis Walker to form the Universal Fastener Company and debuted the clasp locker at the 1893 Chicago World's Fair. By 1913 the company had improved the design to become what we know as the modern zipper.[18]

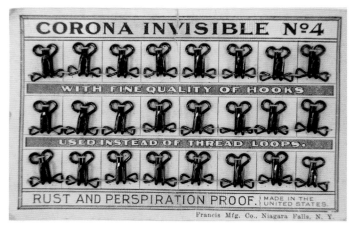

All black hook sets were useful on dark clothing. Each piece is sewn to the card with cotton thread. 3.25" × 6.5". *Collection of the author.*

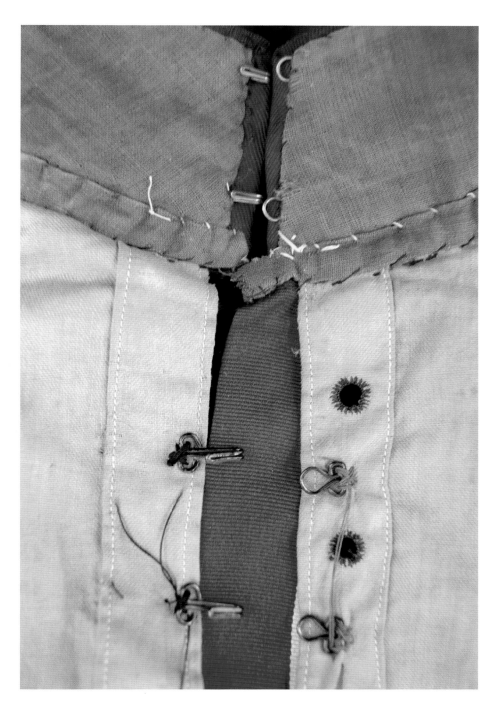

When a seamstress applied the hooks to a garment, it was sometimes done with a continuous length of thread. In this example the eyelets for lacing were also hand sewn. 0.125" eyelet. *Collection of the author.*

# Measuring

Measuring length is an important activity in everyday living. Measuring standards are important for consistency in buying and creating goods, and for making purchases.[1] The earliest examples of measuring devices for needlework were often homemade ribbons marked in ink. Later examples were sometimes marked in embroidery. Some tape measures were made in small home businesses. Long tapes were often wound on a small rod and held in a container shaped like a barrel. The tape was pulled out through a slot in the side of the barrel. The tape had to be wound by hand to retract the tape back into the barrel. To keep the tape from going all the way into the barrel, a small loop, rod, or tab was fixed to the end.

There was variability in many measuring devices. To verify the length, the owner had to compare the ribbon to a wooden measure that may or may not have been accurate.[2]

The United States accepted the "standard yard" in 1856. In 1866 the United States legalized the metric system, but the definition of metric units was still poorly defined. Prior to that, measurements were not standard. One example, the "ell," was a length from the elbow to the shoulder, or the elbow to the wrist. The discrepancies this produced were known and expected.[3] Measures for sewing were often made from ell sticks or yardsticks that varied from the standard. Long wooden measures were often impractical to carry around to settle measurement variations. Pliable tapes of ribbon or cloth were carried but were probably no more accurate than a merchant's stick.

The Industrial Revolution of the late nineteenth century produced a diverse assortment of whimsical and entertaining tape measures. The retractable cloth tapes included features like retractable spring tapes and, by 1870, a button lock to keep the tape extended. Markings combined centimeters and inches to appeal to more markets.

By the 1870s celluloid was improved and successfully used to create attractive molded shapes like flowers, fruit, and butterflies. These tape measures are just as entertaining as they are practical.

Their continued popularity has made them sought out by collectors. They are frequently referred to as figural tape measures.

Tape measures are advertised in the June 1886 Butterick publication called the *Delineator*. The measures were all sixty inches long and ranged in price from five cents for narrow cotton tapes numbered on one side to wider sateen stitch reinforced tapes numbered on both sides for fifty cents. The better-quality measures were promised to last for years in constant use.

An important element for all tape measure manufacturers was the standardization of measures for length. On April 5, 1893, the Mendenhall Order established the American standard for weights and measures as the yard and pound. In 1901 the National Bureau of Standards was founded (whose predecessor was the Office of Standard Weights and Measures of the Treasury Department) and published the calculations for the yard and pound based on calculations of the international meter and kilogram.[4]

In 1959, the international yard and pound were officially recognized by the United States, the United Kingdom, Canada, Australia, New Zealand, and South Africa. A meter is defined as 0.9144 yard and the pound is 0.45359237 kilogram. These standards aided manufacturers in providing consumers with accurate measuring equipment.[5]

American souvenir tape measures were purchased as vacation mementos and were marketed to tourists. Tapes measures have always been popular gifts. They have been used for advertising and were given away as customer premiums. Innovations in measuring devices include folding styles, slide attachments, and spring closures.

Folding rulers are sometimes found with sewing supplies. The rulers are made of wood, ivory, horn, or metal. Material like ivory, bone, and horn shrink over time, distorting the accuracy of a measurement.[6] Some are the same rulers woodworkers used for precision work and then were found useful and practical by the seamstress in the family. Others are designed specifically for small,

Retractable tape measures were hand wound back in their cases prior to the invention of an internal spring mechanism. Silk tapes were sometimes ribbons with inked lines. 0.25" wide tape. *Collection of the author.*

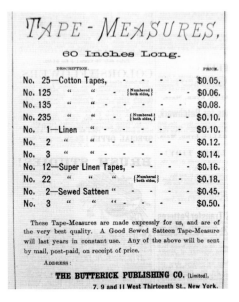

fine needlework. Thin and dainty rulers are easily stored with other sewing tools.

Advertising rulers six inches in length were often used in needlework. Made in wood or celluloid they often feature advertising. The short length made the rulers inexpensive as giveaway promotional items but also a convenient size to keep with sewing supplies.

Sterling hem gauges were made in America circa 1900 in four- and six-inch sizes. Most hems in the early twentieth century were three inches. The hem gauge was shorter and easier to maneuver than a ruler when hemming or altering garments. A slide marks the hem depth so pins could be accurately placed for stitching. American sterling examples from the early twentieth century are usually in the Art Nouveau style.

Tailors used flexible tape measures for fitting menswear. Advertising is often printed on the tape measure. The tapes were made of paper, coated papers, and narrow woven goods. The inexpensive materials made them ideal giveaways for customer premiums.

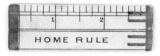

Advertising for 6" rulers directed at the home sewer. The Churngold ruler reads, "For The Lady's Work Basket." Churngold was a butter substitute. The plastic rulers are grained to imitate ivory or bone. The folding ruler on the top is made of paper. 0.5" – 6". *Collection of the author.*

Sterling silver hem gauge with sliding adjustable marker. 0.5" × 5". *Collection of the author.*

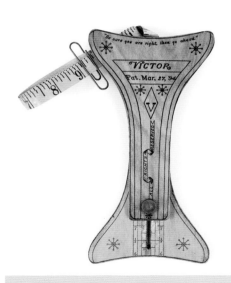

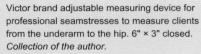

Victor brand adjustable measuring device for professional seamstresses to measure clients from the underarm to the hip. 6" × 3" closed. *Collection of the author.*

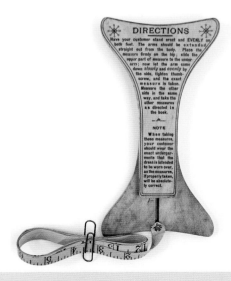

The directions for using the Victor brand adjustable measuring device for professional seamstresses are printed on the back. The user is also instructed to refer to the manual. 6" × 3". *Collection of the author.*

## Marking

Marking textiles has always been important for inventory and ownership purposes. Before textiles were mass produced they were very expensive. Textiles were used for decades, repaired, and remade as needed. Household linens were rotated to minimize wear (or prevent excessive wear). Clear ownership was important when laundry was sent out or household staff managed the textiles. Early textiles were often marked and numbered with embroidery or ink. Discreet small cross stitches, often in red, included one to three letters and sometimes numbers. It is unclear if embroidered numbers represent a year, rotation sequence, or inventory number. Dowry linens were often marked, perhaps to indicate what the bride was bringing to the marriage. Marking customs may have also varied by region and cultural practices.

Children sent to boarding schools had to have their clothing marked. An 1806 Salem Academy for Girls boarding school terms and conditions paper requires, "Every article of clothing they bring along should be marked so as to stand washing." Once at school, the girls were taught plain sewing, which included marking textiles. Instruction in fine needlework required extra tuition and was paid quarterly with all other boarding-school fees. Supplies were charged separately.

Instead of embroidery, clothing and household textiles could also be marked with ink. Numerous inking tools and inking

Assorted cloth tape measures sometimes given away free as advertisements. 0.5" – 120". *Collection of the author.*

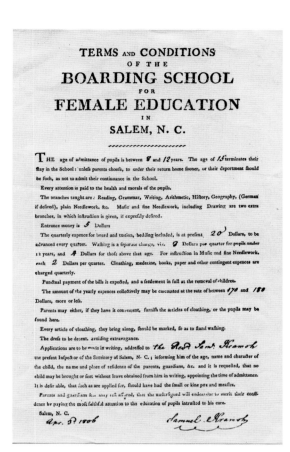

This copy of the "Terms and Conditions of the Boarding School for Female Education" in Salem, North Carolina, was printed in 1806. One of the conditions requires, "Every article of clothing they bring along, should be marked so as to stand washing." In the list of fees, instruction in music and fine needlework was two dollars additional per quarter. 7" × 10". *Salem Academy and College Archives.*

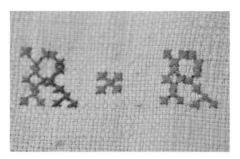

An example of counted-thread cross stitch on linen to mark ownership. The cross stitch is done two threads over two threads. 0.5" per letter. *Collection of the author.*

formulas were available. There were also recipes for making ink in the home. Marking was used to transfer designs for decorative embroidery. Marking was also done for sentimental reasons. In the mid-nineteenth century, ink quilt blocks were popular to commemorate important events and for gifts. The quilt pieces could be inscribed, signed, or stamped, sometimes with added ink embellishment.

Fabric-marking tools include devices that make temporary or permanent markings. Prior to commercially distributed patterns, marking letters and numbers were often drawn by hand. Some counted thread work was learned at very young ages, and no patterns were required. Some designs were copied from existing garments and embroideries.

Marking textiles in ink was important to households for decades. *The Workwoman's Guide* of 1838 provides recipes for linen-marking ink to be made in the home. Recipes in the book include formulas for black, red, green, and blue inks. Also included is a recipe for liquid pounce, the solution needed to prepare the textile for inking. It included a warning that the pounce liquid could also injure the linen if left on too long. Ink was available for purchase; however, the formula for making it at home was well known.

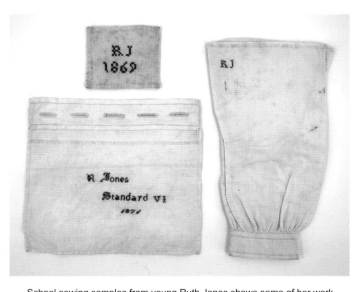

School sewing samples from young Ruth Jones shows some of her work from 1869 to 1871. The samples were often mounted in blank-page books to illustrate the progression and skill each student achieved. Garment pieces, like the sleeve, were done in miniature and are made the way full-size articles are done. Marking textiles was an important first lesson. Ruth was born in Illinois in 1860. 1869 square measures 1.5". *Collection of the author.*

In addition to marking household linens and garments, inking names on cotton for quilt blocks was a popular activity in the nineteenth century. The inked pieces were sewn into quilt blocks. The blocks were given as gifts or exchanged with family and friends. One inking technique was to place the fabric in a linen stretcher and write the name with a dip pen. Unlike a hoop, a linen stretcher has a solid base in the lower ring that provides a solid base for inking. Examples can be found where inking was done by multiple hands, completed by one hand or inked by professional scriveners. *Collection of Florence McConnell*

The 1860 copy of *Ladies Handbook of Fancy and Ornamental Work* advises every lady to excel in the ability to mark well in ink. They reason it prevents loss of clothes of every kind. They advise to be cautious of the ink recipe. Some inks wash out in the first rinse; other inks can eat through the textile, causing holes. Most packaging in marking sets from this era provided instructions specific to the ink packaged in the set. Some required heat set; others warned against it. When ink refills were purchased, not following the process for using the specific ink formula could be devastating to the fabric.

Stencils were an option for marking linens with ink. They were also used to create calling cards. Calling cards were popular with upper-class ladies in urban areas of America from 1840 to 1900. The stencils were sometimes used by soldiers to mark their possessions.[7] Brass stencil cutters had shops where custom stencils were ordered for use by men and women. The stencils were made in many sizes and designs. Metcalf's Stencil Rooms was opened in Boston in 1865. They advertised wholesale and retail stencils for marking textiles, books, and cards. The brass stencils were secured in zinc frames. In addition to a name, buyers could select decorative additions like stars, eagles, botanical motifs, and scrolls. The formulation of ink enclosed with their stencil kit instructed users on how the inked textile should be exposed to heat before washing.

Metal stamps were made in various styles for marking names on textiles with ink. Early examples are made with a wooden handle holding the metal stamp head at the end. Most styles allow the user to switch out the letters and print any names or initials by using a channel for inserting typeset letters. Decorative styles had ovals with relief impressions of doves, eagles, or botanical carvings. These styles also had elaborate screws, which were decorated with a shell motif. To create names, typeset letters are inserted in a channel and secured tightly with a screw at the end of the metal head. Less decorative styles have only the channel for

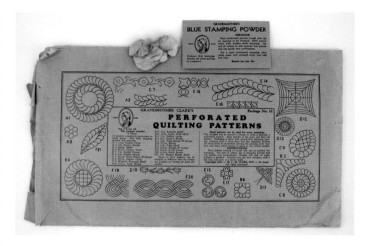

This package of perforated-paper templates includes twenty-one designs on six sheets of paper. The paper is pierced and ready for pouncing with stamping powder. Refills of the blue powder could be purchased for twenty-five cents. The powder was removable unless heat set with a hot iron. *Collection of the author.*

Wooden-handled tracing wheel with replaceable marking wheel. 5.5". *Collection of the author.*

The box for this brass name stencil has the original label advertising Metcalf's Stencil Cutting Room in Boston. They cut stencil plates and sold ink for use on textiles, books, and calling cards. 1.5" × 3". *Collection of the author.*

Custom-made brass stencils for individuals to mark their property in ink. The stencil is placed on the object, and ink is brushed across the surface and then set following the ink manufacturer's instructions. 1.5" – 4". *Collection of the author.*

This painted tin container holds a solid cake of ink and has an empty vessel for water. The indention in the ink is where water was applied to the ink cake, creating a small pool of ink. Brushes were dipped in the ink for use in painting, stenciling, and lettering. 1.25" × 2.25" stencil. *Collection of Florence McConnell*

This wooden box locks to secure the letters and stamps. The sliding tray carries the letters while the stamps are stored under the tray. The stamp heads are plain and hold a single row of letters. 0.25" letters. *Collection of the author.*

letters. Font styles and sizes varied by typeset and were usually not interchangeable.

In November 1879, William Weeden, of Boston, was issued a patent for a metal-plunger-styled linen marker. He licensed his design to William B. Gorham, who boxed it with ink and instructions. In December 1879, Benjamin B. Hill patented one of his many ink stamps. He designed and patented many stamps for home and business use. The B.B. Hill stamp was sold with a boxed set of letters, numbers, an ink bottle, and tweezers. The Gorham and Hill plunger-style linen markers are so similar in design that it is interesting that separate patents were issued thirty days apart.

Carter's Ink Company of Boston received a patent for their ink formulation in 1903. Formula 481 was developed just for indelible use on textiles. The ink was bottled and sold for individual use in addition to being packaged in kits containing bottled ink, pen nib with handle, and a special bevel-edge wooden hoop for pulling the fabric surface taut. Emphasized in numerous places on the packaging are the warnings, "Important! Do Not Use Heat Or Allow Heat To Come In Contact With Fabric Before Washing."[8]

The Ingersoll's Improved Solid Rubber Family Font set is advertised for use as a pocket card printer and linen marker. The label states it is "The cheapest and most durable thing for printing cards, marking books and linen ever known." The kit includes a bottle of unlabeled ink, ink pad, letters in a wooden stand, and a letter holder. The holder accommodates two rows of letters.

If a needle worker had a pattern, unless it was a charted design, it had to be transferred to the ground fabric. One option for marking was the prick-and-pounce technique. The design was traced from the pattern source to a blank piece of paper. Every line was pierced in dots along the line. The piercing tool was either a pin, needle, or sharp stiletto. By the end of the nineteenth century a tracing wheel was available. The pierced paper pattern was placed on the ground fabric. Powder (chalk or charcoal mixes) was

Ink stamps with intricate engraving surrounding the slot where a single row of letters are inserted. The letters and spacers are held in place with a screw adorned with a shell motif. The wooden handle is attached to the metal head. Designs include eagles, flowers, doves, and other sentimental motifs. 2" - 2.5" metal heads. *Collection of the author.*

The Weeden plunger-style marker was boxed with letters, ink bottle, and tweezers. There is a blotter at the bottom of the stamp compartment. Each letter is manually inserted into the marker with the tweezers. 3" square box. *Collection of the author.*

The instructions for the Improved Linen Stamp are glued under the lid. This particular ink required heat-setting treatment to be permanent. 3" square lid. *Collection of the author.*

The Gorham Linen Marker was another plunger-style marker. The Gorham and Weeden plunger-style markers are virtually identical in design and were issued United States patents only four weeks apart. 5" × 3" box. *Collection of the author.*

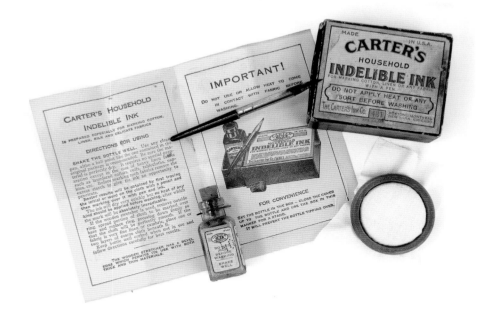

The Carter's ink set includes a dip pen, linen stretcher or hoop, ink, and important instructions. This set requires no heat be used on the finished textile until the ink has dried and the item is washed in cool water. All starch is to be removed prior to inking. 3.5" × 5" box. *Collection of the author.*

The Ingersoll's set has a wooden handle for holding the type. The sets were available in multiple type styles. One end of the box folds down and has an ink blotter. Ink was brushed on the blotter and the stamp was pressed into the blotter. The bottom of the type set in the wooden handle picked up the ink. The inked handle was then pressed down onto linen or paper calling cards. 4.5" square box. *Collection of the author.*

pounced or dabbed over the perforations. When the paper was removed, the little dots of powder left the design on the fabric. Homemade patterns usually had a short life due to piercing for the design transfer.[9]

The 1882 edition of *The Dictionary of Needlework* by Caulfeild and Saward recommends the use of carbonized linen sold in white and blue for pattern transfer. Carbonized pattern transfer was also available in a paper form, which was less desirable. The specially coated surface was placed face down on the front of the textile to be embroidered. The pattern was placed on top and the three layers were pinned together. They recommended the use of a blunt bone or steel knitting needle applied to the design lines like a pencil. The force caused the carbonized treated surface to make a line on the textile. The carbonized material could be renewed by a moderately heated iron to smooth out the lined surface.

In 1886, *The Delineator*, published by Butterick Pattern Company, included an advertisement for a marking set that women could use for marking designs on textiles. There were many ads in the back of the magazine for products related to sewing. The World Manufacturing Company offered readers the chance to earn a solid-gold pocket watch by selling twenty of their textile-marking sets to others.

The 1886 front cover of *The Delineator* magazine, published by Butterick. The newsstand price was 15 cents. Subscriptions were available. 8.5" × 11". *Collection of the author.*

Advertising for ladies to do their own stamping for savings or for profit. Customers were rewarded with a solid-gold watch if they were successful in securing twenty subscribers. It is unknown how many watches were awarded. 5.5" × 7.5". *Collection of the author.*

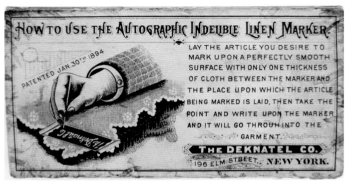

The Autographic Indelible Linen Marker sold for 35 cents in 1894. The side of the package reads, "Requires No Skill To Use." 5.25" × 3". *Collection of the author.*

In 1894 Edward Dodge patented the Autographic Indelible Linen Marker, which retailed for thirty-five cents. It was designed "for marking linen, silk, cotton and all fine fabrics." The label also claims it will not blur or crock, while providing an intense black mark. It also claims no skill is required to use it. A small metal frame held a replaceable inked ribbon taut. The package instructs the user to shake the ink and apply a few drops to the ribbon and rub it carefully with a brush. Lay the article to be marked in a single thickness on a smooth surface. Use the provided pointer from the package and write on the ribbon. The writing is transferred in ink to the textile surface.[10]

The J & J Cash Company was founded in Coventry, England, in 1843, specializing in making ribbons. The Quaker brothers were model employers, philanthropists, and businessmen. J & J Cash moved into manufacturing fabric trims to replace ink marking for clothing. Linen marking with woven initials was produced that was sewn onto clothing for marking ownership. One style includes a machine-produced set of letters that looks like hand cross stitch. The letters were red on white ribbon and resembled hand-applied thread work. The company prospered and eventually opened offices in Norwalk, Connecticut, and later in Los Angeles, California. Retail distributors included Wanamaker's Department Store in Philadelphia.[11]

Cash's Woven Names Tapes were sold in Wanamaker's Department store in Philadelphia. One style of letter was woven to give the appearance of counted cross stitch. 0.375" wide tape. *Collection of the author.*

## Printed Patterns

Prior to the availability to printed patterns, designs were often drawn freehand. In the *South Carolina Gazette*, February 6, 1753, John Thomas advertised, "He will also undertake to teach about 6 young ladies to draw and shade with Indian ink pencil, which may not only seem as an amusement to their genius, but in some respects became serviceable to them in needlework." Printed embroidery patterns were rare and expensive. Embroidery was done and kept for samples; these patterns and stitches were passed from generation to generation.[12] Some notebooks were compiled by teachers and professional embroiderers.

The first printed needlework patterns were sixteenth-century German. Later eighteenth- and nineteenth-century English charted patterns were printed as small folded booklets for use in lace or canvas work. Printed patterns were often traced on canvas or silk to prepare for stitching. In colonial America, stationers and embroiderers sold their services to draw patterns for all kinds of needlework.

Early in the eighteenth century, only the wealthy could afford the first American periodical magazines with embroidery patterns. The content was directed toward the most learned and cultured of the American population. By 1830, more publications directed at the general public were printed. These issues focused on amusement and entertainment. Women's interest magazines published needlework patterns and became a popular source of needlework patterns. At the end of the nineteenth century, there were more than one hundred magazines in the United States, corresponding to the rising rate of American literacy. Many magazines included free patterns, often for clothing or embroidery.[13]

The *American Ladies' Magazine* was purchased by Louis Godey in 1836 and re-created *Godey's Lady's Magazine*. He hired Sarah J. Hale as editor in 1837. They were a successful team for over forty years. They featured only American talent. Hale also published three special issues with work exclusively by women. In 1850 the *Godey's Lady's Magazine* was the largest of any pre–Civil War American magazine.[14] The magazine included sheet music,

*Peterson's* and *Godey's Lady's Magazines* from 1861, 1863, and 1872. Each issue was filled with fiction, fashion, needlework patterns, and numerous other topics to interest a household. The patterns required the maker to transfer and fit the patterns herself. 6" × 10". *Collection of the author.*

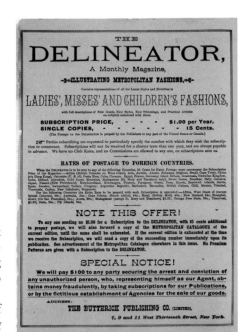

Inside cover of *The Delineator* magazine, sold by the Butterick Publishing Company. The page details subscription conditions and prices. 8.5" × 11". *Collection of the author.*

fiction, fashion, home decorating, and a variety of needlework patterns. The magazine's intent was to inform, educate, and entertain the women of America. *Peterson's Magazine*, a competing periodical, was published from 1842 to 1898, and was designed to sell at a lower price point than rival Godey's *Lady's Book*.[15]

In 1870, James McCall started designing and printing a line of sewing patterns, using a four-page journal: *The Queen: Illustrating McCall's Bazaar Glove-Fitting Patterns*. Management changes and the evolution of the publication content led to the 1897 name change to *McCall's Magazine—The Queen of Fashion*. In 1917, an issue cost ten cents, the equivalent of a cup of coffee. Ownership of the magazine frequently changed, and by 2001 it closed.[16]

Ebenezer Butterick sold reusable clothing patterns for the home sewer in 1863. Ready-made clothing was gaining popularity, and apparel advertisers placed ads alongside milliners' and tailors'. In 1873 Butterick created *The Delineator* magazine, a journal of fashion, culture, and fine arts that included sewing and embroidery. It ceased publication in 1937 to focus on their more profitable clothing-pattern business.[17]

*Ladies' Home Journal* started in 1883 and by 1903 was the first American magazine to reach 1,000,000 subscribers. It started as a double-page insert in *Tribune and Farmer*, titled *Women at Home*, written by Louisa Knapp Curtis. The focus was on housekeeping and family. In 2014 they stopped subscription services and focused on a digital presence.[18]

Charted designs using a cross stitch are called Berlin work and started in Berlin, Germany. The designs were charted on black-and-white graph paper and were hand colored. The designs were sold in individual sheets, making them affordable to the masses. Using wool, the charted designs were worked with tent or cross stitch without the need to mark the canvas. Victorian Romanticism influenced floral designs, biblical motifs, and quotations, including "Home Sweet Home" and "Faith, Hope, Love."[19] The technique gained popularity, getting a global boost in London at the Great Exhibition of 1851. Price, availability, and a time in

The instructions for selecting Butterick sewing patterns have a recurring theme when measuring, "Not Too Tight." They also ask for the age of the misses and girls. 4" × 5.5" ad. *Collection of the author.*

FIGURE NO. 2.—LADIES' COSTUME.—This illustrates Pattern No. 938, price 1s. 8d. or 40 cents.
(For Description see Page 225.)

history when women had more leisure time made Berlin work more popular than ever.

Alternatives to stitching and inking designs were also created during this era. Woodside, New York, resident Bernhard Ulmann incorporated the Bernhard Ulmann Company in 1867. He sold household linens and handkerchiefs with silk-screened embroidery designs from a street cart. He was able to open a retail store in 1870 and expanded into wholesaling in 1875. The company name was eventually changed to Bucilla. The company is still in business today, succeeding with many changes in ownership and business focus.[20]

Embroidery patterns and stamped articles were also available by mail order. The 1895 Montgomery Ward catalog offered numerous needlework supplies. Stamped goods included a variety of household linens with finished and unfinished edges. Linen embroidery thread was offered at an additional fee, with the merchant selecting the colors needed. The patterns were listed as "variety so great we cannot describe them." Prices ranged from five to seventy-five cents each. The customer was to write in with a clear description of their design needs and the purpose for the pattern. A fashionable clothing-pattern catalog was also advertised on the same page for four cents.

Heat-transfer embroidery designs were available from several sources beginning in the early twentieth century. The embroidery design was printed on paper with patented inks that would wash out in the laundry. The single-use paper was placed printed side down on the embroidery ground fabric and ironed. The heat from the iron transferred the design to the fabric. After embroidering, the project was washed and the iron-on markings disappeared. Magazines, pattern printers, thread manufacturers, and needlework specialists all distributed heat-transfer patterns.

One heat-transfer process for embroidery that was patented in the 1920s was called a kaumagraph.[21] Originally, a company in Germany, Kaumagraph franchised their patented heat-transfer process to companies in the United States, Canada, and France. The Kaumagraph name was dual labeled on patterns for companies like McCall's. Consumers had a choice of yellow or blue transfer lines, for use on light or dark fabrics.

Primary evidence is sketchy regarding the beginnings of Vogart Needlecraft Company and their prestamped fabrics. Vogart produced household textiles and unsewn children's clothing with prestamped embroidery motifs in the 1930s. They grew the business with character licensing and exclusive product contracts for retail store chain F. W. Woolworth Company. By 1942 they were also selling iron-on embroidery transfers in paper envelope packages. When interest in embroidery declined, they introduced fabric paints that could be used on all of their designs, hoping to reach a broader consumer base. In 1990 they filed bankruptcy and assets were sold to other companies.[22]

*Aunt Martha's Workbasket Magazine* started in 1935 as a subscription publication that included iron transfers, needlework patterns, and other handicrafts. A yearly subscription was one dollar. In 1942 they dropped "Aunt Martha" from the magazine name to become *Workbasket Magazine*. Early issues advertised all of their patterns and included a quilt block as well as iron-on transfer patterns. After many changes over their 671 issues *Workbasket Magazine* ceased publication in 1996.[23]

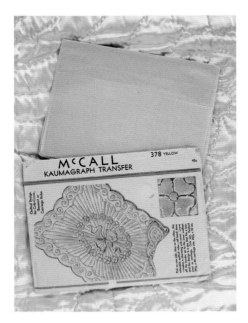

McCall Kaumagraph transfer pattern for a quilted crib cover. The pattern sheets in this example have yellow transfer marks. The pattern and pattern sheets are shown lying on the finished quilt, pink side up. 7" × 11". *Collection of the author.*

Threadwork edging partially completed shows how the linen was marked and used in embroidery. 2" wide bands. *Collection of the author.*

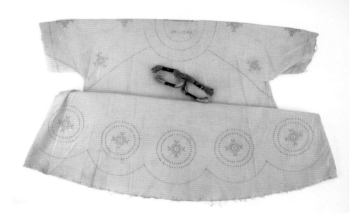

Child's dress with premarked embroidery lines. 20" across. *Collection of the author.*

Three *Workbasket* magazines from 1948. The magazine included many kinds of needlework patterns like knitting, crochet, and quilting. The magazine promoted making articles for sale as fund-raisers for clubs, churches, and schools. 7" × 9". *Collection of the author.*

Plush work six-petal star.
*Collection of the author.*

## Plush Work and Star Templates

Plush work began in France and Holland in the eighteenth century. Sets of metal templates were embroidered over with special locking stitches. When the stitching was completed, the loops were cut, releasing the template. The gauge or template was removed and the stitching process was repeated. The resulting pile was then brushed and shaped, creating a plush finish. Popular Victorian designs were leaves and flowers. The Winterthur Museum has an embroidered chair cover done in colorful three-dimensional plush stitch motifs. While visually interesting, it was most likely uncomfortable to sit on the thick, lumpy creation. When charted Berlin patterns became readily available, some were produced entirely in raised work.[24]

Plush work fell out of favor with most Americans by the end of the nineteenth century. It remained popular with the Amish of Lancaster County, Pennsylvania, through the 1930s. They used the tin metal templates on dark wool ground fabric to create star flower shapes on wool quilts, pincushions, and pillows. They also used needlepoint canvas to stitch layers of built-up wool yarn that was later trimmed away in patterns. The Amish often layered colors of wool yarn so the cut design had a secondary pattern.[25]

Tin templates for use in making plush work stars and flowers. The motif has also been found less often in quilting and applique motifs. *Collection of the author.*

## Quilt Templates

Templates were often made at home for marking designs for quilting. They were made of heavy paper, cardboard, and sometimes tin, wood, and leather. One documented template maker is Jonathan Lowery (1852–1926) of Warwick Township, Lancaster County, Pennsylvania. He signed and dated his templates.[26] Some tin examples are made of recycled painted tin roofing.

Paper templates for use in quilting. The top example was used for a swag border. The blue shape second from the top is called a cable and was used to mark quilting lines. 24". The squares and hexagon were used to cut shapes to piece quilt blocks. The shape on the right was used for applique or quilting motifs. 11". *Collection of the author.*

# Notes

## Introduction

1. Nancy Nehring. *Brief History of C.J. Bates & Son, Inc.*, accessed 6/13/2016. https://lacebuttons.com/?page_id=5340.

2. Ernie Gross. *Advances and Innovations in American Daily Life, 1600s-1930s.* Jefferson, North Carolina: McFarland, 2002; 131.

3. Grant H. Smith. *The History of the Comstock Lode, Nevada Bureau of Mines and Geology.* Reno, Nevada: University of Nevada Press, 1998; 289.

4. Steven Reti. *Silver and Gold: The Political Economy of International Monetary Conferences 1867-1892, Contributions in Economics and Economic History.* Santa Barbara, California: Praeger, 1998; 73.

## Chapter 1: Needles and Thread

1. John G. Rollins. *Needlemaking.* Oxford, United Kingdom: Shire, 2008; 3.

2. Mary C. Beaudry. *Findings: The Material Culture of Needlework and Sewing.* New Haven, Connecticut: Yale University Press, 2006; 45–46.

3. Ibid., pg. 48.

4. Ibid., pg. 73.

5. John Leander. *A History of American Manufacturers, from 1608-1860.* Philadelphia, Pennsylvania: Edward Young & Company, 1864; 504.

6. Rita S. Grossman. *The Arts and Crafts in New York 1726-1776: Advertisements and News Items from New York City Newspapers.* New York, New York: Da Capo Press, 1938; 254.

7. Molly Proctor. *Needlework Tools and Accessories.* London, England: B.T. Batsford, 1990; 14.

8. William R. Merriam. *Census Bulletin No. 191.* Washington, DC: Twelfth Census of the United States, 1902; pg. 9-10.

9. Gay Ann Rogers. *An Illustrated History of Needlework Tools.* Norwich, Great Britain: Fletcher & Son, 1983; 59.

10. William R. Merriam. *Census Bulletin No. 191.* Washington, DC: Twelfth Census of the United States, 1902, pg. 9.

11. Ibid., pg. 11.

12. Nancy Villa Bryk. *Bloomingdale's Illustrated 1886 Catalog.* New York, New York: Dover, 1988; 71.

13. John Blundell. *Ladies for Liberty: Women Who Made a Difference in American History.* New York, New York: Algora, 2011; 83.

14. Jeffrey L. Meikle. *American Plastic: A Cultural History.* New Brunswick, New Jersey: Rutgers University Press, 1995; 58.

15. Helen Sheumaker. *Love Entwined: The Curious History of Hairwork in America.* Philadelphia, Pennsylvania: University of Pennsylvania Press, 2007; 2.

16. Gross Ernie. *Advances and Innovations in American Daily Life, 1600s-1930s.* Jefferson, North Carolina: McFarland, 2002; 146.

17. Mansfield Historical Society. *Industries of Mansfield,* accessed 6/16/2016. www.mansfieldct-history.org/silk-mills-of-mansfield/.

18. Ron Cherry, Entomology Society of America. *History of Sericulture,* accessed 5/12/2016. www.insects.org/ced1/seric.html.

19. North Carolina State University College of Textiles, *Silk in America,* accessed 2/15/2016. https://sites.textiles.ncsu.edu/history/?s=NonotuckSilkCompany.

20. Belding Michigan, *Belding Brothers and Company,* accessed 3/15/2016. www.belding.michlibrary.org/our-history-1/belding-brothers-company-silk-manufacturers.html.

21. *History of Willimantic,* accessed 6/15/2016. www.past-inc.org/Willimantic/overall_history.html.

22. *United States Centennial Reports from Commissioners, Inspectors and Others: Thirty-One Volume 36 International Exhibition 1876 by Commission.* Parliament House of Commerce: Eyre and Spottiswoode, 1877; pg. 589.

23. *History of Willimantic,* accessed 6/15/2016. www.past-inc.org/Willimantic/overall_history.html.

24. Betsey A. Shirley. "History Presented by American Thread," *Bangor Daily News,* August 20, 1975.

25. Bill Ryan. "Industrial Age Ghosts Granted New Lives." *New York Times,* April 11, 1999, accessed 6/10/2016. www.nytimes.com/1999/04/11/nyregion/industrial-age-ghosts-granted-new-lives.html.

26. Elias H. Henderson. *Federal Antitrust Laws.* Chicago, Illinois: Federal Legislative Bulletin Services, 1915; 67.

27. James Elliott Defebaugh. *History of the Lumber Industry of America, Volume 2.* Chicago, Illinois: The American Lumberman, 1907; 100.

28. Fred Aftalion. *A History of the International Chemical Industry: 2nd Edition.* Philadelphia, Pennsylvania: Chemical Heritage Foundation, 2001; 132.

29. DuPont Company History, accessed 06/15/2-16. www.dupont.com/corporate-functions/our-company/dupont-history.html.

30. Norm Cohen. *Folk Music: A Regional Exploration*. Westport, Connecticut: Greenwood, 2005; 24–25.

31. Mary Andere. *Old Needlework Boxes and Tools*. New York, New York: Drake, 1971; 129.

32. William H. Conant, inventor; Bragg Conant, assignee. Improvement in work boxes. United States patent US 214,757, April 29, 1879.


## CHAPTER 2: PINS AND PIN STORAGE

1. Robert K. Barnhart. *Barnhart Concise Dictionary of Etymology*. New York, New York: Harper Collins, 1995; 763.

2. Bureau of the Census. *Twelfth Census of the United States, Census Bulletin Issue Number 191*. Prepared by the Department of the Interior, Washington D.C. June 17, 1902; pg. 8.

3. George S. Cole. *A Complete Dictionary of Dry Goods*. Chicago, Illinois: W.B. Conkey Co., 1892; 287.

4. Bureau of the Census. *Twelfth Census of the United States, Census Bulletin Issue Number 191*. Prepared by the Department of the Interior, Washington, DC. June 17, 1902; pg. 8.

5. Connecticut Daughters of the American Revolution, Trumbull Chapter. *History of Ancient Westbury and Present Watertown from Its Settlement to 1907*. Waterbury, Connecticut: Hemingway Press; 49.

6. Bureau of the Census. *Twelfth Census of the United States, Census Bulletin Issue Number 191*. Prepared by the Department of the Interior, Washington, DC. June 17, 1902; 9.

7. Molly Proctor. *Needlework Tools and Accessories: A Collectors Guide*. London, England: B.T. Batsford, 1990; 56.

8. Eleanor D. Longman and Sophy Loch. *Pins and Pincushions*. New York, New York: Longmans, Green and Co., 1911; 49.

9. M. Stephen Miller. *Inspired Innovations: A Celebration of Shaker Ingenuity*. Lebanon, New Hampshire: University Press of New England, 2007; 145.

10. M. Stephen Miller. *From Shaker Lands and Shaker Hands*. Lebanon, New Hampshire: University Press of New England, 2007; 156.

11. *Cassell's Household Guide Volume III*. New York, New York: Cassell, Petter and Galpin, 1869; 282.

12. Sophia Frances Anne Caulfeild and Blanche C. Saward. *The Dictionary of Needlework Facsimile of 1882 Edition*. New York, New York: Arno, 1972; 207.

13. Katheryn and Donald McCauley. *Decorative Arts of the Amish of Lancaster County*. Intercourse, Pennsylvania: Good Books, 1988; pg. 100.

14. Trish T. Herr. *Amish Arts of Lancaster County*. Atglen, Pennsylvania: Schiffer, 1998; 45–57.

15. Francis and Thesesa Pulszky. *White, Red, Black Sketches of American Society in the United States During the Visit of Their Guests Volume 3*. London, England: Trubner, and Co. 1853; 121-125.

16. Gerry Biron. *Historic Iroquois and Wabanaki Beadwork*, accessed 6/12/2016. iroquoisbeadwork.blogspot.com and www.gerrybiron.com/index.html.

17. Averil Colby. *Pincushions*. New York, New York: Charles Scribner's Sons, 1975; 81.

18. Clarke Hess. *Mennonite Arts*. Atglen, Pennsylvania: Schiffer, 2002; 50, 173.


## CHAPTER 3: THIMBLES AND THIMBLE HOLDERS

1. Mary C. Beaudry. *Findings: The Material Culture of Needlework and Sewing*. New Haven, Connecticut: Yale University Press, 2006; 102–103.

2. Estelle Zalkin. *Zalkin's Handbook of Thimbles and Sewing Implements*. Willow Grove, Pennsylvania: Warman, 1988; 17.

3. Amy K. Smith. *Needlework for Student Teachers, Third Edition*. London, England: London Book Depot, 1894; 12.

4. Edwin F. Holmes. *A History of Thimbles*. Cranbury, New Jersey: Cornwall Books, 1985; 58.

5. University of Nebraska Lincoln, *Journals of the Lewis & Clark Expedition*, accessed 6/01/2016. www.lewisandclarkjournals.unl.edu.

6. Gay Ann Rogers. *An Illustrated History of Needlework Tools*. London, England: John Murray, 1983; 92.

7. Edwin F. Holmes. *A History of Thimbles*. Cranbury, New Jersey: Cornwall Books, 1985; 61.

8. *Simon Brothers Company History*, accessed 5/5/2016. www.simonsbrothers.com/about.html.

9. Gay Ann Rogers. *An Illustrated History of Needle-work Tools*. London, England: John Murray, 1983; 91.

10. Edwin F. Holmes. *A History of Thimbles*. Cranbury, New Jersey: Cornwall Books, 1985; 5, 9.

11. Estelle Zalkin. *Zalkin's Handbook of Thimbles and Sewing Implements*. Willow Grove, Pennsylvania: Warman, 1988; 35.

12. Ibid., 36.

13. Edwin F. Holmes. *A History of Thimbles*. Cranbury, New Jersey: Cornwall Books, 1985; 61.

14. Ibid., 62.

15. Adeline Cordet. *Crocheted Gift Novelties*. East Freetown, Massachusetts: Iva Rose Reproductions, 1916/2008; 6.

## CHAPTER 4: BODKINS, AWLS, AND STILETTOS

1. Molly Proctor. *Needlework Tools and Accessories: A Collector's Guide*. London, England: B.T. Batsford, 1990; 23.

2. Mary Ellen Snodgrass. *World Clothing and Fashion: An Encyclopedia of History, Culture and Social Influence*. New York, New York: Routledge, 2013; 342.

3. Mary C. Beaudry. *Findings: The Material Culture of Needlework and Sewing*. New Haven, Connecticut: Yale University Press, 2006; 82.

4. Charles M. Haynes, Embroidery Stiletto. United States Patent US 917,295. July 3, 1907.

## CHAPTER 5: SCISSORS AND CUTTING

1. Philip R. Pankiewicz. *American Scissors and Shears: An Antique and Vintage Collector's Guide*. Boca Raton, Florida: Universal, 2013; 1.

2. Gay Ann Rogers. *An Illustrated History of Needle-work Tools*. London, England: John Murray, 1983; 110.

3. Alexander Farnham. *Early Tools of New Jersey and the Men Who Made Them*. Kingwood, Texas: Kingwood, 1984; 128.

4. *Clauss: 136 Years of Progress and Innovation*, accessed 5/10/2016. www.acmeunited .com/Company/Articles+Of+Interest.

5. *The Edge of Excellence*, Wiss 125th Anniversary Publication, 1973, accessed 4/7/2016. www .jwissandsons.com.

6. Wiss Heritage, *History and Brand Timeline*, accessed 6/16/2016. www.wisstool.com/ brands-timeline.

7. Louise Austin, Pinking Shears. United States Patent US 489,406. January 03, 1893.

8. *Pinking Shear Patents*, accessed 6/11/2016. www.jwissandsons.com/patents/pinking-shears .html.

9. Thomas B. Doolittle, Doolittle Manufacturing Company. Improvement in button-hole cutters. September 03, 1872, United States Patent US 131,085.

## CHAPTER 6: SEWING ROLLS, RETICULES, BAGS, AND WAIST POCKETS

1. Max Cryer. *Curious English Words and Phrases: The Truth Behind the Expressions We Use*. Wollombi, Australia, 2012; 186.

2. A Lady. *The Workwoman's Guide Facsimile of 1838*. Guilford, Connecticut: Opus, 1986; 215.

3. Civil War at the Smithsonian, *Union Soldier's Housewife*. www.civilwar.si.edu/soldiering _housewife.html.

4. The Reformed Presbyterian magazine for 1864. Google Books January 1855–1876, *Letter from a Friend in America to the Children of the Reformed Presbyterian Church in Scotland*. Sept. 1, 1864; 319.

5. Elsa Barsaloux. *The Priscilla War Work Book*. Boston, Massachusetts: The Priscilla Publishing Company, 1917; 22.

6. Barbara Burman and Seth Denbo. *The History of Pockets*, Victoria & Albert Museum. www.vads .ac.uk/texts/POCKETS/history_of_tie-on _pockets.pdf.

7. Ellen J Gehret. *Rural Pennsylvania Clothing*. York, Pennsylvania: George Shumway, 1976; 73.

8. Mary Andere. *Old Needlework Boxes and Tools*. New York, New York: Drake, 1971; 19.

9. Library of Congress, *Married Women's Property Law*. www.memory.loc.gov/ammem/awh html/awlaw3/property_law.html.

10. Mildred J. Davis. *Early American Embroidery Designs*. New York, New York: Crown, 1969; 128.

CHAPTER 7: SEWING SETS

1. Gertrude Whiting. *Old-Time Tools & Toys of Needlework.* New York, New York: Dover, 1971; 126.

2. Otto Henry Huebel, Pincushion Thimble Holder. United States Patent US 559,032. April 28, 1896.

3. Gay Ann Rogers. *An Illustrated History of Needlework Tools.* London, England: John Murray, 1983; 55.

4. Native American Technology and Art, *Sweet Grass,* accessed 6/1/2016. www.nativetech.org/plants/sweetgrass.html.

5. Frank W. Porter. *The Art of Native American Basketry: A Living Legacy.* New York, New York: Greenwood, 1990; pg. 54.

6. Ibid., pg. 87.

7. Elew John Rogers. Member of the United Houma Nation. *Longleaf Pine Tree Usage by American Indian Tribes of Louisiana.* United States Department of Agriculture Natural Resources Conservation Service, 2012, www.nrcs.usda.gov/Internet/FSE_DOCUMENTS/nrcs141p2_015425.pdf.

8. *Splint Baskets,* www.nativetech.org/basketry/splintweaving.html.

9. *Splint Basketry Traditions,* www.nativetech.org/basketry/splinttraditions.html.

10. Anthony Wonderley. *The Iroquois and Their Neighbors.* Syracuse, New York: Syracuse University Press, 2004; 188.

11. Michael McManus. *A Treasury of American Scrimshaw.* New York, New York: Penguin Studio, 1997; pg. 83.

12. "Food Price Inflation Since 1913," Inflationdata.com.

13. Gay Ann Rogers. *An Illustrated History of Needlework Tools.* London, England: John Murray, 1983; 21.

14. Mary Andere. *Old Needlework Boxes and Tools.* New York, New York: Drake, 1971; 27 and 29.

15. June Sprigg and David Larkin. *Shaker: Life, Work and Art.* Boston, Massachusetts: Houghton, Mifflin, Harcourt, 1991; 211 and 217.

16. M. Stephen Miller. *Inspired Innovations: A Celebration of Shaker Ingenuity.* Lebanon, New Hampshire: University Press of New England, 2010; 136.

17. Ibid., pg. 137.

18. Ibid., pg. 88.

19. Helaine Fendelman. *Tramp Art, a Folk Art Phenomenon.* New York, New York: Stewart, Tabori & Chang, 1999; 40.

20. John Jacob Holtzapffel. *A Manual of Wood Carving.* New York, New York: Charles Scribner's Sons, 1891; 81.

CHAPTER 8: CLAMPS

1. Chas Waterman. United States Patent and Design US 546. February 15, 1853. patft.uspto.gov

2. *Sewing Birds,* The National Museum of American History Collection, Catalog #2004.0116.1, www.americanhistory.si.edu/collections/search/object/nmah_639795.

3. Gay Ann Rogers. *An Illustrated History of Needlework Tools.* London, England: John Murray, 1983; 183.

4. Mary Andere. *Old Needlework Boxes and Tools.* New York, New York: Drake, 1971; 141.

5. Clarke Hess. *Mennonite Arts.* Atglen, Pennsylvania: Schiffer, 2002; 89.

6. Ibid., 73.

CHAPTER 9: THREADWORK: CROCHET, TAMBOUR, KNITTING, TATTING, AND CORDING

1. Lis Paludan. *Crochet: History and Technique.* Loveland, Colorado: Interweave, 1995; 17.

2. Gay Ann Rogers. *An Illustrated History of Needlework Tools.* London, England: John Murray, 1983; 191.

3. Mary Andere. *Old Needlework Boxes and Tools.* New York, New York: Drake, 1971; 115.

4. Anne L. Macdonald. *No Idle Hands: The Social History of American Knitting.* New York, New York: Ballantine Books, 1988; pg. 25.

5. Charles Francis Jenkins. *The Guidebook to Historic Germantown.* Philadelphia, Pennsylvania: Innes & Sons, 1902; 22.

6. Anne L. Macdonald. *No Idle Hands: The Social History of American Knitting.* New York, New York: Ballantine Books, 1988; 5.

7. History.com Staff 2009, *The Fight For Women's Suffrage,* accessed 5/26/2016, www.history.com/topics/womens-history/the-fight-for-womens-suffrage.

8. Anne L. Macdonald. *No Idle Hands: The Social History of American Knitting.* New York, New York: Ballantine, 1988; 180.

9. Ibid., 331.

10. Ellen J. Gehret. *Rural Pennsylvania Clothing.* York, Pennsylvania: George Shumway, 1976; 226.

11. Anne L. Macdonald. *No Idle Hands: The Social History of American Knitting.* New York, New York: Ballantine Books, 1988; 199 and 292.

12. Sylvia Groves. *The History of Needlework Tools and Accessories.* New York, New York: Arco, 1973; 89.

13. Bridget McConnell. *The Story of Antique Needlework Tools.* Atglen, Pennsylvania: Schiffer, 1999; 21, 52.

## CHAPTER 10: HOOPS AND DARNING

1. Helen A. Harmes, Adjustable Embroidery Hoop, United States Patent US744070. November 17, 1903.

2. Lewis Gibbs, Embroidery Hoop, United States Patent US1059143. April 15, 1913.

3. Anna Green Winslow, Boston School Girl Diary of 1771, edited by Alice Morse Earle, www.gutenberg.org/files/20765/20765-h/20765-h.htm#diary.

4. Alfred Steinber. *Mrs. R: The Life of Eleanor Roosevelt.* New York, New York: G. P. Putnam's Sons, 1958; 32.

5. Wayne Muller. *Darn It!* Gas City, Indiana: L-W Books, 1995; 20.

## CHAPTER 11: CLOSURES AND FASTENERS

1. Diana Epstein and Millicent Safro. *Buttons.* New York, New York: Harry N. Abrams, 1991; 14.

2. Ibid., 166.

3. Connecticut Humanities, *Family Ties Bring Together North Branford Industry,* accessed 4/16/2016, www.connecticuthistory.org/family-ties-bring-together-north-branford-industry/.

4. The Waterbury Button Company History, accessed 2/19/2016, www.waterburybutton.com/cart/pc/home.asp.

5. Diana Epstein and Millicent Safro. *Buttons.* New York, New York: Harry N. Abrams, Inc, 1991; 74.

6. Edwin Altee Barber. *Historical Sketch of the Green Point (N.Y.) Porcelain Works of Charles Cartlidge & Co.* Indianapolis, Indiana: Unknown Publisher, 1895; 17.

7. United States Fish and Wildlife Service, *History of Mussel Harvest on the River,* updated June 8, 2006, accessed 5/20/2016. www.fws.gov/midwest/mussel/harvest.html.

8. James Pritchard. *An Historical Analysis of Mussel Propagation and Culture: Research Performed at the Fairport Biological Station.* Ames, Iowa: Clear Creek Historical Research, 2001; 3.

9. Mark Q. Sutton and Brooke S. Arkush. *Archaeological Laboratory Methods: An Introduction.* Greenwood Village, Colorado: Kendall Hunt, 2001; 212.

10. Jeff Ludwig. Historical Researcher, City of Rochester. *Rochester Button Company,* accessed 3/14/2016, www.media.democratandchronicle.com/retrofitting-rochester/rochester-button-company.

11. Mark Q. Sutton and Brooke S. Arkush. *Archaeological Laboratory Methods: An Introduction.* Greenwood Village, Colorado: Kendall Hunt, 2001; 212.

12. Arlene Zeger Wiczyk. *A Treasury of Needlework Projects from Godey's Lady's Book.* New York, New York: Arco, 1972; 148-149.

13. Nancy Nehring. *50 Heirloom Buttons to Make.* Newton, Connecticut: Taunton, 1996; 39.

14. Scovill Fasteners, Inc. *Company History,* accessed 1/16/2016, www.company-histories.com/Scovill-Fasteners-Inc-Company-History.html.

15. Paul Fenton, Resilient Snap Fastener, Scovill Manufacturing Assignee, United States Patent US1832830. November 17, 1931.

16. Frank E. De Long, Garment Hook, United States Patent US492743. February 28, 1893.

17. Elias Howe, Fastening for Garments, United States Patent US8540. November 25, 1851.

18. Gideon Sundback, Separable Fastener, Hookless Fastener Company assignee. United States Patent US1219881. March 20, 1917.

## CHAPTER 12: MEASURING, MARKING, PATTERNS, AND TEMPLATES

1. "Refinement of Values for the Yard and Pound," Federal Register, US Department of Commerce, Doc. 59-5442, June 30, 1959.

2. Gay Ann Rogers. *An Illustrated History of Needlework Tools.* London, England: John Murray, 1983; 121.

3. Ian Whitelaw. *A Measure of All Things.* Cincinnati, Ohio: David & Charles, 2007; 28.

4. "Refinement of Values for the Yard and Pound," Federal Register, US Department of Commerce, Doc. 59-5442, June 30, 1959.

5. Ibid., 5348.

6. Alvin Sellens. *Stanley Folding Rulers*. Fitzwilliam, New Hampshire: Ken Roberts, 1984; 15.

7. Miss Lambert. *The Handbook of Needlework*. New York, New York: Wiley & Putnam, 1842; 85.

8. A History of Victorian Calling Cards, updated 9/4/2011, accessed 3/25/2016, www.daysof elegance.com/callingcards.html.

9. Edward. W. Dodge, Marking Device, United States Patent US 513897, January 30, 1894.

10. Hermann H. Spohn, Laundry Ink, Carters Ink Assignee, United States Patent US741734. October 20, 1903.

11. Cash's Company History, accessed 5/2/2-16, www. jjcash.co.uk/about.php.

12. Mildred J. Davis. *Early American Embroidery Designs*. New York, New York: Crown, 1969; 26.

13. The History of Magazines, accessed 4/12/2016, https://www.magazines.com/history-of -magazines.

14. Anne C. Rose. *Voices of the Marketplace: American Thought and Culture, 1830-1860*. Woodbridge, Connecticut: Twayne, 1994; 75.

15. Frank Luther Mott. *A History of American Magazines 1850-1865*. Cambridge, Massachusetts: Belknap Press of Harvard University Press, 1938; 306.

16. Wikipedia contributors, "McCall's," *Wikipedia*, https://en.wikipedia.org/w/index.php?title =McCall%27s&oldid=746855433 (accessed October 30, 2016).

17. Kelley English, contextualization, *The Delineator Magazine History*, University of West Florida, Virtual Newsstand of 1925, uwf.edu/dearle/ enewsstand/enewsstand_files/Page630.html.

18. Wikipedia contributors, "Ladies' Home Journal," *Wikipedia*, https://en.wikipedia.org/w/index. php?title=Ladies%27_Home_Journal& oldid=754762837 (accessed December 14, 2016).

19. Wikipedia contributors, "Berlin wool work," *Wikipedia*, https://en.wikipedia.org/w/index.php?title =Berlin_wool_work&oldid=720647712 (accessed May 17, 2016).

20. Plaid Enterprises, *The History of Bucilla*, www. plaidonline.com/the-history-of-bucilla/542/ article.html.

21. Winthrop Stanley, Transfer Ink Improvement, Kaumagraph Company assignee, United States Patent 1,573,976. February, 23, 1926.

22. Katherine Whisler, updated 2009, *An Original Transfer Pattern, Vogart Pattern History*, accessed 5/5/2016. www.yellowzeppelin.net/ vogart%20history.html.

23. Workbasket Magazine History, updated 2/3/2008, accessed 4/25/2016, www.theknittershand .homestead.com/Workbaskets.html.

24. Sylvia Groves. *The History of Needlework Tools and Accessories*. New York, New York: Arco, 1973; 95.

25. Trish T. Herr. *Amish Arts of Lancaster County*. Atglen, Pennsylvania: Schiffer, 1998; 45.

26. Trish T. Herr. *Quilting Traditions*. Atglen, Pennsylvania: Schiffer, 2000; 17.

# Bibliography

A Lady. *The Workwoman's Guide Facsimile of 1838.* (Guilford, Connecticut: Opus, 1986.)

Andere, Mary. *Old Needlework Boxes and Tools.* (New York, New York: Drake, 1971.)

Arbittier, Douglas, Janet Elizabeth, and John Morphy. *Collecting Figural Tape Measures.* (Atglen, Pennsylvania: Schiffer, 1995.)

Barber, Elizabeth Wayland. *Women's Work: The First 20,000 Years Women, Cloth, and Society in Early Times.* (New York, New York: W. W. Norton, 1994.)

Bausum, Dolores. *Threading Time.* (Fort Worth, Texas: TCU Press, 2001.)

Beaudry, Mary C. *Findings: The Material Culture of Needlework and Sewing.* (New Haven, Connecticut: Yale University Press, 2006.)

Beaujot, Ariel. *Victorian Fashion Accessories.* (New York, New York: Berg, 2012.)

Bryk, Nancy Villa. *Bloomingdale's Illustrated 1886 Catalog.* (New York, New York: Dover, 1988.)

Caulfeild, Sophia Frances Anne, and Blanche C. Saward. *The Dictionary of Needlework Facsimile of 1882 Edition.* (New York, New York: Arno, 1972.)

Channing, Marion L., and Walter E. Channing. *The Textile Tools of Colonial Homes.* (New Bedford, Massachusetts: Reynolds Dewalt, 1971.)

Colby, Averil. *Pincushions.* (New York, New York: Charles Scribner's Sons, 1975.)

Cryer, Max. *Curious English Words and Phrases: The Truth Behind the Expressions We Use.* (Wollombi, Australia, 2012.)

Davis, Mildred J. *Early American Embroidery Designs.* (New York, New York: Crown, 1969.)

Epstein, Diana, and Millicent Safro. *Buttons.* (New York, New York: Harry N. Abrams, 1991.)

Gehret, Ellen J. *Rural Pennsylvania Clothing.* (York, Pennsylvania: George Shumway, 1976.)

Gengelbach, Darlene J. *Encyclopedia of Children's Sewing Collectibles.* (Paducah, Kentucky: Collector Books, 2007.)

Gottesman, Rita S. *The Arts and Crafts in New York, 1726-1776.* (New York, New York: Da Capo, 1938.)

Gross, Ernie. *Advances and Innovations in American Daily Life, 1600s-1930s.* (Jefferson, North Carolina: McFarland, 2002.)

Groves, Sylvia. *The History of Needlework Tools and Accessories.* (New York, New York: Arco, 1973.)

Gullers, Barbara D. *Antique Sewing Tools and Tales.* (Phoenix, Arizona: Gullers Pictorial Partnership, 1992.)

Hale, Lucretia, and Margaret E. White. *Three Hundred Decorative and Fancy Articles for Presents, Fairs Etc.* (Boston, Massachusetts: S.W. Tilton and Company, 1885.)

Herr, Trish T. *Amish Arts of Lancaster County.* (Atglen, Pennsylvania: Schiffer, 1998.)

Hess, Clarke. *Mennonite Arts.* (Atglen, Pennsylvania: Schiffer, 2002.)

Holmes, Edwin F. *A History of Thimbles.* (Cranbury, New Jersey: Cornwall Books, 1985.)

Houart, Victor. *Sewing Accessories: An Illustrated History.* (London, England: Souvenir, 1984.)

Hughes, Therle. *English Domestic Needlework 1660-1860.* (London, England: Lutterworth, 1961.)

Klamkin, Marian. *Hands to Work: Shaker Folk Art and Industries.* (New York, New York: Dodd, Mead, 1972.)

Lambert, Miss. *The Handbook of Needlework.* (New York, New York: Wiley & Putnam, 1842.)

Lane, Rose Wilder. *Woman's Day Book of American Needlework.* (New York, New York: Simon and Schuster, 1963.)

Lyons, Nick. *Unabridged Facsimile Montgomery Ward & Co. Catalog & Buyers Guide 1895.* (New York, New York: Skyhorse, 2008.)

Macdonald, Anne L. *No Idle Hands: The Social History of American Knitting.* (New York, New York: Ballantine Books, 1988.)

McCauley, Katheryn, and Donald McCauley. *Decorative Arts of the Amish of Lancaster County.* (Intercourse, Pennsylvania: Good Books, 1988.)

McConnel, Bridget. *The Story of Antique Needlework Tools.* (Atglen, Pennsylvania: Schiffer, 1999.)

McCusker, John J. *How Much Is That in Real Money?* (Worcester, Massachusetts: American Antiquarian Society, 2001.)

McManus, Michael. *A Treasury of American Scrimshaw*. (New York, New York: Penguin Studio, 1997.)

Miller, Marla M. *The Needle's Eye: Women and Work in the Age of Revolution*. (Boston, Massachusetts: University of Massachusetts Press, 2006.)

Miller, M. Stephen. *From Shaker Lands and Shaker Hands*. (Lebanon, New Hampshire: University Press of New England, 2007.)

Miller, M. Stephen. *Inspired Innovations: A Celebration of Shaker Ingenuity*. (Lebanon, New Hampshire: University Press of New England, 2010.)

Muller, Wayne. *Darn It!* (Gas City, Indiana: L-W Books, 1995.)

Newell, Aimee E. *A Stitch in Time*. (Athens, Ohio: Ohio University Press, 2014.)

Paludan, Lis. *Crochet: History and Technique*. (Loveland, Colorado: Interweave, 1995.)

Pankiewicz, Philip R. *American Scissors and Shears: An Antique and Vintage Collector's Guide*. (Boca Raton, Florida: Universal, 2013.)

Proctor, Molly. *Needlework Tools and Accessories: A Collector's Guide*. (London, England: B.T. Batsford, 1990.)

Mrs. Pullan. *The Lady's Manual of Fancy-Work*. (New York, New York: Dick & Fitzgerald, 1859.)

Ring, Betty. *Needlework: An Historical Survey*. (Pittstown, New Jersey: Main Street, 1984.)

Rogers, Gay Ann. *An Illustrated History of Needlework Tools*. (London, England: John Murray, 1983.)

Schiffer, Margaret B. *Historical Needlework of Pennsylvania*. (New York, New York: Charles Scribner's Sons, 1968.)

Smith, Amy K. *Needlework for Student Teachers, Third Edition*. (London, England: London Book Depot, 1894.)

Snodgrass, Mary Ellen. *World Clothing and Fashion: An Encyclopedia of History, Culture and Social Influence*. (New York, New York: Routledge, 2013.)

Swan, Susan Burrows. *Plain and Fancy*. (New York, New York: Holt, Rinehart and Winston, 1977.)

Swan, Susan Burrows. *A Winterthur Guide to American Needlework*. (New York, New York: Rutledge Books, 1976.)

Taunton, Nerylla. *Antique Needlework Tools and Embroideries*. (Easthampton, Massachusetts: Antique Collectors' Club, 2007.)

Thompson, Helen Lester. *Sewing Tools and Trinkets*. (Paducah, Kentucky: Collector Books, 1997.)

Thompson, Helen Lester. *Sewing Tools and Trinkets Volume 2*. (Paducah, Kentucky: Collector Books, 2002.)

Ulrich, Laurel Thatcher. *Good Wives*. (New York, New York: Vintage Books Random House, 1991.)

Warren, Geoffrey. *A Stitch in Time Victorian and Edwardian Needlecraft*. (Vancouver, Canada: Douglas David and Charles, 1976.)

Warren, Mrs., and Mrs. Pullman. *Treasures in Needlework Facsimile of 1870 Edition*. (New York, New York: Berkley, 1976.)

Weissman, Judith Reiter, and Wendy Lavitt. *Labors of Love: America's Textiles and Needlework, 1650-1930*. (New York, New York: Random House, 1987.)

Whiting, Gertrude. *Old-Time Tools & Toys of Needlework*. (New York, New York: Dover, 1971.)

Wiczyk, Arlene Zeger. *A Treasury of Needlework Projects fFrom Godey's Lady's Book*. (New York, New York: Arco, 1972.)

Zalkin, Estelle. *Zalkin's Handbook of Thimbles and Sewing Implements*. (Willow Grove, Pennsylvania: Warman, 1988.)

# Index

*American Ladies Magazine*, 223

Amish, 227

Aunt Martha's, 225

Awl, 8, 100, 161-162

Bag, 95, 110, 118, 134-135, 137-146, 162, 167, 202, 207

Bakelite, 26, 88, 181, 199

Bargello, 138

Basket, 36, 38, 62, 73, 89, 90, 92, 134, 137, 141, 160, 162-167, 173, 177-179, 181, 193, 206, 215, 225

Bodkin, 6, 12, 13, 18, 26, 36, 83, 96

Bodkin holder, 98-99

Bone, 100-101, 163, 166, 188-191, 194, 198-199, 206-207, 211, 214-215, 221

Boye, 11, 191-192, 196-197

Brass, 12-14, 48-49, 51, 54, 77, 86-91, 99, 108, 144, 154, 166-167, 169, 171, 175, 184, 187, 199, 206, 218-219

Bristol board, 18-19

Butterick, 214, 221-222, 224

Button, 12, 14-17, 70, 77, 92, 95, 105, 106, 108, 110, 112, 118, 121, 128, 140, 142, 146, 148, 154, 157, 167, 202, 206-211, 214

Cap, 34, 64, 86, 88, 95, 190, 195, 201, 203

Carter's Ink, 221

Cash Company, 222

Celluloid, 9, 35, 88-89, 198, 214-215

Chatelaine, 26, 36-37, 78-79, 89, 91, 154, 160-162

China, 16, 36, 38, 68, 102, 208

Clamp, 6, 58, 173, 182-189, 200, 204

Clauss, 102-104

Closure, 13-14, 16, 19, 26, 29, 52, 54, 90, 96, 112,-113, 125, 127-128, 130, 132, 133, 141, 144, 198, 212, 214

Connecticut, 30-31, 39, 48, 53, 59, 102, 108, 182, 184, 206, 211, 222

Cotton, 12-13, 19, 21, 23, 28, 30-33, 36-37, 41, 47, 56-58, 62-66, 68, 70-71, 73-74, 76, 78-79, 80, 82, 84, 98, 110-111, 113-114, 116-119, 121, 125, 127, 135-137, 142-152, 157, 159, 165, 167, 171, 173, 180, 183, 190, 193, 199, 202, 204, 208-209, 212, 214, 218, 222

Crochet, 12, 14, 30, 45-47, 55, 65-66, 77, 83, 91, 93-94, 96, 137, 145-146, 154, 180, 183, 190-194, 196-197, 211, 226

Darn, 18, 33, 86, 88, 161-162, 167, 201-205, 211

*Delineator*, 214-215, 221, 224

Dutch, 207

Edwardian, 12

Embroidery, 12-13, 15-18, 22, 30, 33, 39, 55-56, 58, 60, 64-65, 67-69, 72, 75, 78-80, 83, 98-102, 118, 120-121, 125-127, 129-130, 136-139, 144, 146, 148-149, 152, 176, 179, 182, 194, 200, 214, 216-217, 223-226

Emery, 12, 13, 29, 45, 58, 60, 62, 74-75, 133, 137, 139-140, 156, 158, 173, 179

Enameled Cloth, 134, 179

England, 8, 26, 30, 48, 60, 102, 208, 222

Eskimo, 133, 135

Fastener, 206, 211-212

France, 190, 208, 225, 227

Girls, 19, 118, 134, 148, 194, 201-202, 204, 207, 216, 224

Germany, 25, 88, 224-225

Godey's, 30, 59, 74, 84-85, 137, 152, 154, 210, 223-224

Hairpin, 53, 190, 192-193

Harley, 203

Hat, 48, 49, 59, 63-64, 93-95, 181, 207

Hem gauge, 216

Henkel, 102

Holland, 227

Hook and eye, 114, 135, 167, 206, 212-213

Hoop, 18, 146, 182, 194, 200, 202, 205, 218-219, 221

Hoop bag, 137, 146

Hoover, Herbert, 24-25

Housewife, 110, 118, 121, 127, 133-134

Howe, Elias, 212

Huswif, 110, 120-121

Ingersoll, 219, 221

Ink, 19-20, 22, 33, 38, 133, 162, 173-174, 214-223, 225

Ivory, 35, 39, 43, 45, 56, 77, 88, 89-90, 100, 160-161, 166, 172, 188-190, 194, 198, 209, 214-215

Kaumagraph, 225-226

Knitting needle, 194-197, 221

Knitting pin, 195-196

Labels, 9, 33, 49, 88, 108

*Ladies' Home Journal*, 224

Leather, 12, 18, 21, 33, 50, 54, 74, 76-77, 83, 86, 87, 89-90, 92-93, 95, 97, 100, 107-108, 110-112, 123, 127, 129-136, 139-141, 145, 154-158, 168, 173, 196, 227

Linen, 18, 31, 33, 54, 57, 61, 74, 78, 80, 82, 111, 113, 116, 120-122, 125, 136-137, 141-144, 147-152, 210-211, 216-222, 225-226

Lucet, 198

Machine needles, 10-11

Magazine, 12, 15-16, 30, 72, 88, 127, 154, 190, 194, 211, 215, 221, 223-226

*Magazine Antiques, The*, 127

Maine, 31, 36, 45-47, 62, 102, 173-174, 182, 227

Marking, 46, 63, 78, 88, 167, 174, 214, 216-219, 221-222, 225, 227

Massachusetts, 8, 30, 37, 202

Measure, 18, 28, 32, 43, 59, 63, 147, 154, 201, 214-216

Military, 118, 121-123, 196, 206

Mother-of-pearl, 34-35, 37, 39, 44, 56, 86, 89, 90, 98, 100, 126, 154, 198

Native American, 22-23, 72-73, 86, 90, 135, 163

Needle, 8-32, 41, 45, 49, 58-59, 61-62, 66-67, 76, 86-90, 94, 96, 110, 118, 121, 130, 134, 154, 156, 158-159, 163, 177, 181, 185, 194, 201, 203-205, 207, 210

Needle book, 12-25, 27, 45, 58, 66-67, 90, 127, 137-139, 141-145, 155, 157, 160-162, 167, 173, 176-179, 196

*Needlecraft Magazine*, 88

Needle lace, 210-211

Needle making, 8

Needle storage, 12, 16, 26, 110, 203

New England, 6, 60, 62

New Jersey, 31, 57, 100, 102, 200

New York, 26, 72, 86, 88, 102, 105, 134-135, 154, 160, 163, 208-209, 225

Ohio, 102, 108, 172

Oil cloth, 134-135

Pasteboard, 18-19, 56, 62, 112, 127, 144, 146, 159, 176-178

Pattern, 12, 19-20, 30, 34, 60, 67, 72-73, 75, 78-79, 81, 85, 88, 90, 93, 98, 100, 105, 110, 120-121, 138, 148, 152, 154, 163, 165, 173, 182, 188, 190, 196, 198, 208, 211, 217, 219, 221-227

Pennsylvania, 15, 20, 21, 26, 58, 60-61, 64-65, 68-69, 71, 78-79, 80, 82, 85-86, 92, 95, 107, 111, 113-117, 120, 125, 133, 140, 147-153, 155, 158-159, 161, 168, 176-179, 184, 185, 194, 199, 227

Perforated paper, 14, 18-20, 218

Peterson's, 15, 223-224

Pin, 8, 17, 29, 41, 45, 48-62, 64-66, 68, 74-76, 83, 85, 89, 95, 118-119, 121, 127, 129, 131, 134, 139, 141-142, 154-156, 158, 160, 167, 170, 177-178, 181-182, 215, 219

Pin ball, 78-85, 161

Pincushion, 15, 22, 29, 39-46, 49-52, 54, 58-77, 83, 85, 89-90, 92, 94, 98, 110, 112, 120-121, 124-125, 127, 133, 135, 145, 154, 156-159, 161-163, 165, 167, 169-178, 182-187, 189, 227

Pin disc, 56-57, 137, 155, 160-162, 180

Pin folder, 54

Pin paper, 49-52, 54

Pin storage, 48, 50, 58

Pine needle, 61, 163, 165

Pinking shears, 105-106

Plush, 18, 68, 73, 152, 227

Pocket, 18, 66, 110, 113, 114, 116-125, 127-128, 130-131, 133-137, 139, 141-143, 145, 147-153, 159, 169, 176-177, 202, 207, 219, 221

Poppet, 52

Porcelain, 12, 52, 86, 98, 208

Pounce, 217, 219, 221

Quaker, 30, 124, 127, 142, 151, 168, 222

Quilt, 19, 55, 68, 78, 82-83, 116, 146, 150-151, 180, 182, 184-185, 217-218, 225-227

Reticule, 110, 137-139, 145, 148, 162

Ribbon, 12-14, 16-19, 21-24, 29, 36-38, 45, 49, 54-56, 60-65, 67, 69-70, 74-78, 80-83, 91, 94-99, 110, 112-113, 117-121, 124-127, 131, 133, 137-139, 141-142, 144-146, 154-155, 157-158, 160-162, 170, 173, 174, 177-179, 181, 197, 210, 214-215, 222

Ring, 12, 14-16, 28, 66, 74, 78, 137, 143-146, 152, 154, 160-162, 198-200, 210-211

Rubber, 200-201, 210, 219

Ruler, 32, 214-215

Sailor, 59, 110, 163, 188

Salem Academy, 216-217

Scissor, 16, 102, 104-108, 119, 125, 130, 133-134, 141, 154-158, 161-163, 167, 169, 181

Scissor rest, 83, 98

Seam ripper, 108-109

Sewing box, 34, 36, 56, 90, 92, 130, 156-157, 163, 167-181, 186

Sewing companion, 108-109, 156

Sewing roll, 60, 90, 99, 110-136, 140, 142, 144, 146, 147, 206

Sewing set, 28, 35, 90, 110, 154-159, 162, 168

Shaker, 36, 39, 45, 46, 62, 83, 127, 160, 173-174

Shakespeare, 110

Shell, 12, 22-24, 26, 56, 58, 61-63, 73, 84, 86, 89, 90-91, 96-98, 100, 154, 181, 188, 194, 198-200, 208-209, 218, 220

Shuttle, 198-199

Silk, 12-16, 18-19, 21-23, 28, 30-31, 33-34, 50-55, 57-61, 64-70, 73-84, 90-92, 95, 98-99, 110-113, 115, 118, 120-122, 124-127, 129-134, 136-139, 141, 145-146, 148, 154, 155-158, 160-162, 164, 169, 173-174, 176-180, 184, 187, 203-205, 215, 222-223, 225

Silver, 7, 19, 26, 34, 36, 65, 79-80, 86, 88-89, 93, 97-98, 100, 102, 154, 160-162, 175, 195, 199, 201-202, 204, 216

Simons, 86

Snap, 13, 17, 96, 110, 127-128, 130, 132, 145, 157, 206, 211

Souvenir, 22-23, 34, 37, 63, 65, 90-91, 96, 135, 198, 214

Spool, 30-31, 33-35, 39-47, 68, 122, 124-129, 133, 154-157, 166-171, 173, 181-184, 189-190, 194, 203

Stamp, 19, 22, 25, 27, 30, 52, 54, 88, 133, 169, 173, 185, 206, 208, 217-221, 225

Stencil, 149, 172, 218-219

Sterling, 26, 34, 36-37, 86, 88, 93-94, 98, 100-102, 156, 158, 160, 162, 195, 199, 201-202, 204, 215-216

Stiletto, 26, 96, 100-101, 154, 219

Sweetgrass, 90, 160, 162-163, 165

Tailor, 8, 31, 59, 102, 215, 224

Tambour, 40-41, 190, 194

Tape, 12, 58-59, 63, 65, 79, 83, 97-98, 111, 118-120, 122, 137, 141-144, 147-153, 167, 169, 185, 187, 212, 214-216, 222

Tape measure, 59, 63, 214-216

Tatting, 30, 66, 137, 198-199

Template, 85, 218, 227

Thimble, 13, 17, 41-43, 66, 86-95, 110, 118, 125-130, 133-134, 137, 140, 142, 145, 154-158, 160-163, 165, 167-169, 177, 180-181, 183, 187, 201

Thimble holder, 41, 89-95, 110, 118, 125, 127, 134, 140, 142, 154-157, 160-163, 165, 167-168, 177

Thread, 9, 12-20, 23, 27-28, 30-34, 36-39, 41-47, 52, 59-61, 64-67, 69-71, 73-74, 76-78, 81-84, 86-87, 98, 100-101, 108, 110, 113, 117-119, 121-122, 124-128, 133, 134, 136-139, 145, 149-150, 154-159, 166-167, 169-170, 173, 176, 181-185, 189-191, 193-194, 196-199, 201-203, 206, 209-213, 217, 222, 225-226

Thread box, 32, 41, 44-45

Thread button, 210

Thread stand, 39, 41-43, 45-46

Thread winder, 17, 30-31, 34-35, 83, 118, 126, 139, 154, 157, 167, 169, 182

Threadwork, 190, 226

Tortoiseshell, 56, 86, 89, 154, 181, 188, 194, 200

Tramp art, 174-176

Transfer, 23, 208, 217, 219, 221-223, 225-226

Tunisian, 190, 192

Unger, 102

US Patent, 10, 26, 30-31, 40-41, 45, 48, 50, 59, 88, 100, 102, 105, 108, 181-182, 184, 195-196, 200, 203-204, 210-212, 219-220, 222, 225

Vegetable ivory, 89, 90, 209

Velvet, 12-13, 21, 42, 44-45, 50-51, 57-59, 61-67, 70, 72-79, 82, 83, 84, 89-92, 108-110, 112, 121, 124, 127-128, 130-131, 133, 136, 144-145, 160, 166, 169, 170, 172, 174-177, 179, 187, 191

Vermont, 121

Victorian, 12, 22, 62, 67, 72, 137, 160, 211, 224, 227

Vogart, 225

Walnut, 43, 44, 52, 58, 61, 89, 187

Waterman, 182-183

Waxer, 36-37, 159, 161-162, 173

Winder, 17, 30-31, 34-35, 83, 118, 126, 139, 154, 157, 167, 169, 182

Wiss, 102, 104-106

Woman's Benefit Association, 24-25

Wool, 11-17, 19-24, 33, 42, 50, 52, 54-56, 58-61, 64, 66-74, 76-78, 80, 82-84, 88, 94, 98-99, 110-114, 117-122, 124-130, 132-133, 135-139, 141, 143-145, 148-150, 152, 157-159, 179, 181-183, 185-186, 190, 196, 200, 202, 224, 227

Woolworth, 225

Work bag, 137, 142-144

*Work Basket Magazine*, 225, 226

Workwoman's Guide, The, 12, 110, 150, 152, 167, 217

Yarn, 28, 31, 33, 46, 47, 60, 67-69, 71, 78, 82-83, 101, 118, 145, 182, 193, 196-197, 201-202, 227

Zipper, 96, 212

Dawn Cook Ronningen is a historian, needle worker, and long-time collector of sewing and embroidery tools as well as antique textiles. She uses her needlework tool collection in her own stitching projects, focusing on historic techniques and designs. She lectures on her collections in the US and abroad, meeting and sharing information with embroiderers, quilters, sewers, and antiques enthusiasts.